Collecting Model Farm Toys of the World

Collecting Model Farm Toys of the World

Raymond E. Crilley
and
Charles E. Burkholder

AZTEX Corporation—Tucson, Arizona 85703

Cover Credits

Left center—Ertl John Deere 5020 modified by Eldon Trumm
Left bottom—Froehlic by Harry Van Woert
Right top—Arcade cast iron McCormick-Deering 10-20, Ertl John Deere
   four-wheel-drive, Strombecker Allis Chalmers (WD-45)
Right center—New Holland combine made in France
Right bottom—Rumley Oil Pull by Irvin

Cover Design: John M. Peckham

ISBN 0-89404-086-3

Library of Congress Catalog Card Number 78-55487

AZTEX CORPORATION, TUCSON, ARIZONA 85703-1046

Printed in the United States of America

Foreword

Most of the companies manufacturing miniature wheeled models include at least one model tractor or crawler. While this seems like an insignificant number, a tractor enthusiast can build quite a collection in a few years.

Model automobiles that represent real ones have far greater collector appeal than ones which are simply toys. Tractor models bearing trade names such as John Deere, International, Allis-Chalmers, Case, Massey Ferguson, White, Steiger, Fiat, etc. all have appeal to individuals who identify with such brands. The purpose of this book is to help collectors, dealers and other interested individuals get a better idea of the wide variety of miniature farm and industrial tractors that were manufactured over the past fifty or more years. Some information on farm implements is also included.

Since information on many model manufacturers is quite limited, or even non-existent, this book does not include an all inclusive list of tractor models, but rather those for which information was available.

Contents

Introduction

Who Collects Farm Models?

Collecting toy farm models is a hobby that is gaining in popularity. This is evidenced by the tremendous demand for obsolete toys at toy shows, flea markets and other places where they may be found. Farm machinery dealers are experiencing a rapid turnover of new toys as are department, variety, and discount stores and other outlets.

Answering the question, "What are farm models?", gets a bit involved. The popular concept would include anything related to farm life. Examples might be farm tractors, implements, horses, cattle, poultry, buildings, crops, landscape items, and, of course, the farmer, his wife and children. There are a variety of farm "sets" still on the market which include all of the above. Obviously, justice could not be done to such a wide variety in just one book, so for that reason, this book is devoted to models representing tractors and allied equipment.

Even this limitation needs further explanation. In the early development of machines, the primary concern was to make the tillage of soil, and planting and harvesting of crops easier for the farmer. After the land was broken and crops produced, it became necessary to get the crops to markets where the consumers could buy them. This made roads a necessity. Some of the machines developed for farm use soon were modified for building roads. Steam traction engines were fitted with smooth roller wheels to firm up roadbeds. The first mass-produced farm tractor, the Fordson, was used widely in road construction and soon was used for other industrial purposes. Even today, practically all the major farm tractor manufacturers include a variety of industrial equipment in their operations. The J. I. Case Company, for decades a leader in the production of steam traction engines and threshers, in recent years markets more industrial equipment than agricultural equipment. There is some discussion of industrial equipment included here since it is so closely related to farm equipment.

While there is mention made and pictures of implements, the major emphasis is on tractors and other power units. While, admittedly, horses must be included with power units, there were not a great number of models of horses and farm implements made. Therefore, this book shall contain only a few references to same. Two early toy manufacturers, Vindex and Arcade, made some very nice cast-iron models of horses and implements such as wagons, manure spreaders, etc.

Getting back to the original question "Who collects farm models?", the answer has to be "A wide variety of people collect farm models." Historically, the vast majority of people, in the area of ninety percent, were actively engaged in agricultural pursuits at the time of the American Revolution. Since that time, farming has become so efficient that only about four or five percent of the population is actively engaged in farming, but another thirty or thirty-five percent are involved in supportive occupations such as the manufacture of farm machinery, fertilizer, feed processing, chemical manufacture, and other occupations which process food produced by farmers and ultimately get it to the consumer.

Obviously one would assume that there would be a good deal of interest in farm toys among farmers themselves. Most farm children like to imitate Dad and use a tractor which looks "just like Dad's", or be a "pint size shadow." After the toys have been lost to the ravages of time, a former farm boy becomes interested in them once again.

During the great depression and dust bowl era, a young farm boy in Kansas spent many quiet evenings making believe that things were better while playing with his Vindex cast iron model of a John Deere model D tractor and prairie combine on the kitchen floor. When told it was bed time, he carefully put his prized possessions away, as these were the only toys his parents could afford to buy for him. The financial demands of the farm business and of a living for the family came before such luxuries as toys.

As the lad grew older, and his responsibilities on the farm increased, his interest in toys faded. Now he could do what he always wanted to do, operate the real tractor. So the toys were destined to a dark corner in the attic. It wasn't until years later after Dad passed away and the now grown lad was searching through the attic for some important papers that he ran across the dusty toys. Immediately memories of his not so easy childhood rushed through his mind. Somehow the memory of playing with the tractor and combine on the kitchen floor stood out. Soon the dusty toys were cleaned up and placed on the fireplace as a permanent reminder of the past. Now that times were better, he could buy some of the other implements that he could not afford then. This farmer soon became an avid collector.

A businessman in a large Midwest city remembers traveling to an uncle's farm to help each summer after school was out. He remembers the long, hard days of farm work, but most of all, he remembers his uncle showing him how to operate the tractor and how tricky that hand clutch was. Years later, perhaps as a reversion to his childhood, or merely as an escape from reality, he decided to try to find models of all the implements and tractors his uncle had. Thus an ongoing search for models began and has since resulted in a collection of several hundred miniature farm models.

Another individual recalls seeing toy model tractors and implements at the farm machinery dealers' booths at the county fair when he was a child. He remembers that his spending money was very limited. He wanted one of those tractor models in the worst way, but all that walking around the fair grounds made him hungry. So hunger overwhelmed the desire for a model tractor and the foot long hotdog and french fries satisfied him then. But how about now? He has a good job and plenty of money for food with some left over. Even though he is now an adult, why not buy a few of those models? He has been collecting for several years now.

Another professional agribusinessman was given an assignment to prepare a television program to explain soil conservation. Now how could he explain soil conservation to people who hardly know what the difference between soil and dirt is? As he pondered his dilemma, he remembered seeing some farm machinery models in a dealer's show window. Why not borrow a few of those models to use as "visuals" for his show? The dealer was very understanding regarding the request. And why not? Here was an opportunity to get his "brand" name before thousands of people, a rather subtle method of advertising. After the program, the agribusinessman decided that perhaps sometime in the future he may need these models for another program. When he returned to the dealer, he decided to purchase them. Later he found a few more pieces and soon interest in a collection began.

The annual farmers' organization banquet table was all set up with a variety of farm-like miniatures. A young member remembered a "manure spreader" model setting in front of the guest speaker's place. Now, whether this was a deliberate attempt to convey a message to "keep it short and sweet" few people will ever know. The speaker had a good laugh over it and, incidentally, the speech didn't take half the evening after all. Somehow the young member remembered this incident and it sparked a desire to collect other models.

A collector from Iowa reports seeing a model of a Minneapolis-Moline

G-1000 in a store. Marveling at its authenticity, he began collecting tractors. His collection now totals over four-hundred models.

A John Deere dealer in Ohio had a complete set of Vindex cast iron models handed down to him through his family. He now adds one of each model John Deere toy made, probably so he can pass them along some day.

Another collector from the Midwest was involved in a charity organization's effort to recondition toys for the less fortunate children at Christmas time. After reconditioning several pieces of model farm equipment, he became interested in collecting them as a hobby.

A vocational agricultural teacher in Michigan traded some newer modern models for older ones to update the ones in the department. He decided to add the current models, not really planning to begin a collection. After accumulating some twenty models, a friend told him about seeing an old cast iron McCormick-Deering 10-20 tractor and thresher in an antique dealer's window. Being skeptical that such a model was ever made, he checked and found that, indeed, it did exist and was for sale for an astounding $80.00. Quite embarrassed about spending so much money on two pieces, he soon learned that the price paid was a bargain and then his collecting effort began in earnest.

A couple having a terminally ill child found collecting a way of getting their minds off the illness by doing some traveling with the child looking for obsolete models.

An engineer was so impressed with the accuracy of the casting details of a small farm model that he decided to collect them for their aesthetic value.

Years ago, some farm machinery dealers would give a toy model to a boy when he accompanied his dad to buy a real model. These models provided countless hours of make believe farming and now rest on their way to collectors' shelves.

M. Howard Karslake, Benfleet, England, proudly displays *one-third* of his collection.

Collecting Farm Toy Models

Once a collector decides that he is indeed, a collector, he needs to decide what he wants to collect. Since the area of farm machinery is quite broad in itself, he should select an area of specialization.

For example, if he has plenty of cash, he may decide to collect only cast iron models. The cast iron era for farm toys extends from the 1920s to 1940 at which time the foundries were converted to production of war items. The well known Arcade Company began to manufacture brake shoes. Sometime during the war, a warehouse containing some of the molds burned and the manufacturing of cast iron toys by that company ended. Some of the other companies that made cast iron models include Vindex, Hubley, Killgore, Kenton, Williams and Dent.

Another way one may decide to specialize is by product name. John Deere, a name associated with farm machinery since 1837, has had a good line of miniatures since the 1920s. Their earliest models were made of cast iron by Vindex. Later, Arcade produced a model of a John Deere "A" tractor and a wagon with a wooden box. After the war, Fred Ertl Sr., founder of the Ertl Company that manufactures so many nice die-cast models today, began producing some John Deere models. By the 1950s, in association with Carter Tru-Scale, he was marketing a line that included tractors, crawlers, plows, wagons, spreaders, grain drills, disks, corn pickers, combines, and others, all bearing the John Deere logo. Today Ertl has extended that line to include industrial equipment and lawn and garden equipment.

International Harvester is another name that has had a wide variety of farm models available since the 1920s. Arcade produced what was then known as McCormick-Deering models. This cast iron line included a very nice team of horses pulling a manure spreader, first on steel wheels, then later on rubber tires. After the war, there were a few die-cast I. H. models produced but a company called Product Miniature produced some rather detailed plastic models until the mid-1950s. After that Ertl began producing die-cast models again. Today, I. H. is one of Ertl's largest customers.

Massey-Ferguson, a company formed by a merger of Massey-Harris and Ferguson in the 1950s, now has an impressive array of tractors in model form. Advanced Products and Topping Models, both made models of the Ferguson during the early 1950s. Fantastically detailed miniatures of the Massey Harris 44 and some implements were made by Ruehl Products. A company called Slik Toys in the United States and one called Lincoln Toys of Canada made Massey-Harris models then, too. Over the past twenty-five years, several toy manufacturers have made miniatures of Massey-Harris, Ferguson or Massey-Ferguson tractors. Most of these companies are outside the United States and include one from India and another from the Union of South Africa.

Undoubtedly in sheer numbers of cast iron models, Fordson ranks first. In addition to a variety of sizes produced by Arcade, companies such as Hubley, Killgore, Kenton and Williams produced Fordson tractors with cleated wheels, rubber tires, smooth steel type wheels and in a wide variety of colors (although gray with red wheels was the "standard" color for the real Fordson in the U. S.). After the introduction of the Fordson in Great Britain by Henry Ford, several toy companies there made models. Dinky, Britains, Corgi and Lesney all have produced Fordsons and continue today, changing the name to simply Ford. In the U. S., Product Miniature made models of the Ford 8-N, NAA (Jubilee), 600 and 900 tractors in 1/12 scale.

Later, Hubley produced several models of die-cast metal, also in 1/12 scale. Now, Ertl is making the Ford models.

J. I. Case models go back to the late 1920s with the cast iron model "L" tractor, a plow, a spreader and a combine. A long time elapsed with no models. Then 1/16 scale models were produced by Monarch and JoHan. Since about 1963, Ertl had been making the Case models.

In the Allis Chalmers line, a limited number of cast iron models were made by Arcade in three different scales. Hubley or Dent made a model of cast iron also. In 1950, American Precision Products made a 1/12 scale model of the model "C" tractor. Later Product Miniature made a HD-5 crawler with Baker blade. A WD-45 tractor and a D series plastic kit were made by Strombecker in association with Kelton and Kaysun Plastics.

White Motors Inc. now owns controlling interest in the companies that formerly produced Oliver, Minneapolis-Moline and Cockshutt tractors and equipment. These three lines of tractors have had a variety of toy manufacturers including Arcade, Auburn Rubber, Slik Toy, Lincoln Toy, and of course, Ertl. Two different companies made Minneapolis-Moline models out of wood during World War II. Although quite crude compared with cast iron or die-cast metal, these wooden models undoubtedly served the purpose when other materials were unavailable.

In the industrial line, Caterpillar had a variety of manufacturers too. Early ones were made of cast iron, die-cast metal and plastic. Two German firms are producing excellently scaled models for the market today.

Some of the collectable brand names made outside the U. S. include Beauce, Belarus, Deutz, Eicher, Fendt, Fiat, Hanomag, Kohctpykto, Leyland, Mercedes-Benz, Porsche, and SAME.

There are many brand name farm models made in very limited numbers. For example, a Lantz Cutter Colter plow model was made years ago. Three New Idea models: a corn picker, a spreader and a mower, were marketed in 1950s. A cast iron Wallis tractor was sold about 1930. A few patent models and salesman's samples have found themselves on collectors' shelves. A couple of individuals are currently making new "old timers" including a hefty model of a Twin City 60-90 tractor.

In the United States today, the most popular size of farm models seems to be the 1/16 scale. This simply means that for each sixteen inches the real model is, the miniature will be one inch. This reduces the size of tractors to a range of about eight to fourteen inches for regular farm style tractor models. Many American models were made to a smaller 1/20 scale both before and after World War II. A variety of scales are available now. Some of the more popular scales other than the 1/16 include a larger 1/12, mostly the Ford line, and smaller 1/20, 1/25, 1/32, 1/43, 1/50 and 1/87. Anything less than 1/100 is extremely small and hardly any detail is permitted. Some collectors may decide to specialize in one size range such as 1/16 or 1/43.

Earlier, cast iron models of the 1920s through 1940 were mentioned as an area of specialized collecting. A younger collector may want to specialize in models he was familiar with such as those made from 1950 to 1960, or 1960 to 1970, etc.

In addition to cast iron, a collector may want to collect only models made of die-cast metal, plastic, or wood, etc. There were several models on the market in plastic kit form.

With all the talk of specialization, it should be pointed out that what a collector decides to collect should be of his choosing and within his own limitations. Many collectors do not limit themselves and instead collect anything related to farming.

The life-like features of some of the farm models are amazing. Many feature items like operable steering, a turn of the steering wheel operating the front wheels. Some have wide front axles which oscillate like the real ones. During the 1950s, International Harvester models featured the famous two point, fast-hitch. The little drawbar could be removed and a plow or disk could be mounted in its place, making the tractor and implement one integral unit. Before that, the famous three-point-hitch was developed. Several toy models had this feature. And, of course, a tractor would not be a tractor without some type of towing hitch that permitted wagons, plows, spreaders and a variety of other implements to be attached.

Many of the latest models feature safety cabs on the tractors that protect the operator in case of overturning. Dual rear wheels for better flotation have been added and front end weight brackets are found on some models. Even four-wheel-drive, giving power to the front wheels as well as the rear wheels, is featured on some models. Very little detail is lost. For example, the triangular safety emblem called the SMV (Slow moving vehicle) is included on some models.

Another important factor in the realism of farm models is correct color schemes. A John Deere in any other colors than green and yellow is almost obscene. A notable exception is a few of the early cast iron implements which were made before the standard green and yellow was adopted. Another exception was the so-called color-key lawn and garden tractors which were introduced in red, yellow, orange and blue with white trim. Consumer reluctance to buy anything with colors other than the traditional John Deere green and yellow doomed the color-key scheme and it was dropped by Deere and Company.

Ford changed its official pattern from the gray and red of the Fordson to the all gray of the 9-N. Then the gray and red was revived for the 8-N and a few succeeding models. With the introduction of the 4000 and second series 6000 models, the color pattern changed to gray and blue, which is still used today. All along the way the toy models had the color pattern conforming to the official colors.

To add to the realism of these models, a variety of implements were available. For those who are not familiar with such implements, a brief discussion will follow.

Probably the most common implement is the wagon or trailer. Depending what part of the country you hail from, the terms are used interchangeably. In the Midwest, any wheeled implement used for hauling, be it two wheeled or four wheeled, is called a trailer. Generally though, one with two wheels is called a trailer while those with four wheels are called wagons. There are wagons and trailers for special uses including those made with flat beds for hauling hay, fertilizer in bags, rocks and other like materials. Others, wider at the top than the bottom, were made for hauling grain and were called flair wagons. A variation of that concept is the modern gravity box which permits unloading of grain through a hopper-like chute. Other wagons were modified in design to handle bulky material such as silage, also called ensilage. A forage harvester chopped the corn or grass into tiny pieces and blew it into a trailing wagon or one towed along side the harvester. These have built-in unloading mechanisms.

A variation of the wagon is a manure spreader or simply, spreader, as it is commonly known. It is equipped with a conveyer and a spreading mechanism. These are used to spread animal wastes on the fields to replace some of the fertilizer and organic matter lost when a crop is removed. The latest spreaders are more like a tank with a mechanism that permits the spreading of liquid wastes.

Another important piece of equipment on a farm is the plow. It is equipped with from one to twelve or more "bottoms," (a name given to curved pieces of steel which turns the soil over burying the trash on the surface and exposing raw earth). This process helps kill existing vegetation by smothering it and hastening decomposition so that fertilizer can be released for the next crop. It also helps aerate the soil and provide better water penetration.

After plowing, the soil must be "fitted". This is the process of breaking the lumps so that a suitable seed bed is established. The degree of fineness depends upon which crop is to be planted. The finer the seed, the finer the soil needs to be. The most common implement used is a disk, sometimes spelled disc. It is composed of a series of round cutting blades and may be a single or tandem design. A tandem disk has one set of disks following another set and throws the soil in two directions. Sometimes a roller follows the disk to further break up the soil. A spring-tooth harrow or spike-tooth harrow, sometimes called a "drag," is used for the same operation. A float is simply a wooden plank which one drags across the soil to further pulverize it.

After preparing the soil, a planter of some type can be used. One type is called a grain drill and it plants grain, such as wheat or oats, in rows close together. Another type is called a corn planter or row crop planter. The corn, soybeans, etc. are spaced farther apart in rows ranging from twenty to thirty six inches. Fertilizer, weed and insect chemicals can be applied with some planters at the same time. The third type of planter is a transplanter. It is used for planting plants already partially grown such as tomatoes, cabbage, or even trees.

Cultivators are used to work up the ground between rows. These can be mounted on the front or rear of the tractor.

The early machines used to harvest grain were the reaper, a mower-like device, and thresher which separated the grain from the straw. Later these two were replaced by the combine which performed both operations at the same time.

Corn is harvested by a machine called a corn picker. This removes the husks from the corn and deposits the ears, via an elevator, in a wagon. Modern combines can be used to harvest corn by using a corn "head". Allis Chalmers has a toy model with an interchangeable set of heads.

To aid in the back-breaking chore of handling manure, a hydraulically operated loader was developed for the tractor. While most of these mount on the front of the tractor, a few are mounted on the rear.

Equipment for handling hay include the mower that cuts it, a rake for gathering it and a baler for compressing it into cubes for easier handling. The early type of rake was called a dump rake, while the later rake was called a side delivery and placed the hay in long rows called windrows. Both of these were used to fluff up the hay so that the wind could dry it better. Before the invention of the pick-up baler, a device called a hay loader was used to elevate the hay up onto the wagon. The most modern pick-up balers have throwers which actually throw the bales into the trailing wagon. Several new balers that make large stacks or loaves of hay weighing a couple of tons have been introduced. Along with these are special loaders or trailers to permit handling of these giant parcels of hay. Hay elevators are used to carry bales into the storage area.

Where To Find Models

The best place to find current farm models is at local retail farm machinery dealers. Most of the dealers stock a good supply of models, especially at Christmas time. If you don't find what you want, ask him if he would order some.

Farm supply centers are another good source of current models. Some department and variety stores sellfarm toys, but this will vary widely. Discount stores usually have a few models.

Obsolete models are more difficult to find. Occasionally, one may find a few older models at some of the outlets listed previously. However, here is where the scratching begins. Antique shows, flea markets, Salvation Army stores, Goodwill stores, rummage sales, basement or garage sales and bazaars sometimes yield older models in reasonably good condition. If you are handy, a few repairs or touching up a bit makes a damaged model look practically like new.

Hobby shops provide another good source of models, especially smaller scale and foreign models. Some shop owners make every reasonable effort to obtain models wanted by customers. However, don't expect them to stock items for which there is a very limited market.

If you live in a town or city, treat yourself to a real experience and travel out to the country to a farm auction. Older farm models often turn up at these sales. However, take heed, it is easy to get carried away at an auction and you may find yourself with a truck load of other goodies which may be difficult to get into the trusty V. W.

Some collectors have even resorted to going door-to-door in an effort to locate long sought after models. While this is time consuming, it could result in some nice models for the shelves.

Advertising in local or regional newspapers, antique or hobby papers and magazines, trade magazines, etc. may result in locating some models. Check out other advertisements as they may contain what you seek. When replying to an advertisement, be sure to enclose a self addressed stamped envelope. This does not insure a reply, but increases the chances of getting one.

Now if you want to fill up those empty shelves in a hurry, just fill your wallet with cash and attend one of those ever popular toy shows. These are held in various regions of the country and bring together dealers and collectors from a wide area and with a variety of interests along the toy lines. If you have duplicates, bring them along and do some swapping.

A collector must keep collecting in its proper perspective. Remember, the fun of a collection is in the collecting. You can meet wonderful people who share interests similar to yours and lasting friendships can grow from this hobby. Set a reasonable limit on how much money you will spend, or invest, if you will, and stick with it. Don't get caught up to the degree that you spend money you shouldn't spend. You can very easily end up in the doghouse if you spend the grocery money for a toy. To some people who share your enthusiasm, these are priceless gems. To others, these are just toys, or Heaven forbid, junk!

Your Choice of These

FAMOUS CASE TOYS

These are perfect miniatures of the famous Case Tractor, Case three-Furrow Tractor Plow, and the Case Combine.

Given with your own subscription or as a reward for securing subscriptions of your neighbors to Farm Mechanics Magazine.

TOY CASE THREE-FURROW PLOW
—Length 11½ inches, Width 3½ inches, Height 3¾ inches. Painted in full Case colors—Red with green wheels, aluminum coulters, shares and lever handles. Equipped with a wire hook for attaching to tractor.

TOY CASE TRACTOR—Length 7 inches, Width 3¾ inches, Height 4¼ inches. Painted in full Case colors—Gray with red wheels— Nickeled pulley and manikin.

Given free with your own subscription at the regular price of $1.00 for three years; 36 issues, or you can secure this toy by obtaining a 3-year subscription from your neighbor.

Given free with your own subscription at the regular price of $1.00 for three years; 36 issues or you can secure this toy by obtaining a 3-year subscription from your neighbor.

TOY CASE COMBINE— Length 13 inches. Width 12 inches, Height 7½ inches. Painted in full Case colors— aluminum, trimmed with red. has red wheels, engine. and header reel. Header reel turns when combine is pulled. Equipped with a wire hook for attaching to tractor.

Given free as a reward for securing three 3-year subscriptions to Farm Mechanics at our regular price of $1.00 each.

How to Claim Your Toys

Select the toy you want. Read carefully the instructions about what you have to do to get the toy you select.

Mail the full amount you collect for subscriptions with the request for toys. Write your name and address and the names of the subscribers you secure carefully, so that there will be no doubt about the spelling of either the name or the town. You need not be a subscriber to Farm Mechanics to qualify for any of these toys. You can obtain as many toys as you want by securing the number of subscriptions necessary to qualify for each toy.

The coupon is for your convenience.

Arcade Manufacturing Company

The forerunner of the Arcade Manufacturing Company was a small concern known as the Novelty Iron Works which was founded in Freeport in 1868 by two brothers, E. H. and Charles Morgan. The first factory was on the corner of Chicago and Jackson Streets.   Business was conducted from this location for nearly 20 years, occupying two small brick buildings and employing ten people.

The old buildings were torn down in 1874, and a new building erected on the same site. Pumps, windmills, iron pavements, store fronts, and a variety of castings were made by the company.

In 1885 the business was discontinued, and the Arcade Manufacturing Company was organized. Soon afterward, a new factory was erected in the southeast part of Freeport, the operation continuing until 1891.

In that year the company moved again, this time taking possession of a building that had recently been vacated by the Emory and Williams Canning Company. The building burned to the ground in 1892, and the company faced a deficit of $20,000 beside a stock loss of 40,000 coffee mills that were burned.

Another factory site was purchased, and the newly platted section of Freeport became known as the Arcade Addition. Here the company erected it offices and foundries. In 1893 L. L. Munn became a partner in the firm and its principal stockholder.

Products made by the Arcade Manufacturing Company were coffee mills, hinges, screen door hinges, stove pipe dampers, stove lid lifters, cork extractors, cork screws, and numerous small notions and novelties. A large number of children's toys were also manufactured, such as toy coffee mills, miniature trains, swings, doll carriages, etc. Cast iron Farm toys were probably not made before 1920, although other toys were.

In 1946 the Arcade business and buildings were purchased by the Rockwell Manufacturing Company of Buffalo, New York, and Arcade

became a division of that business. Rockwell continued to operate at the Arcade location until 1954. Modern Plating Corporation now occupies the premises.

Carter Tru-Scale

The Carter Tru-Scale line of farm toys began in 1946. That was the year that Carter ceased production of "spiders" for the Brearley Bathroom Scale Company. Mr. Joseph H. Carter made a decision to invest some $70,000.00 for dies and materials to manufacture farm toy models. Soon he teamed up with Mr. Fred Ertl and the Eska Company who marketed Carter's toys consisting mainly of implements, and Ertl's line of farm tractors.

In addition to manufacturing all the implements for John Deere and International, Carter manufactured truck models for I. H. as well as some implements for other farm machinery companies. One of Carter's innovations was a toy miniature chain saw that he developed for Textron's Homelite Division. He also patented the free steering type of toy tractor sold under the Tru-Scale logo.

In 1965 Carter ceased production of models for major machinery companies and marketed all his products under the Tru-Scale name. In 1970, the year before Carter sold out to the Ertl Company, he manufactured a million and a half dollars worth of models.

Mr. Carter is now retired and enjoying his favorite hobby, rock collecting.

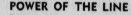

CARTER TRU ⊕ SCALE 1967

POWER OF THE LINE

Tractors and new products power Tru-Scale line to larger and larger sales. Composite up-to-date styling and the only complete line of implements makes Tru-Scale the line to buy and stock.

401 TRU-SCALE TRACTOR
Magic No-Scuff steering is just like power steering. Die cast metal and steel with poly tires. Red baked enamel and ivory wheels. Length 8½" x 4¾" x 4½". Individual visual cartons. 12 to shipping case. Weight 26 lbs.

890 TRU-SCALE DELUXE TRACTOR
Big rugged latest model tractor. Steering wheel turns front wheels. Tru-Scale quality with available attachments. Length 9" x 5½" x 5½". Packed in individual new visual carton. 6 per master. Weight 17 lbs.
890-1 Red   890-2 Green   890-3 Yellow

891 TRU-SCALE DELUXE FWD TRACTOR
A beast of a tractor for the big jobs. Simulated four wheel drive. Steers by steering wheel. Strong die cast metal and steel construction. Length 8½" x 5½" x 5½". Packed in individual new visual carton. 6 per master. Weight 20 lbs.
891-1 Red   891-2 Green   891-3 Yellow

701 TRACTOR
Smooth detailed die cast tractor, with rubber tires. Yellow with aluminum grill. Length 5½" x 3½" x 3½". Packed 12 to corrugated carton, 36 to shipper. Weight 23 lbs.

419 TRU-SCALE HAY RAKE
Pick up fingers drive hay to make windrows just like the real machine. Crank to adjust for height. Length 7½" x 7½" x 3". Packed 12 to master. Individual visual cartons. Weight 13 lbs.

420 TRU-SCALE SPREADER
New latest scale model spreader. Lever to shift to neutral gear. Red with white fenders and wheels with cleated rubber tires. Length 12¾" x 3½" x 3½". Individual cartons — 12 to shipping case. Weight 13½ lbs.

CARTER TRU-SCALE CO.
ROCKFORD, ILLINOIS 61101

Your Choice of These
FAMOUS McCORMICK-DEERING TOYS

These are perfect miniatures of the famous McCormick-Deering Tractor, the Farmall Tractor, McCormick-Deering Plow, McCormick-Deering Thresher, McCormick-Deering Spreader, and the International Truck.

Given with your own subscription or as a reward for securing subscriptions of your neighbors to Farm Mechanics Magazine.

McCORMICK-DEERING MANURE SPREADER—Made of cast iron, has hook on tongue for attaching to tractor; horses are removable. Length over all 15 inches; length of wagon box 9 inches; width 3⅝ inches; height 3 inches. Finished with red body, nickeled gears, blue gear guard and seat with a yellow tongue. Black horses trimmed in gold. Beaters revolve when spreader is pulled.

Given as a reward for securing two 3-year subscriptions to Farm Mechanics Magazine at the regular price of $1.00 each. Your own subscription cannot be included.

TOY INTERNATIONAL RED BABY DUMP TRUCK—Made of cast iron with rubber tire wheels; has red body with nickeled man, rachet crank and hoist which operates the dump body. Length 10¾ inches, 4½ inches high, 3½ inches wide.

Given as a reward for securing two 3-year subscriptions to Farm Mechanics at the regular price of $1.00 each. Your own subscription cannot be included.

TOY McCORMICK-DEERING THRESHER—9½ inches long; length with stacker extended 16½ inches; width 2⅞ inches; height 5¾ inches. Painted in green with nickeled wheels and stacker, red grain pipe, entire thresher trimmed in gold. Stacker extends and is movable. Grain pipe swings out. Hook on front axle for attaching to tractor.

This McCormick-Deering Thresher given as a reward for securing one 3-year subscription to Farm Mechanics at the regular price of $1.00. Your own subscription cannot be included.

TOY McCORMICK-DEERING TRACTOR—Made of cast iron with flexible axle. 7¼ inches long, 3¾ inches wide and 4¼ inches high. Painted in regular McCormick-Deering colors—Battleship Gray with Gold stripes and Red wheels; driver in polished metal.

Given with your own subscription to Farm Mechanics at the regular price of $1.00 for three years; 36 issues; or you can secure this toy by obtaining a 3-year subscription from your neighbor.

TOY McCORMICK-DEERING PLOW—Made of cast iron with hook on tongue for fastening to tractors, 7¾ inches long, 3⅝ inches wide and 2⅞ inches high. Finished in regular McCormick-Deering colors. Aluminum painted plow shares and discs with Red frame and Yellow wheels.

Given with your own subscription to Farm Mechanics at the regular price of $1.00 for three years; 36 issues; or you can obtain this toy by securing a 3-year subscription from your neighbor.

TOY FARMALL TRACTOR

TOY FARMALL TRACTOR—Made of cast iron and finished in regular McCormick-Deering colors. Gray body, red wheels and nickeled man. Length 6 inches, width 4⅞ inches, height 4⅝ inches.

Given with your own subscription to Farm Mechanics at the regular price of $1.00 for three years; 36 issues; or you can obtain this toy by securing a 3-year subscription from your neighbor.

Use This Blank to Secure Toys

FARM MECHANICS MAGAZINE,
407 South Dearborn Street, Chicago, Illinois.   Nov. 30

Gentlemen:

Send me by mail, postage prepaid, the McCormick-Deering Toy (write in name of toy)..............
....
and Farm Mechanics Magazine for three years (36 issues), for which I am enclosing the regular subscription price of $1.00 each

Send Toy to:

Name ....

Town ....

R. F. D. ....State.....................

Send Farm Mechanics to:

Name ....

Town ....

R. F. D. ....State.....................

Name ....

Town ....

R. F. D. ....State.....................

How to Claim Your Toys

Select the toy you want. Read carefully the instructions about what you have to do to get the toy you select.

Mail the full amount you collect for subscriptions with the request for toys. Write your name and address and the names of the subscribers you secure carefully so that there will be no doubt about the spelling of either the name or the town. You need not be a subscriber to Farm Mechanics to qualify for any of these toys. You can obtain as many toys as you want by securing the number of subscriptions necessary to qualify for each toy.

The coupon is for your convenience.

Your Choice of These
FAMOUS JOHN DEERE TOYS

THEY ARE PERFECT MINIATURES OF THE JOHN DEERE LINE OF FARM EQUIPMENT

HOW TO CLAIM YOUR TOYS—Select the toy you want. Read carefully the instructions about what you have to do to get the toy you select. Mail the full amount you collect for subscriptions with the request for toys. Write your name and address and the names of the subscribers you secure carefully so that there will be no doubt about the spelling of either the name or the town. You need not be a subscriber to Farm Mechanics to qualify for any of these toys. You can obtain as many toys as you want by securing the number of subscriptions necessary to qualify for each toy. The coupon below is for your convenience.

No. 1—TOY JOHN DEERE GAS ENGINE—Mounted on a four-wheel hand truck. Length 5½ inches, width 3 inches, height 3½ inches. Painted in full John Deere colors—Green trimmed with Gold lettering, pulley and fly wheel trimmed in Aluminum; front wheels turn under skid.

Given with your own subscription to Farm Mechanics at the regular price of $1.00 for three years; 36 issues.

No. 3—TOY JOHN DEERE TRACTOR—Length 6½ inches, width 4 inches, height 4 inches. Painted in full John Deere colors—Green with Gold lettering, Yellow wheels, Aluminum steering wheel, Nickeled fly wheel, pulley and driver.

Given as a reward for securing one 3-year subscription to Farm Mechanics at the regular price of $1.00 for three years; 36 issues. Your own subscription cannot be counted.

No. 2—TOY TEAM OF HORSES—Length 4½ inches, width 3¾ inches, height 4¾ inches. Painted in Black with Aluminum trim, furnished with a cotter pin for attaching horses to tongue of wagon, manure spreader or hayrack.

Given with your own subscription to Farm Mechanics at the regular price of $1.00 for three years; 36 issues.

No. 11—TOY JOHN DEERE COMBINE—Length 16 inches, width 12½ inches, height 8¼ inches. Painted in full John Deere colors—Aluminum, trimmed Green with Gold lettering, Yellow wheels, Green engine and reel. Cutter bar slides, header reel and straw spreader revolve when combine is pulled. Equipped with a wire hook for attaching to tractor.

Given as a reward for securing five 3-year subscriptions to Farm Mechanics magazine at the regular price of $1.00 for three years. Your own subscription cannot be counted.

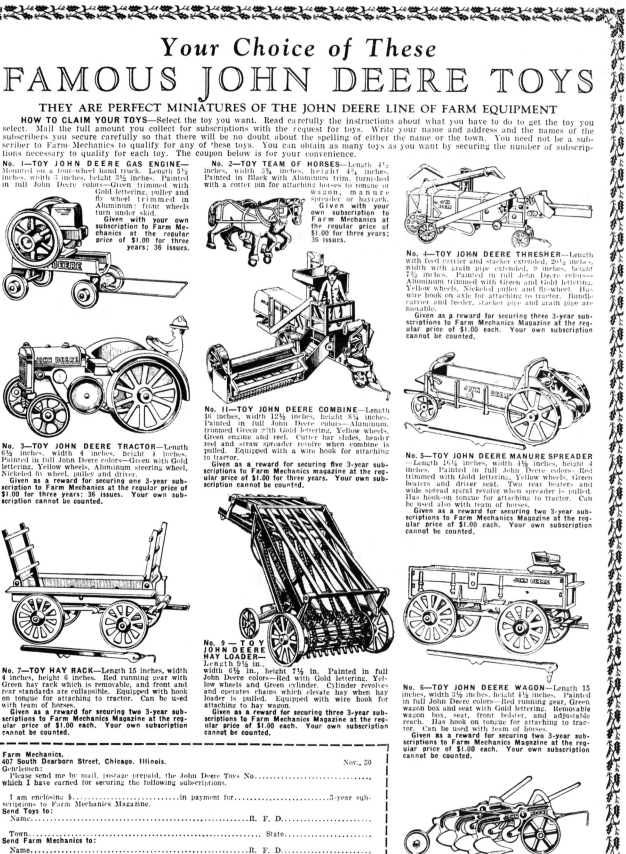

No. 7—TOY HAY RACK—Length 15 inches, width 4 inches, height 6 inches. Red running gear with Green hay rack which is removable, and front and rear standards are collapsible. Equipped with hook on tongue for attaching to tractor. Can be used with team of horses.

Given as a reward for securing two 3-year subscriptions to Farm Mechanics Magazine at the regular price of $1.00 each. Your own subscription cannot be counted.

No. 9—TOY JOHN DEERE HAY LOADER—Length 9½ in., width 6½ in., height 7½ in. Painted in full John Deere colors—Red with Gold lettering, Yellow wheels and Green cylinder. Cylinder revolves and operates chains which elevate hay when hay loader is pulled. Equipped with wire hook for attaching to hay wagon.

Given as a reward for securing three 3-year subscriptions to Farm Mechanics Magazine at the regular price of $1.00 each. Your own subscription cannot be counted.

No. 4—TOY JOHN DEERE THRESHER—Length with feed carrier and stacker extended, 20½ inches, width with grain pipe extended, 9 inches, height 7½ inches. Painted in full John Deere colors—Aluminum trimmed with Green and Gold lettering, Yellow wheels, Nickeled pulley and fly-wheel. Has wire hook on axle for attaching to tractor. Bundle carrier and feeder, stacker pipe and grain pipe are movable.

Given as a reward for securing three 3-year subscriptions to Farm Mechanics Magazine at the regular price of $1.00 each. Your own subscription cannot be counted.

No. 5—TOY JOHN DEERE MANURE SPREADER—Length 16¼ inches, width 4½ inches, height 4 inches. Painted in full John Deere colors—Red trimmed with Gold lettering, Yellow wheels, Green beaters and seat. Two rear beaters and wide spread spiral revolve when spreader is pulled. Has hook-on tongue for attaching to tractor. Can be used also with team of horses.

Given as a reward for securing two 3-year subscriptions to Farm Mechanics Magazine at the regular price of $1.00 each. Your own subscription cannot be counted.

No. 6—TOY JOHN DEERE WAGON—Length 15 inches, width 3½ inches, height 4½ inches. Painted in full John Deere colors—Red running gear, Green wagon box and driver seat with Gold lettering. Removable wagon box, seat, front bolster, and adjustable reach. Has hook on tongue for attaching to tractor. Can be used with team of horses.

Given as a reward for securing two 3-year subscriptions to Farm Mechanics Magazine at the regular price of $1.00 each. Your own subscription cannot be counted.

Farm Mechanics,
407 South Dearborn Street, Chicago, Illinois.   Nov., 30
Gentlemen:
Please send me by mail, postage prepaid, the John Deere Toys No.....................
which I have earned for securing the following subscriptions.

I am enclosing $.....................in payment for.....................3-year subscriptions to Farm Mechanics Magazine.
Send Toys to:
Name...R. F. D..........

Town.. State..........
Send Farm Mechanics to:
Name...R. F. D..........

Town.. State..........

Name...R. F. D..........

Town.. State..........

Name...R. F. D..........

Town.. State..........

No. 10—TOY JOHN DEERE TRACTOR PLOW—Length 10 inches, width 4¾ inches, height 3¾ inches. Painted in full John Deere colors—Green trimmed with Gold lettering, Yellow wheels, Aluminum Coulters, shares and hand hooks on levers. Equipped with a wire hook for attaching to tractor.

Given as a reward for securing one 3-year subscription to Farm Mechanics Magazine at the regular price of $1.00. Your own subscription can not be counted.

Assembly line operation.

Of the many toy manufacturers in the world over the past fifty years, only a few have survived. One of those surviving companies is The Ertl Company of Dyersville, Iowa; a manufacturer of farm and construction toys. The Ertl Company's history and growth is a remarkable success story.

Back in 1945, Fred Ertl, Sr., a molder for a Dubuque factory, was not working because of a strike. Unable to find another job and having the responsibility of supporting a wife and children, Ertl hit upon the idea of making toy cars, tractors and airplanes for sale in the community.

He melted metal in the furnace of his home and poured the metal into sand molds. His sons assembled the toys and his wife and the boys painted them.

The little business did so well that Ertl decided to make it a full-time project. In 1947 he moved the business from his home to a westside Dubuque building. Several additions to the original building followed.

When the company ran out of space again, the Ertls decided to build a new factory. The Dyersville Development Corporation convinced the Ertls that the eastern edge of Dyersville was the place to build.

Production began in Dyersville in July, 1959, with 50 employees and 16,000 square feet of space.

Eight years later, in December, 1967, the company became a subsidiary of the Victor Comptometer Corporation, guaranteeing security and growth for the company and international distribution of products: die-cast metal toy replicas of nationally know farm tractors, trucks and construction equipment, a line of "Ertlkins" pre-school toys and "Blueprint Replica" plastic model kits.

As Ertl grew, the necessity of having another type of toy to market along with their die-cast ones became evident. In February of 1974, Ertl acquired the "Structo" toy division of the King-Seeley Thermos Co. This opened a new field to Ertl in the toy market and "will," in the words of Fred, Jr., "become as big a part of our operation as the die-cast toys."

The old plant has expanded 10 times to its present size of 165,000 square feet. In the spring of 1975 a new 240,000 square feet plant opened a short distance away on a 40-acre plot. The combined capacity of the plants results in a daily production of over 20,000 models and an annual consumption of over 2,000,000 pounds of aluminum and 750,000 pounds of zinc. Ertl currently employs 650 people.

The division currently makes and markets more than 300 different products and all but a few are replicas.

Along with the trucks, tractors, wagons and plows, the toy line in-

Castings being electrostatically painted in a spray booth.

Ertl's first tractors.

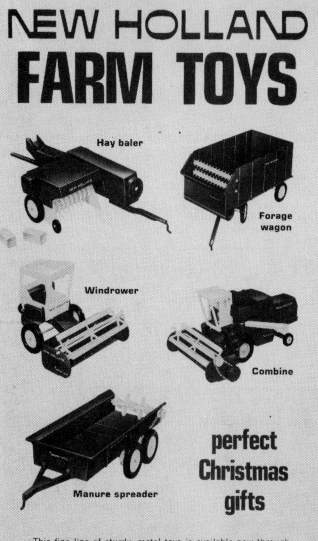

cludes crawler-loaders, chain saws, combines, rakes, spreaders, tandem discs, grain drills, lawn and garden or farm sets, hay balers, portable and auger elevators, animals, graders, gantry cranes, contractor sets, sport cars, boats, fire, rescue and emergency trucks, and bull dozers. Last but not least is their largest toy, the riding tractor—a toy which tots can ride like a tricycle.

Close working relationships with companies such as International Harvester, John Deere, Massey-Ferguson, Ford, Allis Chalmers and J. I. Case assures the consumers of not only great play value, but precise detail with each new model released.

Precise attention to detail is a major factor in the success of The Ertl Company. Their construction and farm models are accurately scaled to 1/12, 1/16, 1/25, 1/32 or 1/64 sizes. Only a few of the parts are not truly to scale so that additional play value is derived from them. In past years, the manufacturing of a typical farm tractor scale model required a total of over fifty individual parts with over forty separate assembly operations.

The Hubley Company (Gabriel)

Mr. John Hubley established a factory in 1894 to manufacture cast iron toys in quantity. Previously, for a short time, they had been produced in a carriage factory in Lancaster, Pennsylvania.

The Hubley Company made cars, cap pistols, fire engines, highway construction equipment, farm equipment, trucks, and a variety of other toys.

By 1940, cast iron toys rapidly became a thing of the past due to rising transportation cost, foreign competition and a general uncertainty of the future because of the pending war. By 1942, Hubley became almost one-hundred percent involved in the war effort, turning out more than 5,000,000 M-74 bomb fuses by the end of the war.

After the war, the baby boom produced a lucrative market for toy manufacturers. With many of the Japanese and German toy factories destroyed during the war, the need became even greater. Later during the Korean conflict, aluminum and steel prices increased in price while zinc decreased. This brought about a greater utilization of zinc in the toy industry. It was also easier to die-cast than some other materials. Shortly after, plastics really came into their own and were widely used in the toy industry.

Today Hubley is a part of Gabriel Industries, Inc. which manufactures the famous Gilbert Erector sets, Chemcraft sets, Gym Dandy home playgrounds and other toy lines.

Lansing Foundry Co. (Slik), Slik Toy and Lee Foundry

The Lansing Foundry Company began manufacturing the Slik Toy line of farm models about 1946 in Lansing, Iowa.

In 1956, Mr. Leon Hosch, superintendent of the foundry for the Lansing Company, bought out the foundry division and continued manufacturing the Slik Toy line, but now in New Albin, Iowa. The Lansing Company continues to manufacture buttons and other lines but has discontinued toy manufacture.

Mr. Hosch's present business, known as Lee Aluminum Foundry and Manufacturing Co., continues the Slik Line as well as Lee Toys. Another division known as Iowa Casting is part of his business.

During the late 1940s, the Lansing Company manufactured toy castings which were sold to Lincoln Toys of Canada in an unfinished form since the duty on unfinished products was much more favorable than finished. Two of the tractor models sold by Lincoln Toys but manufactured by Lansing were the small row-crop tractor with the MM on the sides (this represented the Minneapolis-Moline R tractor) and the Farmall M style tractor. Both were sold also as Slik Toys.

The Lansing Foundry Co. made the Olivers including the 70 model which was quite similar to the Arcade 1/16 Oliver 70 that was made in cast iron. Lansing's models were cast in aluminum only. Lansing also made the Minneapolis-Moline U row-crop tractor.

The Lee Foundry continued the small MM row crop as well as the wide front axle MM Jetstar and 445 models in 1/32 scale.

Underwood Engineering Co. (Fun-Ho)

The early history of this toy manufacturing company in New Zealand is quite sketchy due to a fire that destroyed most of the company's records in 1940.

Cast aluminum toys were first manufactured in 1941 as a sideline in a small non-ferrous foundry formed in 1940 to make components for a firm engaged in manufacture for the war. The first Fun-Ho models were mostly copies of cast iron toys including an Oliver Orchard tractor still offered on the toy list in 1975. Changes have been made in the production of wheels and other improvements and additions have been made over the many years of production. The company is so confident of the durability of their toys that they offer to take back old ones for refinishing.

In 1963 zinc alloy toys were introduced. The list has grown from the original nine to over thirty-five. Two miniature tractors are included among the Mobil Midgets. Many farm tractors and implements, as well as industrial equipment and cars and trucks are included in the regular line.

Mr. H. J. Underwood is the owner of Underwood Engineering Company, manufacturer of the Fun-Ho lines.

9914X HAYMASTER SET
Our finest set of quality toys. Set includes tractor (9824), hay loader (9820) mower (9819), and wagon (9817), all the equipment needed for haying. Assorted color combinations in display type set box. Packed one-half dozen per carton. Shipping weight 13 lbs.

9917X TRACTOR & WAGON SET
An outstanding combination, metal tractor (9824), and steel farm wagon (9817). Attractively boxed in display type carton. Packed one dozen per shipping carton, 16 lbs.

LANSING COMPANY INCORPORATED
Lansing, Iowa, U. S. A.

Boy AND TOYS Today!
MAN AND MACHINES
Tomorrow!

This little fellow says emphatically . . . "These are My Toys" . . .
It's natural for him to say this, and he's the capitalist of tomorrow . . .

He may decide to be tomorrow's farmer *or* clerk *or* business executive *or* mechanic *or* scientist or almost anything he wants to be. But that's not the most important thought right now . . .

This is . . .

He can be the capitalist of tomorrow because our *competitive enterprise* system says he will be free to work where and when he will, to save, to invest, to spend. He will choose his work for his own particular kind of satisfaction. He will save for his own self-interest, but that helps everybody. He may invest to his own advantage and that makes work for others. For there is now, *and must continue to be,* incentive! An incentive that is *realistic* . . . that *creates* . . . that helps produce more.

We at Minneapolis-Moline hope to do business with this young American. We hope to help him grow . . . and in turn his growth will help our growth . . . and our growth will again create more and better oppor-

tunities for more people.

This is the chain reaction of good living that the *competitive incentive* system brings out . . . And our *competitive enterprise* system is the *incentive system* . . . the American way . . . WHERE ability and the willingness to work and to produce, still earn a deserved dividend . . . WHERE competition stirs everyone to do his level best.

The world has never known a better system or plan of progress for all mankind.

Let's guard this way of life . . . our American Heritage. It's been mighty good to a lot of people—and if we take care of it, *the best is yet to come.* The most important thing about America is that it is the land of hope, of promise, and of progress for our children.

Our part in the American parade of progress is the manufacture of a complete line of Modern Farm Machines, Visionlined Tractors and Power Units for modern farming and industry.

Sold and Serviced by MM Dealers and Distributers Everywhere

MINNEAPOLIS-MOLINE
MINNEAPOLIS 1, MINNESOTA

MM MINNEAPOLIS-MOLINE MODERN MACHINERY

PHOTO: PETER DANT

"Just Like Dad's!" *By M. Estle Brown and Merle Betts*

Solve the toy problem with working models of your favorite brand of farm machinery.

Rᴇᴀʟɪsᴍ in toys is the trend today. And what can be more realistic to a farm boy than rugged, working models of the same equipment his dad uses. These toys are identical with their life-size counterparts right down to the maker's name and color. They include tractors, combines, manure spreaders, wagons, plows, rakes, harrows, balers and mowers. Many can be taken apart and reassembled over and over again. It's even possible to get repair parts. Some of the toys are plastic and some metal. Prices range from 60 cents for a plastic wagon to $3.75 for a metal combine with working parts. In most cases, you'll find these toys available from your regular farm-equipment dealer.

Junior feels he's doing his share when he pedals a riding-size tractor like this around the place. For ages three to eight. Price range is $20 to $30.

Country Gentleman *December 1954*

Companies Manufacturing Farm & Industrial Models & Countries

A.H.I.—Hong Kong (HK)
A.M.T. (Aluminum Model Toys)—USA
A.R. France—France (F)
Advanced Products—USA
Aero Manufacturing Co.—USA
Airfix—Great Britain (GB)
Alfinson—USA
Allemagne Plasty—W. Germany (D)
Alps Toys—Hong Kong (HK)
Aluminum Model Toys (A.M.T.)—USA
American Prescision—USA
Animated Toy—USA
Arcor—USA
Apthkya—U.S.S.R. (SU)
Arnold—W. Germany (D)
Arcade—USA
Arthur Hammer—W. Germany (D)
Auburn Rubber—USA
Aubrubber—USA
Atma—Brazil (BR)
Auguplas-Minicars—Spain (E)
Avon—USA
B—Japan (J)
BJW (Wardie)—Scotland (GB)
Barclay—USA
Banner Plastic—USA
Barr Rubber Products—USA
Benbros—Great Britain (GB)
Ben Bros.—Great Britain (GB)
Betaltin—W. Germany (D)
Bing—W. Germany (D)
Brio—Sweden (S)
Britains—Great Britain (GB)
Buby—Argentina (RA)
Budgie—Great Britain (GB)
Buddy-L—USA
Bukh—Columbia (CO)
Burkholder, Charles—USA
C.D.—France (F)
C.K.O.—U.S. Zone, W. Germany (D)
C.I.J.—France (F)
C.I.J. Europarc—France (F)
Carter (Tru-Scale)—USA
Chad Valley—Great Britain (GB)
Champion—USA
Charbens—Great Britain (GB)
Cherryca Phoenix (Taiseiya)—Japan (J)
Chico—Columbia (CO)
Clifford—Hong Kong (HK)
Copy Cat (Varney)—Great Britain (GB)
Cordeg (Universal)—Hong Kong (HK)
Corgi—Great Britain (GB)
Corgi Jr.—Great Britain & Hong Kong (GB & HK)
Cortland—USA
Cox, Charles—USA
Crescent—Great Britain (GB)
Cragston—Japan (J)
Cursor—W. Germany (D)
Daisy—USA & Canada (CDN)
D.C.M.T. Lonestar—Great Britain (GB)
Design Fabricators—USA
Densil Skinner—Great Britain (GB)
Diapet (Yonezawa)—Japan (J)
Dinky—Great Britain
Doepke—USA
Dol-Trac—USA

Dugu—Italy (I)
Eccles Brothers—USA
Ehersol, Alvin—USA
Eidai Grip Zechin—Japan (J)
Ertl (Eska Certl)—USA
Eska Certl—USA
Espewe—W. Germany (D)
Ezra Brooks—USA
Forma-Plast—Italy (I)
Fun-Ho (Underwood Engineering)—New Zealand (NZ)
Gabriel (Hubley)—USA
Gama—W. Germany (D)
Gamda—Israel (IS)
Gay Toys—USA
Gescha—W. Germany (D)
Grip (Eidai)—Japan (J)
Gray, Robert (Pioneers of Power)—USA
Guisval—Spain (E)
Hubley (Gabriel)—USA
Husky—Great Britain (GB)
Ideal—USA
Lmpy (Lone Star)—Great Britain (GB)
Irvin's Model Shop—USA
Jadali—France (F)
Joal—Spain (E)
JoHan—USA
Jordon Products—USA
Joustra—France (F)
Jue (Minimac)—Brazil (BR)
Jurgensen, Earl—USA
K—Japan (J)
Kaysun Plastics—USA
Kansas Toy—USA
Kelton—USA
Kenton—USA
The King Company—USA
L.B.Z.—U.S. Zone, W. Germany (D)
Killgore—USA
LaHotte St. Nicholas—France (F)
Lansing (Slik)—USA
Lee Toys (Slik)—USA
Lesney (Matchbox or Moko)—Great Britain (GB)
Lincoln Specialities Ltd.—Canada (CDN)
Lionel—USA
Lion Molberg—Netherlands (NL)
Lions Brothers—?
Lonestar (Impy)—Great Britain (GB)
Lucky—Hong Kong (HK)
M.P.C.—USA
M.S.—W. Germany (D)
M.W. Empire Made—Hong Kong (HK)
Majorette—France (F)
Major Models—New Zealand (NZ)
Marklin—W. Germany (D)
Marx—USA
Matchbox (Lesney or Moko)—Great Britain (GB)
Mercury Lit'l Toy—USA
Mercury—Italy (I)
Micromodels—New Zealand (NZ)
Mettoy—Great Britain (GB)
Minic Triang—Great Britain (GB)
Minimac (Jue)—Brazil (BR)
Midget Toys—France (F)
Mini-Auto—W. Germany (D)

PINT-SIZED SHADOW

Many a farmer has a pint-sized shadow that tags him all over the farm . . . shrilly repeats his pet words . . . dresses like a tiny twin. Like most little boys, he can't wait to grow up. The thing he wants most in the world is to be a farmer just like his dad.

Old-fashioned farming, with its never-ending toil, often shattered this childhood dream—sent the boy off to the city to work his fortune. Today, it's easier to keep him on the farm. Better crops and improved farming practices have boosted yields and farming profits. Modern John Deere power equipment has taken over much of the muscle work, and

chopped hours from the old dawn-to-dusk work day.

No wonder more and more farm boys are staying with the land—realizing a childhood ambition to follow in their fathers' footsteps. This is a good sign. These young farmers will hasten the fuller mechanization of our agriculture, pioneer new farming practices, and bolster vital food production.

Yes, labor-saving, profit-making farm equipment is helping to raise our most valuable crop—young Americans who love the land. In such hands the future of our agriculture, and of America, will be secure.

John Deere
MOLINE · ILLINOIS

Four-Wheel-Drive Tractor

Here's a scale model of the biggest John Deere Tractor . . . the tough one that gets through the wet and muddy places, over the humps and rough spots, pulling big implements on rolling land or on the level.

Two-unit, hinged design lets the toy make short turns. Oscillating front axle to step over bumps; deep-lugged rubber tires. Hitch for pulling other toys. The 4-Wheel-Drive Tractor is 13½ inches long. 8 inches high with simulated Roll-Gard cab. No. 510

Tractor-Disk Set

Four-Wheel-Drive Tractor and Level-Action™ Disk make a great big-job toy set. Disk frame of cast aluminum folds in middle to move through narrow, playtime "gates." Carrying wheels can be raised for travel, lowered for work. Plastic disk blades make tracks in loose dirt or sand. No. 586

9

Companies Manufacturing Farm & Industrial Models & Countries

Mini-Dinky—Great Britain (GB)
Mini Gama—W. Germany (D)
Miniluxe—France (F)
MOD AC—USA
Modelle Toys (Doepke)—USA
Moko (Lesney)—Great Britain (GB)
Monarch Plastic—USA
Morgan Milton Limited—India (IN)
N.Z.G.—W. Germany (D)
Nacoral—Spain (E)
Norev—France (F)
North & Judd—Sweden (S)
Old Time Toys—USA
P.M.I.—Union of South Africa (ZA)
Paya—Spain (E)
Peetzy Roco—Austria (A)
Peter Products Co.—USA
Peterson's Model Shop—USA
Pippin (Raphael Lipkin)—Great Britain (GB)
Pioneers of Power (Robert Gray)—USA
Pioneers of Power II (John & Kathy Gray)—USA
Politoys—Italy (I)
Processed Plastics Co.—USA
Product Miniature Co.—USA
Quiralu—France (F)·
R.W. Modelle (Ziss)—W. Germany (D)
Raphael Lipkin (Pippin)—Great Britain (GB)
Reindeer—Union of South Africa (ZA)
Revell—USA
Rex—W. Germany (D)
Rosko—Japan (J)
Ruehl Products—USA

Sankyo—Japan (J)
Saunders Swader—USA
Scale Craft—Great Britain (GB)
Scale Models (Dyersville Die-casting)—USA
Schuco—W. Germany (D)
Shinsei—Japan (J)
Siku—W. Germany (D)
Slik Toys (Lansing or Lee)—USA
Solido—France (F)
Souhrada, Charles—USA
Spot-On (Triang)—Ireland (IRL)
Structo—USA
Strombecker—USA
Sun Rubber—USA
T.C.O.—W. Germany (D)
T.N.—Japan (J)
Taiseiya (Cherryca Phoenix)—Japan (J)
Tiny Car—Brazil (BR)
Tekno—Denmark (DK)
Thomas Toys—USA
Tomica—Japan (J)
Tomte—Norway (N)
Tonka—USA
Tootsietoy—USA
Topping Models—USA
Triang (Spot-On)—Ireland (IRL)
Trol—Brazil (BR)
Tru-Scale (Carter)—USA
Tudor Rose—Great Britain (GB)
Umex—Austria (AU)
U.S.U.D.—Czechoslovakia (CS)
Underwood Engineering (Fun-Ho)—New

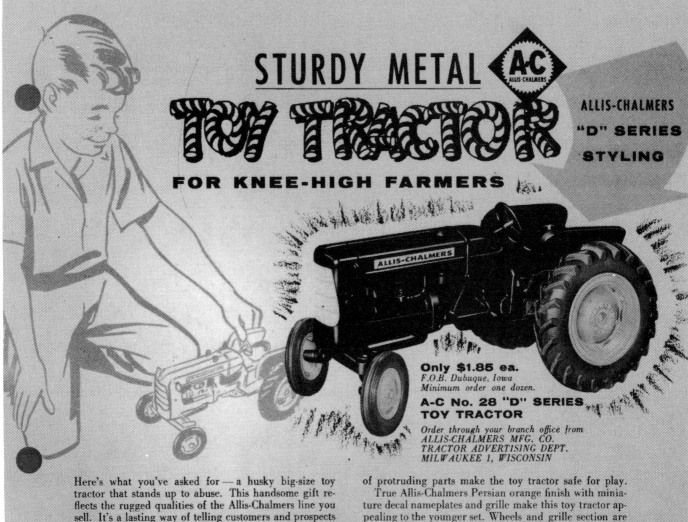

Refinishing Models

During the process of collecting farm models, collectors often discover that certain pieces are difficult to locate or if found, may be in a "played with" condition. Paint may be badly chipped, decals scratched or missing, wheels and other parts broken or missing. Many times the collector will restore one of these models in poor condition and add it to his collection to fill the vacant space on his shelf until a better model is found.

There are pro's and con's as to the "refinishing of models." Some collectors feel that restoring a model devalues the piece as a collectors item since it does lose some if its "originality." some even deplore the thought of refinishing any model. This feeling seems to be more common among those collectors whose interests are mainly in cast iron pieces.

I'm sure all collectors would agree that having pieces in their orginal condition—paint, decals, and without replacement parts is highly desirable.

Unfortunately, as the number of farm model collectors increase, it becomes increasingly more difficult for new collectors to find all the possible models in "mint" original condition.

To Refinish or Not to Refinish

At this point, the collector needs to decide if he would rather have "vacant" spots in his collection until a near mint piece is found, or refinish a damaged model to fill that slot (until) he does find a better replacement, or leave the damaged model in its present state to be added to the collection.

If the collector feels a good restoration would be the direction to go, there are several techniques that could be used to "dress up" tattered models.

The first step in refinishing is to decide if the decals are in good enough condition to be masked over and saved. The water transfer type decals are referred to here. Refinished models that do not have good identification decals look "bare" and lack eye appeal. A model in fair condition having a nearly complete decal set, may be more desirable in the "as is"condition than when repainted if replacement decals of the original type are not available.

Restored models having had the original decals masked over when repainted usually result in having a "blotched up" appearance due to some differences in the shades of the new paint vs. the aged paint that partly shows through the "brand name" decal. However, if replacement decals are not available and the model is greatly lacking paint, then masking over the original decal may be the best procedure.

If replacement decals are available, either excess ones obtained from the model manufacturer or replacement decals made by individuals, then complete stripping of paint and decals should be done.

Stripping

All paint and decals should be removed down to bare metal to obtain the most desirable refinished model. Painting over old paint results in indentations where ever the old paint may have been chipped.

Old decals and paint can be removed by 1. Carefully sanding or steel wooling, 2. Use of a chemical remover, or 3. Blast with a commercial type blasting cabinet. Before using one of the three methods, rubber tires or wheels should be removed. Heating rubber tires in hot water aids in removing them from their rims.

When using sand paper or steel wool, it is usually difficult to get into cracks and crevices. Sand paper may also remove some metal.

Chemical removers allow for easier removal of paint in cracks and crevices, however some may not like the "messy" handling of these materials.

Blasting cabinets provide quick, easy removal of paint and decals down to bare metal. It easily gets into cracks and crevices. When using a blasting machine only non-abrasive material such as microscopic glass beads should be used. Use of sand would wear away the metal along with the paint.

One limitation of blasting cabinets is their availability of use and high cost of purchase. Many industrial and mechanical courses offered in high schools and vocational-technical schools now have blasting cabinets to clean parts.

Repainting

True color implement paints give the best appearing refinish job. Purchase of pressurized spray cans of paint in the desired color of the model being repainted can be obtained from farm equipment dealers. Even though true implements colors are used, a shade difference will result due to the brighter color of the new paint vs. the darkened color of the aging paint on models in original condition.

The method of painting will affect the appearance of a finished model.

Spray painting will give a smooth, glossy finish. Pressurized spray cans or the newer and more costly hobby air brush may be used. Painting with a bristle brush usually results in a finish having unevenness or brush streaks.

"Dipping" may be considered as a possible means of applying new paint. Excessive drips of paint and thickness of finish may result in a loss of desirable appearance.

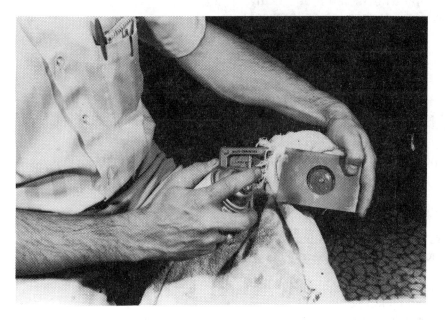

Masking

Those parts not intended to be painted may be masked off with masking tape or a liquid masking material available from some hobby shops. Paper or metal templates may also be used.

When using masking tape, be sure the edge of the tape is pressed down to make contact all along the edge preventing paint from seeping under the tape. A sharp razor blade or hobby carving knives may be used to trim along edges following desired contours.

Caution should be practiced when removing masking tape from a previously repainted area (such as a two tone refinishing job) to prevent lifting of the paint with the tape.

Liquid masker is applied with a brush, forming a rubber latex film upon drying which is peeled off after painting.

Templates made from paper, cardboard or thin metal may be used to shield those areas where spray paint is not desired. The center part of solid type wheels and tires can easily be spray painted by cutting a circle the desired size of wheel center to be painted. Spray painting gives a more original appearance and smoother, more even application of paint than brush-applied paint.

Those wheels having rubber tires over metal wheels can most neatly be refinished by removing the rubber tire. Care is needed to prevent damage to sides of the tire.

Decaling

Application of decals gives the model its realistic appearance. Decals of the correct color and style make the model "come alive."

The primary problem with decals is their availability. Original decals for older models usually cannot be obtained from the manufacturers. Decals for current or just out-of-production models sometimes can be purchased from the manufacturer.

Since decals are not always available, a few collectors have gone to great expense and time to have replacement decals made to match the original one as near as possible.

To make decals, one can hire a commercial company. This usually requires a minimum quantity of several hundred, usually more than one can use and sell to other collectors.

A collector may also hire professional services to have some of this technical work done such as the photography and making of the silk screen used to produce the decals. Once the silk screen is made, almost anyone can produce the decals.

The materials needed to print from a silk screen would include: the silk screen having the correct image for the decals being made, special water transfer type decal paper or "Mylar" type adhesive material used to print the decal image on and special decal paint or desired colors. These materials may be obtained from most silk screen printing businesses or they can order them from their supplier.

Several steps are needed to print the decal. First, a thin layer of clear material is applied to the paper to form a base. After drying, the decal image is applied and must be allowed to dry. If the decal is of a multi-color type, each color constitutes a separate printing stage which is followed by a drying period. After the final print is applied and dried, a coat of clear is again applied to protect the print and give the decal some "body." After the final clear coat dries, the decal is ready to be trimmed to size and applied.

Models made of cast iron and some of cast aluminium save time, and have raised letters to identify the "brand" name. These can easily be made to stand out by simply applying the proper color paint to the raised part of the letters with a small brush, rubber roller or a rubber blotter.

The Massey-Harris 44 by "Ruehl" has indented letters and numbers for the name and model number. These can easily be made to stand out by using your finger with some John Deere yellow paint and wipe across the indented name area, forcing the paint into the indented letters. Carefully wipe excess paint off from around the letters before it dries. This step should be done after the red has been sprayed and allowed to dry thoroughly. The result is a nearly original appearance.

Repairs and Replacement Parts

In addition to repainting and decaling, sometimes repairs are needed. Broken cast iron pieces may be brazed together, carefully, with the excess brazing ground or filed off; or epoxy glue does a neat holding job on both cast iron as well as pot metal and die-cast materials. Before using epoxy, a clean surface around the area to be mended is necessary. Used pieces such as front and rear wheels, steering wheel, drivers and etc. can often by obtained from another junk model.

A few individuals have available for sale various replacement parts such as drivers, wheels, bundle table and straw shoot for cast iron McCormack-Deering threshers and pressed steel seats. Often one or more of these persons has his wares available at various toy shows.

A special comment should be mentioned at this point. No one likes to have been the victim of a misrepresented purchase or trade. When a collector offers for sale or trade an item that has been altered in any way, such as a repaired break, repainted, replacement parts, it is fair and honest to inform the purchaser or person involved in the trade, of the alterations. Collecting is great fun and many new friends are made. However one can become quite upset when he learns he just traded some valuable piece in trade for something that he thought was genuine and later learned it had been altered. Honesty is always the best policy.

Modifying Models

Since the early days of the farm tractor, small scale replicas of the more popular makes and models of tractors have been made. Early models were made of cast iron while later ones were made of a variety of materials including; plastic, slush mold (pot metal), tin and the popular die-cast of aluminum and zinc primarily used in today's models. The die-cast models lend themselves best to modification. Even though there were many scale models of farm tractors from the past to the present as illustrated by this book, not every make and model of tractor made for farmers had a corresponding miniature model of it available.

Having a desire to fill in the gaps with models of tractors used by farmers, but not produced in miniature as a toy or scale model, collectors have used their own ingenuity and skills in making from scratch a complete new model or by making alterations to available models resulting in interesting variations of that model.

Modifications of models usually involve:
1. Changing from metal lug wheels to rubber tires.
2. Adding exhaust stacks and/or air cleaners.
3. Adding or removing cabs.
4. Making wide front axle version of a row-crop model.

Some collectors have also altered machinery models to represent another variation of that particular piece of equipment.

With the increasing number of farm model collectors, the future of modifying models can only be expected to increase as collectors with new ideas apply their skills to come up with interesting variations.

To acquaint the reader with some of the variations and modifications possible, the authors have selected the following pictures with a short explanation of how the variation was made.

Ertl John Deere D modification

Ertl John Deere D modification by Robert Condray

Ertl John Deere D modification by Earl Jurgenson

Ertl John Deere D modification by Earl Jurgenson

Robert Gray John Deere GP modification

Ertl John Deere 4020 modification

Ertl John Deere 4020 modification

Ertl John Deere 4020 modification

Ertl John Deere 4020 modification (notice the front mounted batteries)

Ertl John Deere 4020 modification (notice the rear weights and the "wheelie" bars)

John Deere 4430 modification (cab removed and four wheel drive wheels in front)

Arcade John Deere A modification (wide front axle)

Ertl John Deere 60 modification (wide front axle)

Farmall M Conversion

A John Deere with a wide front axle added

A trio of John Deeres with wide front axles added.

A John Deere A with levers added.

A John Deere with cab removed and four wheel drive added.

Ertl John Deere 730

Robert Gray McCormick W-9 converted to rubber

Carter Tru-Scale forage harvester modification (painted John Deere green & yellow) and Ertl John Deere Chuck Wagon modification (extensions).

William Hotz of Iowa has taken several models in the IH "66" series and done some paint trimming as well as adding the black strip decal making these variations that Ertl has not produced. Bill, a farmer, modifies these Ertl tractors during the winter when "things are slow." The real black strip IH "66" series was only in production for a short time before being replaced by the "68" series.

Modifications by the authors unless otherwise noted.

Making Models of Early Farm Tractors

Since all makes and models of farm tractors weren't produced in miniature form, a few talented collectors used their skills in making, from scratch, a complete new model of an earlier farm tractor. Usually only one of a kind is made for the collector's own collection. However, in a few cases the models were put into production and made available to other collectors. Examples of the latter would be Pioneers of Power (Robert Gray), Pioneers of Power II (John Gray), Irwin's Model Shop, Old Time Toys, Alvin Ebersol, Charles Souhrada and Earl Jergensen.

The interest in older models of farm tractors is evidenced by the requests to toy manufacturers such as the Ertl Company, to have reissued older models made several years ago. Also the interest in the Ertl John Deere model "D" and the early "Fordson" tractors tends to substantiate the interest in older models.

As the number of collectors increases, it may become more feasible for other collectors to offer their original models for mass distribution, provided reproduction costs can be recovered and a suitable margin earned.

Following are some selected examples of models made by various collectors that represent early farm tractors. These models are considered "originals" since they were not produced in miniature form during the period of time the tractor they represent was made and sold.

The models below are by Harry Van Woert.

Wooden Froelich

Wooden Waterloo Boy

Wooden Dain John Deere

Wooden Dain John Deere.

Some rather enterprising individuals have created a new sport. They have taken 1/16 scale Ertl tractor models and fitted them with either Cox .049 or .051 model airplane engines and have their own mini-tractor pulls.

It was just a few years ago that the 1/1 scale real tractor pulling contests became recognized as a serious sport. It is not uncommon for a farmer to invest $20,000 or more in a tractor, then add several modifications that produce more horsepower, and not use the tractor for any farmwork but only for pulling contests. The fever got so severe that these pullers organized themselves into an association for the promotion of the hobby. The National Tractor Pullers Association headquartders is located in Upper Sandusky, Ohio. They have individual state affiliations through-out most of the country.

Not to be outdone, the hobbyists formed their own mini-tractor pulling associations. Rules for mini-pulling are found at the end of this section.

Neither The Ertl Company nor the Cox Company builds mini-pulling tractors, although both support the hobby with trophies and prizes. American Model Design, 2603 South Glenwood, Springfield, Illinios 62704 or Mid-East Model Tractor Distributors, P. O. Box 267, Christiansburg, Ohio 45389 or P. O. Box 2524, Mansfield, Ohio 44906 can supply hobbyists with models ready to pull. Various components and a pulling sled can also be purchased for making a "home-made" mini-puller.

The pulling sled is designed to perform just as the real one does. It uses the weight transfer principle whereby the greater the distance pulled, the greater the weight transferred to the sled.

A micro-mini tractor pull can be held anywhere; indoors or outdoors, provided there is adequate room for the pulling table, work tables for the pullers and separate seating area for the spectators.

A contest can include all or any combination of the tractor weight classes. These classes are limited to stock classes of 3 pounds, 4 pounds, 5 pounds, and 6 pounds and also a 6 pound hot rod, if desired.

The materials needed for a contest are as follow:
    2 ft. X 16 ft. wood pulling ramp (3 ft. high is desired)
    scales
    weight transfer sled
    16 foot tape measure
    ice pick
    wood sticks
    carpenter's square
    hitch height gauge
    durameter (tire hardness gauge)
    entry forms (no., name, address, tractor, distance, place)
    distance recording forms (numbered according to entries)

In addition:
    tables and chairs for the pullers' area
    table at each ramp for starting tractors
    officials' table
    public address system

When entries are taken for each class, each tractor is consecutively numbered. This number is for identification only. The puller is given a numbered slip of paper for each class on which his distance is recorded. He presents this form to the ramp official at the time of his pull.

When the officials are ready, the pullers may begin starting their tractors. There is no designated pulling order. By using the starting table the pullers can regulate their pulling order. When the sled is free, whoever starts his tractor first can hook on and pull. The pulling order is simply regulated by the strarting of the tractors.

When the sled stops moving, it is picked and the distance measured. The distance is marked to the front center of the skid plate. To aid in measuring, it is advisable to nail the tape measure to the top edge of the ramp and then use the carpenter's square to read the distance where the sled was marked. This is then recorded on the puller's distance form which he then takes back to the official's table. At this time, the tractor is officially weighed and checked for measurements and if the tractor passes inspection, the distance is recorded. If something is not within the limits, the pull is disqualified.

Generally, a contest with one pulling ramp can be operated with four people.

One person to watch the guiding of the tractor and record the distance on the puller's form.

One person to watch the sled and mark the point where the sled stops. He also returns the sled for the next puller as the previous measurement is being taken.

One person must record the entries and then later records the pulled distances.

One person must officially weigh and measure each tractor after it pulls.

Anyone of these people can be the official judge of the contest, or another person can be appointed for this officiating. If a larger number of tractors are expected to be at the pull, then an additional four people would be necessary to operate a second ramp.

As in all tractor pulls, the winner of each class is determined by the greatest distance pulled. If more than one has a "pull through" then it is necessary to add additional weight and have a "pull off" to get a winner.

NATIONAL MICRO-MINI-TRACTOR PULLERS ASSOCIATION RULES AND REGULATIONS

SECTION I—GENERAL

1. All judges' decisions are final. Misconduct will cause disqualification.

2. All pit and track areas must contain only pullers and officials; no spectators.

3. Each tractor may be entered in more than one class, but only once in each class.

4. First puller of each class has option to pull over for his official pull pending his immediate decision. No pull overs in a pull-off.

5. Contestants will be allowed two attempts and four feet to start the sled. Official pull is when the skid plate crosses the four foot mark.

6. Pull measurements are to be taken from the front center of the skid plate. Full pulls are 15' on the standard 2' X 16' wooden track.

7. Excessive fuel spillage will be cleaned from the track between pulls with a towel as necessary.

8. Any part of the tractor tire or sled leaving the track during a pull will have the distance measured to that point.

9. Tractors are to be guided by touching only the front side of the tractor with a pencil or flat stick in a vertical position. Any pushing, battering or pulling of the tractor will cause the puller to be disqualified. The purpose is to guide the tractor in a straight line only. No zig-zagging or s-ing will be allowed.

10. Fuel open (use caution). Each puller is responsible for his own safety as well as spectators.

11. Hitch height must be no higher than 1-1/4" to top of drawbar. Hitch cannot be closer than 1-1/8" from back of hitch hole to center of rear axle. Hitch must be mounted solid to the tractor. Pulling point (hole) may not be more than 1/4" from back edge of the drawbar. Pulling point must be rigid, and parallel to the ground. Hitch must be made from 1/16" material thickness, minimum.

12. No radio controlled tractors will be allowed.

13. All pullers will be given a maximum of five (5) minutes time limit to have their tractor in operation from previous last pull of the class.

SECTION II—STOCK

1. All stock tractors must originate from farm tractor models 1/16th scale. They must keep their tractor-like appearance which includes seat, steering wheel, hood, etc. Each tractor must have stock wheel base plus or minus 1/4". Front end height can be altered but not radically such as inverted front axle.

2. Motor to be no larger than .051 reed valve only. No rotary valve, diesel, or electric allowed in stock class. No dual engine tractors in stock class.

3. Tractor must be pulled by no more than two (2) rear wheels. No duals, no track type tractors and all tires are to be ERTL, 1/16th scale with no additives, fillers or softeners of any kind. Tires may be turned down to pullers preference (tractor type tire to start). No exceptions. Tires may be cleaned with rubbing alcohol ONLY. Tires are subject to be checked by a durometer with a minimum reading of 62.

4. Weight classes will be set at 3#, 4#, 5# and 6# optional. Officials may run any combination of classes.

5. Front weights cannot extend further than 1 1/2" from frontmost part of the tractor including weight bracket. Rear weights cannot extend behind rear wheels. Any thing (weights, nuts, etc.) that falls off of the tractor during a pull will result in the pull being measured at that point. Weight must be distributed equally on the rear axle.

SECTION III—HOT ROD

1. Hot rod tractor models modified to pullers' plans. Maximum length may not exceed 12" from center of rear axle to the frontmost part of the tractor which includes front weights.

2. Tractor must be pulled by no more than 2 rear wheels. No duals, no four wheel drives, no chains and no track type tractors.

3. Tires may be of pullers design but may not have larger than 6" diameter. Tread design and width are open. No adhesive substances permitted such as: Liquid Tire Chain, Liquid Rosin, Glue and etc.

4. Weight classes will be set at 6#

5. Motor(s) may not exceed .20 total displacement. Puller must show proof of motor size prior to class entry.

6. Hot rod tractors must run seat and steering wheel.

Recently a class for four-wheel-drive micro-mini tractors was established.

As you'll read later about the three Ertl farm tractor kits, my first thoughts about them were, more or less, "what are you gonna do with a tractor?"

Ertl has brought out two very interesting kits of what is probably the most basic field implement, the plow. Don't turn your nose up at a kit of a farm plow. When I was quite young, my father's uncle was a Massey Harris dealer and I spent many days at his barn, which served as his garage. At that time most plows were two and three bottom, quite simple, with a beam and a hitch. This is not the case now. With the tremendous rise in horsepower for tractors, the use of diesel engines, etc., the modern day plows are far from being simple. As a matter of fact, the John Deere catalog shows no less than 18 different plows.

The two plow kits are the John Deere 2350-2450 Moldboard Plow and the International 700 Series Automatic Moldboard Plow. Even though the two kits appear to be the same because both are six bottom plows, cutting six furrows at the same time, they are really quite different. Not being a farmer nor an expert on plows, I wouldn't like to stick my neck out too far with technical information on either one of them. I do know that both are hydraulically controlled and in the following material I'll show you how to put the hydraulic hook-up on the tractors. Both have a steering mechanism to help make a shorter turn at the end of the field. The International, being an automatic, has the additional advantage that if a rock or other debris is hit, each individual moldboard will raise up until it is clear of the obstruction. Each of these plows is well suited to go with their respective tractors and will hook right up to them. As I mentioned before, the only thing that Ertl failed to supply in the tractor kits was hydraulic hook-up points. The addition of a plow behind one of these tractors makes an interesting display piece in itself and to quote from the Ertl instruction book, (yes, eight pages) "together the 4430 tractor and John Deere moldboard plow offer great diorama modeling possibilities." This is exactly what I have in mind for both of my units.

Both of these units are fairly easy to build and only require that you read the instructions *well*, work slowly and carefully, and make sure you have let the glue dry well before you go on to the next step. I think that I put about four to six hours work into each of them, starting in the evening and finishing them the next evening, including painting. Assembly was easy enough and no big problems were encountered during the building of either one. Ertl left enough material on the pins that require heat swaging but if you're not familiar with this process, I would suggest that you practice a little, as if you paint your model you will find that you have to work close to some painted surfaces. I use a trigger operated soldering iron with a very small flat point in it and usually heat it up good, then release the trigger and touch the pin until I think it has flared enough to make a nice snug fit. I then try the movement right away and if the two parts happen to have stuck slightly they will loosen right up. One hint on gluing the steering parts together on both of the kits—apply just a little Vasoline to the shaft itself and use just a minimum of a tube type of glue on outer pieces. This will minimize chances of getting all three parts stuck together.

As I stated, I painted both of the plows. For the International, I used Testor's No. 1103 Red and for the Deere, Testor's No. 1124 Green. Now I know that that green will cause a ripple of controversy. However, I've tried to stick with colors that are generally available to all model builders. I'll readily agree that the most realistic color would, of course, be John Deere touch-up. My problem here is availability. Besides being hard for most modelers to get, I've found that implement paint generally tends to be quite heavy and will cover detail. Actually, the Testor's green isn't all that far off and if you use an airbrush you could add either some darker green or black, and come up with a very close match. The wheels on the Deere were painted with Testor's yellow and on the International with Testor's metallic silver. Coulter units on both were painted gloss black with the spring done flat black. The plows themselves were brushed with flat black, but the supports or legs that they were glued to (part 20G on the Deere, 16R on the International) were done in the color of each unit, green or red. On the International, I painted the cylinders for the plows (part 11WT) flat white with a small amount of gloss white mixed in it. I did not feel that any paint was necessary on the tires as they look quite a bit like new rubber when assembled and mounted.

There are pieces of tubing supplied in the kits for hydraulic lines. It is a nice small diameter tubing that is quite flexible and looks right when it is installed. I made couplings on these lines with short pieces of 1/16th K&S tubing which slide into the outlets that I had installed on the tractors.

A Trio of 1/25th Workhorses

Ertl Kit No. 1H1466

When the first of these three rather unique kits arrived on the scene, I was rather dubious about just what could be done with a kit of a large farm tractor. However, after a close examination of the kit, the International 1466, and then building one, I found that I was really looking forward to the next two kits, the John Deere 4430 and the Massey Ferguson 1155, and had decided that maybe Ertl had something here after all. Now after building all three of the tractors, and plows for two of them, I'm convinced that here are some kits that are really fun to build, interesting when finished and a good change of pace.

Believe it or not, there is a lot of detail that can be added to any of the three. Combined with one of the plow kits, you could try your hand at a small diorama type of setting, complete with freshly turned furrows. You could build any of the three kits as open jobs, or with just a roll bar. However, most of the modern day farmers probably prefer the nice heated, air conditioned, sound proofed cab, with AM-FM radio and stereo eight track tape player, to being sun burned and frost bitten—but the possibilities are there.

As I said before, these kits make an interesting change of pace and one of their best points is their unbelievable ease of construction. Ertl has gone to great lengths to assure an easily assembled kit with easy to follow instructions. The molding of the kits is extremely good, almost without fault, except for some minor mold lines here and there and no working hinges for the cabs. This last problem we'll discuss later however. The really nice thing about these kits is that with a half decent paint job and some careful brush work on details you will have yourself a totally different, beautiful model of some extraordinary machinery with little or no hassel.

Let's take a look at each of these tractors. The first, the International 1466, is, according to IH, their biggest rubber-tired and what we'll call regular tractor. The kit at first appears to be larger than 1/25th scale but checks out quite accurately. Each individual color or tree is wrapped in its own poly bag in the kit and each kit contains a spec sheet of the real machine. Of interest to us (other manufacturers should note) is the fact that the points of the attachment of the parts to the trees are very small, thereby reducing to a minimum risky cutting and smoothing of the parts.

For painting this kit, all you will need are spray cans of red, white and Testor's silver. The silver is for the rear rims and Testor's is the only silver that dries to the proper sheen, chrome silver being too bright, and candy undercoat too gray. If necessary, you could use a flat aluminum and carefully brush the rims but the spray cans will do a better job in this instance.

Glue the rims together right away when you open the kit, and make sure you glue them well as they must be able to put up with quite a bit of pushing and pulling when putting the tires one. This is true of all three of these kits. A possibly helpful hint on the tires is to remove the sprues from the inside of them, then place them near, not on, but *near* a light bulb and leave them there until the bead, or part that holds the tire to the rim, gets warm and flexible. Then slide the cooler side of the tire over the rim first, followed by the warmed-up side. This heating will make the job of getting the tire on many times easier. I've used this method of installing these tires on all three of my tractors and it sure beats the struggle that you'll have if you don't heat them. At this same time, you should check the fit of the rims on the axle, as this fit is extremely tight on the International.

On this kit decide just how far you want to go with your detailing before you go past Step No. 3 of the instructions. When I got to this point I decided to remove all of the cast-on detail on the engine and replace it with various sizes of tubing and wire. If you go beyond this point you won't be able to remove many of the lines, etc., from the engine. The piece of literature that Ertl supplies with the kit is excellent for doing this and shows just where the different lines and hoses should go. Actually the hardest part of the job is removing the cast-on parts. Decide just what you want to remove and drill holes where the line or whatever goes into the block and then cut, file, or saw away the part you're removing. I've found that a No. 11 Exacto, a good sharp chisel point blade, and an assortment of jewelers files are all you need for this kind of work.

Since you have already drilled the holes, it is fairly easy to insert the wire in one of them and then bend it to shape, following the photos supplied in the kit. The trickiest job on this engine is, of course, the fuel injection lines from the distributor-type pump at the left front of block to the injection port area of the head, which is right beside the valve cover on the left side also. However, the kit photos show you, very clearly, how these lines run.

The injection pump can be made from a piece of the kit runner. If you don't think you can drill the six holes individually, then just drill one larger hole and glue six wires into it. In this instance I would recommend the use of a soft aluminum wire over anything else since these six lines follow a rather twisty path. You'll notice in the kit photos that the lines are paired into three groups after they leave the pump: one front pair, one center pair and one pair to the rear. As a last bit of detail here, you can use a small piece of thin styrene sheet, about 1/32nd of an inch by 1/16th of an inch and drill two holes toward the ends of each piece to use as separators, which

you can see in the photos also. Once you have the lines installed you can use a small drop of white glue to represent fittings.

When I got around to the front of the tractor, I decided I just had to open up the grille, and though this was a time-consuming job the results were worth it. It is not at all hard to do, but requires patience and a square or triangular jewelers file. I first drilled a hole through the center of each of the openings of the grille, using progressively larger drills, until the hole was almost as large as the opening was high. From here, it is a matter of *very carefully* filing the opening without actually touching the bars of the grille. After painting your basic red, the frame and bars should be painted with a good aluminum color, as should the frame and center part of the area around the head lights. The small area where the head lights are installed should be flat black. You'll see this on the front of the instruction book. If you have some very fine screen, you can attach a piece behind the grille since the real tractor appears to have a very fine mesh dust collector to keep things out of the radiator.

I mentioned earlier that painting should be all *red* on the outside of the tractor. Any of the parts that are cast in the rather yellowish-white in the kit really should be given a coat of gloss white. On the inside of the cab it becomes slightly more complicated, though still easy enough to do. The interior sides and window frame areas should also be gloss white. The boot area around the dash should be flat black. Control handles at the dash are flat silver with gloss black handles. Foot pedals are red, the steering wheel gloss black, and I've included a drawing showing the proper colors on the dash itself. The floor mats should be a very dark, flat gray and the padding on the inside of the fender wells, flat black. The seat cushions should be a semi-gloss black and the seat frame gloss black. The hydraulic control quadrant and the two handles beside the seat are red with black handles. On the roof of the cab, the frame around the head liner should be a dark gloss gray and the head liner on the center of the roof should be the same color gray, but flat. The air filter and air conditioning outlet grilles toward the front of the cab roof should be painted gloss black.

Something that really should have been included in the kits, but wasn't, is the hydraulic couplers. This is very important since a lot of modern farm equipment is operated hydraulically. This is an easy detail to add and it makes the plows look a lot more realistic when hooked up behind the tractor.

On the International, there are two couplers at the rear of the tractor. It is a very simple matter to make working couplings. I used K&S aluminum tubing but you could do the same job in a number of ways. It just happens that the tubing is the easiest. The K&S tubing is made so that one size fits into the next. The smallest size is 1/16th inch and can be crimped onto the end of a piece of wire which in turn can be inserted into the tubing that is supplied in the plow kits.

I eyeballed my hookups for size, and since they turned out looking good, I'll pass their dimensions on to you. They measure 1/4th inch high, 1/8th inch wide and 1/4th inch deep. I made mine by gluing two pieces of 1/16th inch thick plastruct sheet together, but anything you can come up with that will give you a block of that size will do nicely.

You'll need two of these blocks. Next, drill two holes in each one of your blocks. See photo 3, which will give you the best idea of the location of these hook-ups. After you drill these four holes, which should be 3/32nds of an inch in diameter and all the way through the block, you should be able to either force or slide a piece of 3/32nd inch tubing into the holes. When you have the two pieces in the block, you can cut them off carefully leaving only a very little bit of the tubing extending past the outer surface. Once you have the tubes all in place, round off the ends of the two blocks as you see them in the photo. Paint them and install them on the tractor, but make sure you have a good bond when you glue them as you only have a small part of their area to use.

A nice addition to any of the three tractor kits is a set of dual tires on the drivers. The only problem that will be encountered in doing so will be the use of two kits, as you'll need the tires, wheels and rims from a second kit. I much prefer the looks of the tractors with the dual wheels as it adds a look of massiveness to the model. On the IH model you must assemble the outside hub to the inside position of the rim, just reversed from the instructions, in order to get enough room on the axle to fit the second wheel on.

Ertl Kit No. 8005   John Deere 4430

Once again, the point must be raised that a fine looking model can be built from the kit without any modification at all. The 4430 is a good looking tractor with a modern design and good clean lines. The kit is molded in a good color, close to the actual John Deere green, but looks too plastic if not painted. Even though you could use actual John Deere touch-up paint, I chose to use a common hobby paint for plastic—Testor's No. 24 green. Even though not quite the right shade of green, it dries to just about the right color, is much easier to get than the touch-up paint and is a lot easier to apply. Since there is no primer necessary and you only need a coat to color the model, no detail is lost. Because it makes assembly much easier, it is better to build sub-assemblies and paint them, than assemble them after the paint has dried. On the John Deere, assemble steps 1, 2, 3, 8, and the tool boxes in 10, and then go on.

For more realism, on just a small part, pay attention to part No. 8CL in step 6. Careful examination will reveal that there is a frame around the two clear bowls. I first drilled a hole through the back part of this piece (near the engine) which would allow a piece of wire to be fitted through. The framework was painted green and the bowls were tinted with an amber color to represent fuel. Just small details like this will help to produce an outstanding model.

Next, fuel injector lines were added from the pump, part No. 63G, to the six indentations on the head using a fine wire. This is inserted in holes drilled in the top of the fuel pump, then neatly bent and cuved to fit into holes drilled approximately 3/4ths of the way up each of the indentations. These fuel lines are very neat on the real thing and should be done as neatly as possible on your model also. After the lines are on, a small touch of white glue will do nicely as fittings. Other than these fuel lines, the only other necessary lines are an oil line from the oil filter, part No. 29B, up and across the top of the engine to the small area between the exhaust and intake turbo's.

On the left side of the engine the only lines you need to add are the two air conditioning hoses. One of these hoses shows clearly in the left side view of the tractor on the front of the instruction booklet. Part No. 43B is the air conditioning compressor and you'll notice a small projection on the rear of it. Drill a hole that will accept a wire with insulation stripped off it. Look closely at the picture and try to match the size of your wire with something else that shows on the tractor. For instance, the hose is about the same diameter as the thickness of the steps. Drill another hole the same size in the back of the compressor, just below the projection. The upper hose can be installed from the projection back and curving down, and disappear into the frame rail under the cab. The second hose should curve under the compressor and run forward, once again disappearing under the radiator. Actually, it would run into the air conditioning condenser in front of the radiator.

Inside the cab just about everything in sight is flat black. I painted the control, part No. 44B, gloss black; the assembled control island, gloss black; dashboard face, flat black with gloss black instruments and steering wheel. On the roof inside, all of the air and heat controls and outlets, radio and tape deck are gloss black. On the outside, everything below the drip moulding to the bottom of the windows is flat black. Parts Nos. 23, 24, 25, 26, 27 and 28 are also flat black. Back on the inside, lever No. 18Y was painted yellow and all round knobs on the console are red; the others gloss black. The tail light lenses are, of course, red, and all of the roof marker lights and signals are amber. The fuel filler cap, the front one, should be red, the water filler, black. Windshield wiper arms should be flat aluminum.

The last and final addition to the John Deere is the hydraulic hookup points. The John Deere is slightly tougher, but not too bad. On the 4430 there are three outlets and luckily, they are easy to install. The accompanying drawing shows the shape of the outlets and the dimensions given are only for an idea of the proper size. Be careful that you don't make them larger though, as they will appear to be way off scale. Hold the size down as small as you can work with and they will look better. Use 3/32nds of an inch aluminum tubing and you'll have a working coupling.

On page four, step 5, of the instruction book, there is a good drawing of the rear of the tractor. Locate the point where the link for the hitch, Part No. 76G, is in the center. One outlet goes approximately 1/16th of an inch to the *left* of that point, and just slightly above. One outlet goes just slightly to the right of the center and in line with the left side outlet. The third outlet goes directly over the one on the right side. If you have a breather pipe in your spare parts box, you can glue it between the link mounts and the outlet on the left side. Check the drawing for location of all parts.

The Massey Ferguson seemed to be a slight step up from the IH and John Deere tractors, almost as if Ertl has been going through a learning process on the farm kits. The fit of the parts seemed to be a little better and the whole kit, though seemingly more complex, went together better than the two earlier kits had. At the time the model shown in the photographs was built, I'd had a rather hard time laying my hands on a piece of literature with color pictures of the real thing. As a result, I made a couple of mistakes when painting. I knew that the engine, main frame and front axle were a silver-gray but I didn't know that they were as dark as they are. Actually, you could use a gunmetal and then put a gloss coat of some sort over it and be fairly close. The roof of the cab should be painted a gloss white and the rest of the machine red. It's an easy matter to then pick out what should be painted flat black. Final decoration is easy because of the truly excellent decals that Ertl provides for all three of these kits.

As I mentioned earlier, this kit seemed to be more complete in detail. As a result, I only added fuel injection lines and air conditioning lines. The set-up for the air conditioning lines is basically the same as on the JD. Two hoses go into the back of the compressor, part No. 29S, which should be painted a semi-gloss black. One hose runs from the compressor to the top of the condenser in front of the radiator, the second to the fire wall and a third hose runs from the bottom of the condenser to the fire wall. Of course, this is rather simplified. These hoses would be clamped and hung along the top of the engine.

The fuel injection lines on the Massey, though out in the open more so than either the IH or JD, are a bit of work. There are eight of them on this engine. Use the smallest diameter wire you have available to you and a wire that will bend easily yet hold its shape. The fuel injection nozzles are easily spotted, looking almost like spark plugs, between the valve covers and the exhaust manifolds. If you look closely at the picture on the front of the instruction book, you will notice that the two *end* injector's fuel lines run around the outside of the valve cover, while the two center injector's fuel lines come through the opening between the two valve covers. The fuel injection pump is molded with eight fittings on the top and all that is required is to carefully drill a hole to take your size wire in each of these eight projections. It is easiest to do this if you first make sure that the tops of these projections are as flat as it is possible to make them. Either file them slightly or cut them slightly with your hobby knife. Taking your time and working carefully can't be over-stressed when doing work like this. The same procedure is used on the eight fuel injectors on the heads. Looking at the picture on the cover of the instruction book, you'll note these lines are very neatly bent and clamped, and this neatness should show on your model also. You'll find by starting at the pump (in the center of the engine), installing one wire at a time and working out to the nozzle on the head, that each wire can be bent and twisted as needed, finally being glued in the hole you drilled in the nozzle. Try not to mar or mangle the wire too much as it will detract from the appearance.

I decided since there really wasn't much detail to add to this tractor, I'd replace the molded plastic grille with a very fine screen. Brass screen, used to filter water from gasoline, is available in hardware stores and can be found in 4" x 6" and other size sheets. Get the finest you can locate. The first step is to remove the MF emblem from the molded grille, part No. 92B. Though I did this, it is *not* necessary to do it. Actually, it will look just as good if you cut out only the areas above and below the area where the headlights and emblem are. These areas were cut out very carefully using a jeweler's saw and the removed pieces were saved. I then located a piece of scrap plastic that was as thick as the indentations in the pieces cut out of the grille. A piece of the screen material was then cut to the proper width and roughly twice as long as the opening. The piece cut out of the grille was then clamped in a vise and the screen laid on top of it. Holding the screen so that it would remain stationary, the piece of plastic was used to press the screen down into the depressions of the original piece. After forming the screen, any final bending could be accomplished with a pair of long nosed pliers. (*Make sure* the screen material has a good close fit in the opening.) A very small bead of "five-minute epoxy" was laid in the opening and the screen then put in place, just as the epoxy started to set. By waiting until it had started to set there was less chance of forcing it out and into the screen. A little bit of care when doing something like this will pay off with a neat looking job. If you remove the emblem, after the grille piece is painted flat black the emblem can be epoxied back in place.

The interior is painted in the following manner. The seat, dash board, floor mats and inside of the fenders are all flat black. The steering wheel is gloss black. Part No. 103B, with the exception of the instrument panel, is the same color you painted the engine and frame. The inside of the cab is the same red as the outside with a flat black headliner. The instruments are touched with gloss black. All levers are touched up with flat aluminum and the knob of each one with gloss black. The large lever just to the right of the steering wheel, part no. 28S, has a red knob on it.

As I mentioned before, the detail on the MF seemed to be more complete than on the other two and this is true with regards to the hydraulic outlets. Check the bar across the top of part No. 24S. You'll notice there are four small raised discs on the bar. These are the outlets. The same method of making the couplings with aluminum tubing is used here, by simply drilling four holes where the raised discs are and gluing the short pieces of 3/32nds tubing in place.

The instruction book states you can use tape to make working hinges and it is recommended in all three of the tractor kits. I personally have never liked the tape hinges as they tend to become brittle in time, and break. I wanted to have working hinges though, so the nice interior detail could be shown off. All three of these kits can be hinged in the same manner so the following can be applied to all three. There are very small brass hinges on the market. The particular ones used on these tractors are HO railroad items. They are intended as barn door hinges but, as luck would have it, are almost exactly the same size as the cast-on fakes of the kits. On whatever cab you are working with, locate the molded-on hinge on both the cab itself and the door. Cut away the hinge and very carefully file an opening in both the door and the frame (cab) that the hinge will fit into easily. Be careful not to make this opening too deep or too large, but just a nice snug fit when the hinge is slid into it (see drawing). File the opening as neatly as possible. Slide the hinge into the opening and then bend the two sides of the hinge and glue or epoxy the hinge neatly on the inside. Some minor adjustment might be necessary after the glue or epoxy sets. The doors, you will find, are a very close fit. You will probably find that the two legs of the hinge will have to be shortened. This can be accomplished easily by carefully cutting the brass with a good sharp pair of cutters.

Another feature of all three of these kits are the clear windows. Ertl has done a really nice job on them and they have a raised molding around the window. With a little time and care, these moldings can be easily painted a flat black. Use a flat, pointed brush of whatever size you're most comfortable with. A brush with long bristles is best, as the bristles hold more paint and you can go farther with each "fill" of the brush. Rather than trying to use the point of the brush, lay the brush on its side at a slight angle and just pull it along slowly. Any paint that happens to get on the window itself can be erased by very carefully scraping it away with a sharp, clean toothpick. A little practice will help, and by the time you paint all the windows for the three tractors you should have the technique pretty well mastered. Good luck!

Special Custom made model tractor, plow and anhydrous ammonia
plowdown outfit—United states Steel, Fertilizer Division

Advantages to plowing down
(UsS) Anhydrous Ammonia

This unit is custom-designed for plow-down
application of anhydrous ammonia. Each
saddle tank holds up to 200 gallons of ammonia under pressure. This is enough to
supply the applicator-delivery system with
100 to 125 pounds of nitrogen per acre for
a half-day of continuous operation. Tanks
and valves are positioned for proper weight
distribution and safety in ammonia transfer
and application.

Plow and fertilize in one operation
Less soil compaction
Saves time and labor
Promotes decomposition of plant residue
Places nitrogen dee...
Provides ideal dist...
Easily assimilate...

4

This tiny model of an antique style steam traction engine is extremely well detailed. The tractor represents a 1925 Allchin 7-32, the 7 referring to the drawbar horsepower rating and the 32 referring to the pulley horsepower for belt work. The miniature was first made in 1955 by Lesney and was numbered Y-1 in its Models of Yesteryear series.

Allchin 7-32 Steam Traction Engine   ALL-1

Like ALL-1, this miniature represents the Allchin 7-32 traction engine. However, it was released in 1976 as a metal kit by ABS Models. The canopy is optional.

Allchin 7-32 Steam Traction Engine   ALL-2

One of Robert Gray's Pioneers of Power, this represents an old style standard Allis-Chalmers tractor and resembles the model A. Mr. Gray first made this "oldie" about 1971, first of cast aluminum, then later of Korloy, a material resembling cast iron in weight and texture. The real Allis-Chalmers A was made during the early 1930s.

Allis-Chalmers (A)   AC-2

Only three inches in length, this is one of many cast iron tractor models made by the Arcade Company of Freeport, Illinois during the 1930s. The driver is cast in with the halves of the tractor.

Allis-Chalmers (U) AC-3

Similar in design to the AC-3, this miniature tractor was also made by Arcade. However, it measures five inches in length and was available with a bottom dump earth hauler. It has the Allis-Chalmers name in raised letters along the sides whereas the smaller one does not.

Allis-Chalmers (U) AC-4

So called "row crop" tractors were designed to make cultivation of row crops such as corn easier. This is a model of a very early row crop tractor and represents the WC model of the Allis-Chalmers line. Rubber tires were introduced in the middle 1930s and made road travel between fields much easier. The driver is cast in with the tractor and the name appears in raised letters.

Allis-Chalmers (WC) AC-5

This miniature A-C tractor also represents the WC model but is made in a larger scale. It measures seven inches in length. The driver is cast separately and is nickle plated. A decal bearing the Allis-Chalmers name replaces the raised cast in letters.

Allis-Chalmers (WC)   AC-6

This tractor representing an Allis-Chalmers WC also was manufactured by a different toy company. It is almost the same size as AC-6, but has letters cast in along the sides of the hoods showing the Allis-Chalmers logo. It is red and has a separately cast, but painted driver.

Allis-Chalmers (WC)   AC-7

While not officially labeled as an Allis-Chalmers tractor, this rather inexpensive plastic model sold in variety stores is a rather good likeness of a model WC. The driver is molded in with the tractor. It was made by Auburn Rubber Company.

Allis-Chalmers (WC)   AC-8

Allis-Chalmers (C)   AC-9

Just before 1950 Allis-Chalmers introduced the model C, a small tractor designed primarily for row crop work. Many are still being used on farms today. The miniature pictured here was made to the 1/12 scale by American Precision Company. Because of its larger scale, this miniature appears to represent a larger tractor model when compared with some of the previous miniatures.

Allis-Chalmers (WD-45)   AC-10

This miniature represents one of the most popular tractors ever made by Allis-Chalmers. It is the model WD-45. Made of plastic, it was very well detailed and was available with a barge wagon, also made of plastic.

Allis-Chalmers D-Series   AC-11a & AC-11b

At one time this miniature tractor model was offered in kit form on a cereal box for one box top and fifty cents. It was also available as a completed model. This Strombecker model was quite detailed even down to the hand clutch which could be moved back and forth. It represented the D series of Allis-Chalmers tractors.

A rather scarce model, this plastic model of the Allis-Chalmers HD-5 Diesel crawler was made only for a short time around 1955 by the Product Miniature Company. It is orange in color as are most of the early A-C tractors. The tracks were made of rubber.

Allis-Chalmers HD-5 Diesel Crawler   AC-12

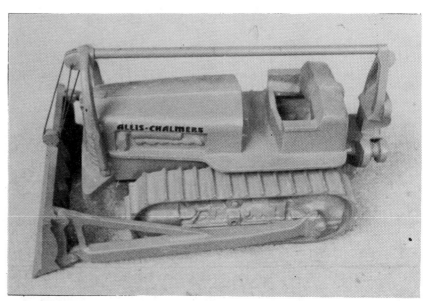

This miniature shows the "noggin knocker," an overhead pipe which carried the cable that lifts the front mounted BAKER blade. If the driver stood up too tall, he soon learned why the pipe was nicknamed "noggin knocker." This solid cast miniature was made as a paperweight and had solid cast tracks.

Allis-Chalmers HD-5 Crawler   AC-13

A later companion to AC-13, this model of the improved Allis-Chalmers HD-5 crawler with BAKER blade was solid cast as a miniature paperweight. The blade was lifted with side arms by hydraulic power supplied by a pump operating off the engine power. Both AC-13 and AC-14 were earlier models than the AC-12 model.

Allis-Chalmers HD-5 Crawler   AC-14

Photo Not Available
See Page 23
Photo On Right

One of the first three tractors made by the Ertl Company in Dubuque, Iowa—this row crop Allis-Chalmers tractor is quite similar to the Arcade AC-5 model shown previously. This one, however, is made of cast aluminum rather than cast iron. It was made for just a short time after World War II.

Allis-Chalmers (WC)   AC-15

Allis-Chalmers D-Series   AC-16a
Allis-Chalmers D-Series II   AC-16b

After a period of nearly fifteen years, Ertl began making models of Allis-Chalmers tractors beginning with this D-series in 1960. This one had "working" steering that would turn the wheels on its wide front end. This first variation can be identified by the black trim around the radiator grill and name on the sides of the hood.

A minor change in the grill decal and side trim makes this one representative of the D-Series II. The wheels are now an off-white color instead of orange.

Allis-Chalmers D-Series III   AC-16c

This replica of the Allis-Chalmers D-Series III finds the headlights missing and an identification decal running nearly the full length of the hood sides.

Designed to make chores around the lawn and garden easier, Allis-Chlmers introduced their B-110 tractor in 1967. The Ertl Company also introduced this miniature which even had "working" steering.

Using the same basic casting as the AC-17a, Ertl simply changed the decal and made this B-112 the updated version of Allis-Chalmers lawn and garden tractor. A scale model mower added underneath, a blade attached to the front and a trailer hooked to the rear made this a versatile miniature representing the real thing.

Allis-Chalmers B-110 Lawn & Garden Tractor   AC-17a
Allis-Chalmers B-112 Lawn & Garden Tractor   AC-17b

Extensive modification by Allis-Chalmers resulted in a more powerful and stylish "would-be" farmers' friend. This series of lawn and garden tractors was introduced in 1972 and Ertl quickly followed with release of the miniature shown here.

Allis-Chalmers Lawn & Garden Tractor   AC-18

The 1960s began a trend toward larger tractors to handle more acres in less time. One of Allis-Chalmers' entries included the 190 tractor. The first Ertl A-C 190 miniature was released in 1965 and had metal wheels while the very slight variation released in 1966 has plastic wheels. (AC-19b). A feature of the real tractor was the location of the fuel tank behind the driver's seat.

Allis-Chalmers 190   AC-19a

Allis-Chalmers 190XT   AC-20

A higher horsepowered model replaced the 190 in 1969 and was numbered 190XT. Ertl used basically the same casting but omitted the cross bars on the grill just as did Allis-Chalmers on the real tractor. The design of the fenders was changed also. The XT designated the addition of a "turbocharger" to obtain greater power. A. C. was one of the first manufacturers to add "trubos" to engines.

Allis-Chalmers 190XT Series III Landhandler   AC-21

With a name that would rival any thoroughbred, it became obvious that Allis-Chalmers, with its 190XT Series III Landhandler, was serious in its bid to share the market of larger tractors. Shown also was a greater concern for operator safety with the Roll Over Protection System (ROPS) and protection from the elements with the attached canopy. Larger flotation tires were added too, as shown on this Ertl model.

Allis-Chalmers Big Ace   AC-22

Competitive spirit is not limited to those engaged in athletics. For years farmers have enjoyed friendly competition in the form of horse or pony pulling contests. In recent years tractor pulling contests have become very popular. The miniature shown here is a modified Allis-Chalmers 190XT and has been transformed into a "Super Rod Pulling Tractor" by the Ertl Company.

In 1972 Allis-Chalmers introduced this flashy model labeled the 200. Notice the addition of front end weights, an exhaust stack and an air cleaner stack. The 200 replaced the 190 series in the A-C line.

Allis-Chalmers 200   AC-23a

A new design, a new color scheme and greater horsepower is in keeping with the "bigger and better" theme of the farm equipment business. This Ertl miniature model of the A-C 7030 was introduced in 1974 and is identical to the miniature 7040 introduced a year later, except for decal differences.

Allis-Chalmers 7030   AC-24a

Safety and comfort are combined in this Allis-Chalmers 7050 model. In addition to the cab, this model had more horsepower. Ertl used the same tractor casting but added the cab. Except for decals, it is virtually identical to the 7060 introduced a year later. Because of consumer safety regulations, some of these toy models came without the air cleaner stack on the front of the hood.

Allis-Chalmers 7050   AC-24c

Allis-Chalmers 12G Crawler-Loader   AC-25a

This is the first Ertl miniature crawler representing an Allis-Chalmers industrial tractor. First introduced in 1967, this one had rubber tracks and an operating loader. It was painted industrial yellow.

Fiat-Allis 12G-B Crawler-Loader   AC-25b

In 1975, Fiat of Italy bought a controlling interest in the Allis-Chalmers industrial line. At this time a decision was made to change the name to Fiat-Allis and the model number was changed to 12G-B. This Ertl miniature is identical to AC-25a.

Allis-Chalmers HD-16 Crawler with Blade   AC-26

This plastic scale model replica of a rather large Allis-Chalmers industrial crawler was used several years ago as a load for a Lionel flat freight railroad car. It represents the HD-16 crawler with bulldozer blade.

Allis-Chalmers Scraper Pan   AC-27

Articulated in the middle, this piece of industrial equipment was designed to load from the bottom, haul, then spread the load of dirt. The plastic miniature here is a companion to the A. C. HD-16 as the railroad-car load.

Allis-Chalmers 260 Scraper Pan   AC-29

Nearly six inches in length, this orange scaper pan model represents the Allis-Chalmers 260. It was made by Lesney of England, manufacturer of the famous Matchbox line of die-cast miniatures. The fine detail includes an operating bottom and articulated steering.

(Allis-Chalmers D-Series)   AC-30

This "toy" tractor has the familiar lines of the D series Allis Chalmers tractors. It is twelve inches long and made by Empire. The driver is molded into this plastic tractor.

Avery   AV-3, AV-2, & AV-1

This group of three Avery tractor models includes two originals and one reproduction. The one on the right is a Hubley first made around 1920. The Avery name is cast on the sides. The one in the center is reportedly an Arcade according to some publications, but the similarities to the Hubley are remarkable. The cast aluminum model on the left was made in the early 1960s by Peterson's Model Shop.

B. M. Volvo 800   BMV-1 or BMV-2

The manufacturer of the famous Volvo automobile also makes a farm tractor line. Here the line is represented by this miniature B. M. Volvo 800 tractor. This model has been marketed under two different manufacturing or marketing names, first Husky, then Corgi Junior. Both are practically identical and made to a very small 1/66 scale.

B. M. Volvo 800   BMV-3

A more recent model of the B. M. Volvo 800 is represented by this plastic toy miniature. Equipped with a protective cab, it measures nearly five inches in length.

Bates 40 Steel Mule   BAT-1

The Vindex Company of Belvidere, Illinois made several minatures representing models of less well known lines than John Deere, Case, etc. such as this Bates 40 Steel Mule crawler. This rare model was made around 1930 and solid cast with small roller wheels under the non-functioning tracks.

The similarities between this crawler and the Beauce tractor are more than just coincidental. Both shared the same body and came as a kit which could be converted from a wheel tractor to a tracked crawler tractor. The crawler, however, was known as a Flandre rather than the Beauce.

First made in 1948, this farm type wheel tractor is marked Solido on both sides. That is the name of the toy manufacturer, but it is modeled after the Beauce tractor. Many of the early toys coming from Europe had clockwork mechanisms and this French model is no exception. There were a variety of implements available to attach to the tractor.

Flandre   FLA-2
Beauce   BEA-1

One of the very few farm tractor models coming from the U. S. S. R. is this rather recent Belarus (Byalarus) 420, a four wheel drive tractor. Very well made with excellent detail, the miniature is manufactured of plastic. The cab is detachable and the front wheels can be steered. The model represented here was probably made in France by Minalux.

Belarus (Byalarus) Four-Wheel Drive   BEL-1

Blaw Knox Crawlers   BK-1 & BK-3

Most of the Dinky toy line is made of die-cast metal and this miniature Blaw Knox crawler is no exception. It first appeared in the Dinky catalog in 1948 and had a removable driver and rubber tracks. A later version had an attached blade. In 1951 this miniature Blaw Knox crawler was released. It was made of die-cast metal, to a 1/38 scale. In the early days of Lesney, before the introduction of the famous Matchbox line, the company name was Moke.

Blaw Knox Bulldozer   BK-2

This Dinky Blaw Knox toy model is the exception to the die-cast metal rule. It was manufactured of plastic, probably for the export market. It features a bulldozer blade and has the Dinky number 961 rather than 561 (BK-1).

Buffalo-Pitts Steam Traction Engine   BUF-1

The romance of the steam era is brought back to memory with this miniature of a Buffalo-Pitts steam traction engine. Although representing a turn-of-the-century machine, it was only in 1974 that Robert Gray of Iowa released this version. Almost nine inches long, Gray made this toy of the material called Korloy which has the same weight and similar characteristics as cast iron. Gray also had a model thresher and water wagon to accompany the tractor.

Buhk D-30 Diesel   BUH-1

From Columbia, South America comes this rather recent miniature Buhk D-30 Diesel utility tractor. Its number is 17 and is made by Chico Toys. The body and fenders are lime green while the hood and wheels are red.

Case (L)   CAS-1

Made of cast iron by the Vindex Company of Belvidere, Illinois around 1930, this rather rare model represents the Case Model L. This would be considered a standard style tractor, having non-adjustable wheel spacings. This toy had a chrome plated driver; the driver illustrated here is not the correct one.

Case (L)   CAS-2

During the late 1960s and early 1970s, a cast aluminum reproduction of the Vindex Case (L) was made by Old Time Toys in Illinois. It was gray with orange trim.

Tractors with the wheels together under the radiator are frequently referred to as "row crop" models because they were easy to operate when cultivating crops such as corn. This particular Case model was the DC and the miniature was made in plastic. The version with no fenders was made in 1950 while the second version with fenders came a year later.

Case (SD)   CAS-3a & 3b

A new era in stream-lining of farm tractors is evidenced in this model of a Case Casomatic (800). Not only was the styling very different, but the J. I. Case Company introduced a type of "automatic" transmission in this series of tractors. This miniature was made in the late 1950s by JoHan, famous for its 1/25 scale promotional model automobiles.

Case Casomatic (800)   CAS-4

The hood styling of this 1030 with the lights is the same as the Casomatic model, but that is where the similarities end. This model is what might be referred to as "wheatland" style of tractor is similar to the older "standard"'style. The fenders cover more of the rear wheels and operator's platform which cuts down on the dust problem. This miniature is the first Ertl model of a Case tractor. A similar version of the "930" was also made.

Case 1030 Comfort King   CAS-5b

A noticable difference between this tractor and CAS-5b the fender design. Instead of being round, these are flat on top. This miniature also has a front end weight.

Case 1030 Comfort King   CAS-6

In late 1969, J. I. Case Company introduced a new concept in operator comfort and safety in their "70" series of tractors. The model shown here is an Ertl and features a removable cab. The cab design features a built-in roll over protection frame.

Case 1070 Agri-King   CAS-7a

"Dual" are designed to provide better flotation and greater traction in soft ground. This also causes less soil compaction resulting in better root growth.

Case 1070 Agri-King/Duals   CAS-7b

Case 1070 Agri-King Demonstrator   CAS-7c

Specially painted to attract attention, this particular model represented a demonstrator model that each local dealer had enabling him to have farmers "try it out." At the end of the demonstration season, it was sold to some local farmer. This particular model called the Golden Harvester was used for only one season.

Case 1070 Demonstrator 451 Cubes   CAS-7d

Commonly referred to as the "BLACK KNIGHT," this style demonstrator replaced the earlier version. The name comes from the greater amount of black paint. It also had gold colored trim. Refinements included an increase in the cubic inch displacement of the engine, resulting in greater horse-power.

Case 1270 Agri-King   CAS-8a

This Ertl miniature represents the Case 1270 Agri-King tractor. The castings making up this miniature are slightly larger than those making up the other 1070s.

Case 1370 Agri-King 504 Turbo   CAS-8c

The horsepower race continues with more cubic-inch displacement in the engine of this 1972 model. It represents a Case 1370.

Case (1370) Agri-King   CAS-8d

In 1974, Tennaco Inc., the parent company of J. I. Case purchased controlling interest in David Brown Ltd. of England. At that time, the management decided to abandon the traditional beige and orange Case colors and blend the David Brown line into the Case line. Therefore, this model was painted "Power Red and White."

Case (1370) Agri-King/Cab   CAS-8e

Similar to 8d, this model has larger wheels and a safety cab added.

Case (1570) Agri-King Spirit of 76   CAS-8f

In commemoration of the Bicentennial of 1776, J. I. Case chose to celebrate with this specially painted red, white and blue "Spirit of 76" model. There were a light blue and dark blue variations. There were actually a limited number of real Case 1570 tractors issued as Spirit of 76s. Ertl also made a limited number of miniatures.

Case Steam Traction Roller   CAS-9b

This beautifully made antique style Case steam traction roller miniature model was manufactured and sold by at least three different model shops: White's, Peterson's and Irvin's, all at different times. The scale is 1/25. Available as a three piece set which also included a thresher and water wagon, it was representative of the earliest style of "tractor" made in the late 1800s and early 1900s.

Case-David Brown 995   CAS-10

After the merger of David Brown Ltd. and J. I. Case under the Tennaco organization, the Dinky toy company in England changed the paint scheme to match the real Case-David Brown counterparts. See also David Brown.

Case-David Brown 1412   CAS-11

A transitional model, this miniature representing the Case-David Brown 1412 was made in West Germany by NZG. The very precise 1/25 scale model features a roll over protection system and front end weights.

Case (1412)   CAS-12

Made also by NZG and quite similar to the CAS-11, this miniature has no roll over protection system or weight stack, nor does it have the David Brown name. The 1412 model number is missing as well.

Case (2670) Traction King   CAS-13

Representing the largest tractor in the Case line, this miniature is made to a relatively small 1/40 scale. The real tractor has both four-wheel drive and four-wheel steering. It can actually travel sideways.

Case 580C Construction-King   CAS-14

A 1976 miniature die-cast model of the Case 580C Construction King was made by NZG of West Germany. In addition to having a different color pattern, this miniature was made to a smaller scale than either CAS-18 or CAS-19.

Case (2670) Traction King in Lucite Prism   CAS-15

While hardly a toy model, this interesting specimen is solid-cast in gold color and enclosed in a clear lucite prism. Several different views of the tractor can be seen by looking at the prism from different angles. The entire prism only measures 2 1/2 inches in height.

Case Bulldozer   CAS-16

An industrial crawler from England, this model is made of die-cast metal by Lesney, manufacturer of the Matchbox line. This one is 2 1/2 inches long.

Case Bulldozer   CAS-17

Very similar in design to CAS-16, this Lesney Case miniature is built to a slightly larger scale. Measuring about an inch longer than CAS-16. It was used as a load on Matchbox King Size truck model.

Case 580 Construction-King   CAS-18

Departing a bit from strictly farm tractors, we find a tractor fitted with a backhoe and loader. Industrial yellow in color, this Case 580 Construction King was made of plastic in Hong Kong around 1967. It has excellent detail and many "working" features.

Case 580B Construction-King   CAS-19

Another industrial miniature made for J. I. Case, is this Case 580B Construction-King. This die-cast metal model was made by Gescha of West Germany and also had many "working" details.

Case 750 Bulldozer   CAS-20

This interesting miniature Case 750 crawler has a blade that moves up and down as it travels along, powered by batteries. It has rubber tracks and was made of plastic in approximately 1/16 scale by a company in Hong Kong.

Case-David Brown 1412   CAS-21a

The Corgi line of miniatures manufactured in Wales now has this 1/43 scale model of the Case-David Brown 1412. The model is red and white with a black roof on the cab. Notice the front end weights.

Case-David Brown 1412/J-F Combine   CAS-21b

A later variation of the Case-David Brown 1412 was this one having a J-F combine harvester. The unusual feature of this model is that the combine is mounted on the tractor rather than being towed behind. This feature permits use of the tractor engine to power the combine rather than having a separate engine.

The detail in this miniature 1929 Case CC is very good. This very limited issue, made by Earl Jergensen, is 1/16 scale. Notice the "non-functional" steering arm above the front wheel pedestal.

Case CC   CAS-22

Shown here are two of the 1/64 scale models made for Ertl in Asia. The one on the left is the Case Agri-King while the one on the right is the Massey-Ferguson 2800.

Case Agri-King   CAS-24 & Massey-Ferguson 2800   MF-39

Miniatures of tractors most frequently are intended to be toys but some were made as paperweights, display pieces, salesman's samples, etc. This one is actually a Ronson cigarette lighter. Made many years ago, it represented a Cletrac crawler tractor, a company that was absorbed by Oliver, now a part of the giant White Corporation. The picture was provided by model collectors, Graham and Michelle Miller of England.

Cletrac Crawler   CLE-1

Clark Bobcat M-700   CL-1a

A relatively new machine on farms is the four-wheel skid loader. This well detailed 1/24 die-cast miniature represents the Clark Bobcat M-700. It was made by Gescha of West Germany.

Clark Melroe Bobcat Loaders   CL-1a, CL-1b, CL-2

Shown here are three versions of the Clark Melroe Bobcat steer loaders. On the left is the first version made in 1975. The center one is a variation having a white ROPS instead of the black one. Both of these were made by Gescha of Germany. The loader on the right is a slightly smaller one numbered 533 rather than M-700 and made by Gama of Germany.

Cockshutt 30   COC-1

The striking similarities between this miniature and the Co-op E-3 (CO-1) are more than coincidental. After the co-op effort of the farmers faded, the Cockshutt Company of Belleview, Ohio began marketing the tractor under their own name, Cockshutt. This model represents the "30" model and was made by Advanced Products. It is red with yellow wheels.

A later version of the Cockshutt by Advanced Products is this one which probably represents the 540. This wide front end model is all tan rather than red and yellow like the previous model.

Cockshutt (540)   COC-2

Another Cockshutt 30 miniature was made in Canada by Lincoln Specialties. While it is the same scale as the Advanced Products model (COC-1), it has a wide front axle.

Cockshutt 30   COC-4

The Cockshutt Company moved its headquarters to Canada just before 1960. Later it became affiliated with the Oliver Corporation. In Canada the Oliver tractors were sold under the Cockshutt logo as is shown in this Cockshutt 1850 tractor. It is basically identical to the Oliver 1850 except that the color is tan and red rather than green and white. This miniature is an Ertl product.

Cockshutt 1850   COC-5a

A slightly later version of the Cockshutt 1850 is this red and white model. Except for color, it is identical to COC-5a.

Cockshutt 1850   COC-5b

The detail in this 1/16 plastic scale model Cockshutt is excellent. This model 30 features a wide front axle.

Cockshutt 30   COC-6

Described as a "Colorado" by an antique dealer from France, this model, minus its rubber tracks, was made in model form for only a few years. Quiralo, its manufacturer, was only in business for the years 1957 to 1959. It is made of a rather light aluminum-like material and has a clockwork mechanism.

"Colorado" Crawler   COL-1

An example of a product resulting from cooperative efforts of farmers is this Co-op tractor. The economic slowdown after World War II found farmers in the United States in difficult financial condition. Efforts to join together to form co-ops for buying and selling became widespread. This 1/16 scale model represents the Co-op E-3 tractor.

Co-op E-3   CO-1

Before the introduction of David Brown into the United States, and the eventual acquisition by the J. I. Case Company, the tractor line was quite different. In 1954 its model 25D was recreated in miniature by Densil Skinner of England. Shown here is a tremendously detailed miniature which was cast in many separate parts which could be disassembled and reassembled.

David Brown (25D)   DB-1

During the early 1960s, the David Brown tractor line was restyled and given a tri-color paint pattern consisting of a brown engine and transmission, red hood and fenders and yellow wheels. The model on the right is also a 990, but a later version. It is brown and white with a cab. The model in the rear is a Case-David Brown 995 and is red and white.

David Brown 990   DB-2, DB-3 & Case David Brown 995   CAS-1

David Brown Cropmaster   DB-4

The David Brown Cropmaster tractor shown here is an earlier model than the 25D (DB-1). Notice the excellent detail including the shield around the driver's platform. Also, an unusual feature of this Densil Skinner masterpiece is the double seat that provided a safe place for a passenger.

David Brown Cropmaster   DB-5

A model tractor? A puzzle? A prize in a corn flakes cereal box? The answer to all three questions is "yes." This six part, one and a half inch plastic miniature can be disassembled then reassembled. It is patterned after the David Brown Cropmaster tractor of the early 1950s.

Deutz 60BS   DE-2

This German Deutz 60BS miniature was made around 1962 by Schuco. It is a tiny 1/90 scale but has good detail.

Deutz, a German based company, now markets its products world wide. In the early 1960s, a toy model manufacturer made this plastic model of a Deutz DM-55. It is a kit and four inches long. This rather unusual model is considered to be quite rare even though it is of rather recent vintage. It was manufactured in Brazil by Trol.

Deutz   DM-55   DE-4

Deutz tractors have been famous for the air-cooled engines they are fitted with. Around 1970 the Ziss R. W. Modelle line produced an 06 Series Deutz tractor in this form. The colors are dark green hood and fenders, gray engine and transmission and orange seat. In 1975 the green color was lightened while the gray gave way to brown and the seat was changed to red. The 1/30 scale model is made of die-cast metal.

Deutz 06 Series   DE-5a   DE-5b

The addition of a comfortable cab and four wheel drive is shown in this 1976 model Deutz made by Gama of Germany. The cleated front tires indicate that engine power turns these as well as the rear tires for greater traction, especially in soft wet ground. (See also Intrac)

Deutz D100-06   DE-8

Deutz Intrac 2005   DE-9a

A rather new innovation in farm tractors is this German-made Intrac system by Deutz. The foreward control design of this tractor enables it to be used either with rear or front mounted implements, or a combination of both. For example, a hay rake could be mounted on the front while a baler could be towed from the rear. This five and a half inch model, made by Gama, was released in 1976. It is of four wheel drive design.

Deutz Intrac 2005 with Bed   DE-9b

The same Deutz Intrac with a "bed" on it.

Deutz Intrac 2005 with Semi-dump trailer   DE-9c

A Deutz Intrac with a heavy duty semi-mounted trailer.

Deutz Intrac 2005 with Sprayer Tank   DE-9d

This variation of the Deutz Intrac 2005 with a sprayer tank has a sprayer boom added by an inventive collector. Notice how it is attached to the front three-point-hitch.

Deutz   DE-10

These tiny 1/90 scale plastic miniature were made by Wiking of Germany. Identical except for color, these two miniature Deutz tractors were made in the 1950s. One is red with white wheels while the other is gray with white wheels.

Deutz   DE-11

Here are two later versions of the Deutz tractor by Wiking. Like the previous models, these are also made to the tiny 1/90 scale.

This Gama miniature of a Deutz represents a four-wheel-drive tractor. Notice the front weights.

Deutz   DE-12

Few miniature tractor models from Eastern Europe are made, but pictured here is one of the few. This nine inch long "tin" or stamped steel model was made in Hungary and represents a four wheel drive Dutra D-4K-B tractor. A rather unusual feature of this toy is the loop type hitch on the rear serves as a crank to wind the clockwork mechanism.

Dutra D-4K-B   DU-1

Another four-wheel drive tractor is this Eicher, made in West Germany. Made of die-cast metal and plastic to about a 1/20 scale, it features a lifting or foreward tilting hood permitting easier engine accesibility. It was made in model form by M. S.

Eicher Four Wheel Drive   EI-1

This miniature represents a rather interesting tractor, the Field Marshall. Manufactured in England, it had but a single, large cylinder and produced a unique sound when in operation. The miniature 1/43 model was first made in 1952 by Dinky of Great Britain. Notice the metal wheels and tires as well as the driver.

A slightly newer variation of the Field Marshall by Dinky has rubber tires on metal wheels. The driver has been recast and painted to create a more realistic image. There are several color and other minor variations of this Dinky model.

Field Marshall   FM-1a
Field Marshall   FM-1b

Small portable gasoline engines were quite popular on farms before rural electricity was available. These one to ten horsepower engines were used to power corn shellers, butter churns, cream separators, windmills for fanning grain, etc. The model on the left is an Arcade made about 1930 while the one on the right is a reproduction by Old Time Toys (Pioneer Tractor Works).

Fairbanks-Moorse Z Gasoline Engine   FMO-1 & 2

A companion model to the Fendt Geratrager is this four wheel drive Fendt. It, like the Geratrager is made by Cursor in the 1/43 scale. It has very good detail and is die-cast. The name "Veith" appears on the tires.

At first glance, one might think a mistake had been made with this "tractor." In place of an engine and hood up front, there is a bed for hauling items. This miniature Fendt Geratrager was made in Germany by Cursor. Obviously it was designed for specialized use and not an ordinary farm tractor.

Fendt Geratrager   FEN-3
Fendt Four Wheel Drive   FEN-4

Fendt Favoris Turbomatic by Cursor   FEN-6

Precise detail describes this Fendt Favoris Turbomatic made by Cursor of W. Germany. It features a four-wheel-drive and cab. The die-cast model is made to an accurate 1/43 scale.

Ferguson (30)   FER-1
Ferguson (30)   FER-2

After the famous hand-shake agreement between Henry Ford and Harry Ferguson ended, each marketed his tractor under his own name. This miniature, although not bearing the Ferguson name, is typical of several toy models patterned after the Ferguson 30 or 35 tractor. This one is made by Benbros of England and has a separately cast driver.

Very similar in design as FER-1, this Moko miniature is about one-half inch longer, measuring three and one-half inches. The driver was also cast separately, but a feature that differentiates the two is the movable front axle on this one. It was made in the early days of the Lesney Company by its forerunner, Moko.

Ferguson (30)   FER-3

A toy company in England famous for its extremely well detailed models was one called Chad Valley. Around 1955 it produced an excellent model of a Ferguson 30. The front wheels could be steered and the hood tilted foreward to reveal the engine details. An unusual feature was the color scheme. The tractor was painted green and had red wheels while most "Fergies" were all gray.

In the United States a company called Topping Models produced a very well detailed plastic model of the Ferguson 30. This one, made around 1954, even had a three point hitch and could be fitted with an accompanying disk plow. Disk plows were often preferred to conventional moldboard plows because of their superiority in covering surface trash such as corn stalks or grain stubble.

Ferguson (30)   FER-4

In 1948 another toy company in the United States called Advanced Products began making a model 30 Ferguson. It also had a three point hitch, but no accompanying implements. This 1/12 die-cast metal model had a fiber solid cast set of front wheels tires.

Ferguson (20)   FER-5

A 1/43 model of a Ferguson 30 was first made around 1954 by Tekno of Denmark. This little red model with tipping hood can be easily identified by the rather unofficial looking "Ferguson" name strip splashed across the top of the hood. It was also available with a set of miniature implements.

Ferguson (30)   FER-6

Ferguson 30   FER-8

Although plastic model kits became quite popular in the last decade, there were some around in the 1950s. This Airfix kit assembles into a Ferguson 30 model. The real model Ferguson 30 was numbered TE-30 (European) or TO-30 (American). This model is the TE-30.

Ferguson (30)   FER-10

From "down-under" New Zealand comes this likeness of a Ferguson 30. It is about four and a half inches in length. The colors are blue, silver and yellow.

Ferguson (35)   FER-11

Another model coming from New Zealand, and being made by Fun-Ho is this later model Ferguson 35. This rather upright version is solid red with black plastic wheels tires. It measures six and one-half inches in length.

Fiat Concorde 700-S   FIA-1

Although Fiat is famous for its production of automobiles, it also manufactures farm tractors and construction equipment. The home offices are in Italy but Fiat has manufacturing plants in many other countries. This well detailed replica, first made around 1971, was produced by the miniature model company Buby, of Argentina.

Fiat 550   FIA-2

This 1/30 scale model of the Fiat 550 tractor was made in 1966 by an Italian firm known as Dugu. The 550 was a very popular model in the Fiat line. This miniature even had the three point hitch as did the real tractor.

Fiat   FIA-3d

This miniature represents a Fiat before the restyling that resulted in the design of the 550. It was first built around 1961 and was available with a variety of attachments. The color is orange with white wheels.

Fiat 550   FIA-4a
Fiat 600   FIA-4b

Another Fiat 550 made to the 1/30 scale is this model manufactured by Ziss, R. W. Modelle. although quite similar in appearance to the FIA-2, it can be identified easily since it is considerably heavier. It was manufactured around 1970 in Germany.

A simple decal change results in this variation, a Fiat 600. In real life it would represent a slight increase in horsepower and other improvements. It was first released with the 600 logo in 1973.

Fiat 780   FIA-5a
Fiat 880DT Four Wheel Drive   FIA-5b

A relatively new firm making miniatures is one called Forma-Plast of Italy. This Fiat 780 is an excellent piece of die-casting with just a bit of plastic trim. It was released in 1976.

An interesting variation is created by modifying the front axle converting it to a four wheel drive. This 880DT model is also made by Forma-Plast of Italy. It has a three point hitch as does FIA-5a.

Fiat 40CA Crawler with bucket   FIA-6a

A rather tiny 1/60 scale model Fiat 40CA crawler was made by another German firm called Siku. This one has a bucket loader on it.

Fiat 40CA Crawler with blade   FIA-6b

Instead of a bucket, this Fiat 40CA has a blade. It was also made by Siku of Germany. Both FIA-6a and FIA-6b Fiat crawlers were used as part of a load for a Siku tractor-semi-trailer miniature.

Fiat FL-10 Crawler-loader   FIA-7a

This Fiat FL-10 crawler loader model has excellent casting detail. It was made in West Germany by Mini-Auto. Being scaled to 1/24, it is larger than any of the previous Fiat models. In 1975, Fiat bought a controlling interest in Allis-Chalmers construction division. A variation of this miniature carries the Fiat-Allis logo, representing the resulting merger.

Ford (9-N)　FOR-1

With the introduction of the 9-N model in 1939, Ford Motor Company changed the name of their tractor line from Fordson to simply, Ford. This 6 1/2 inch cast iron model was made by Arcade around 1940. One variation came with a three point hitch plow just as did the 1/1 scale tractor.

Ford (9-N) with Earth Hauler　FOR-2

This Arcade Ford tractor is quite similar to the FOR-1 except that it had a special hitch for the earth hauler that came with it. Like the FOR-1, it had a cast-in driver and a wide front end.

Ford (9-N) Row Crop　FOR-3

Although the Ford Tractor Division never marketed a 9-N in the tricycle or row crop style, the Arcade Company made a model of one. While not specifically labeled a Ford, the lines are unmistakably those of the 9-N Ford, except for the narrow front end. This model is just half the size of FOR-I and 2.

Ford (8-N)   FOR-4

In any collection of miniature farm tractor models, one thing that stands out is the size of the Ford tractors compared to others. The Fords are, for the most part, 1/12 scale while most others are a smaller 1/16 or less. An explanation advanced is that Ford did not want their tractor to be known as the "small" tractor. This plastic model was made in the early 1950s by Product Miniature Company.

Ford NAA Jubilee   FOR-5a

In 1953, the Ford Motor Company celebrated its 50th Anniversary. That year it introduced a new tractor model named the NAA or better known as the Jubilee model. This 1/12 plastic replica was alsomade by Product Miniature Company. It, like the 8-N, had the famous three point hitch and was available with a miniature Dearborn two bottom plow.

Ford 600   FOR-5b

A slight variation of the NAA is this model of the Ford 600. It replaced the NAA and began the numbering system which Ford still uses to identify its tractor models. Careful examination of this Product Miniature model will reveal headlights which are not on the Jubilee model.

Ford 900 Row Crop   FOR-6

Another Product Miniature 1/12 scale model is this Ford 900 row crop. Compared with the 600, the most obvious difference is the greater height and location of the front wheels directly under the radiator. This design made cultivation of row crops, such as corn and soybeans, much easier. This tractor was introduced by Ford in 1955.

Ford (8-N)   FOR-9

Made only from 1957 to 1959, this die-cast aluminum toy model tractor strongly resembles the Ford 8-N. It was made in France and was available with implements such as a mower, a rake or a wagon. The five inch long model with several color variations was made by Quiralu.

Ford (8-N)   FOR-10b
Ford (8-N) with Loader   FOR-10a

A second variation of the Tootsietoy Ford 8-N was without the loader. Instead of being all red, this one was red and silver (gray) more closely duplicating the paint pattern of the real Ford 8-N. The Tootsietoy Fords were available through variety stores, department stores and other retail outlets.

An American company, Doust, selling their products under the name Tootsietoy, produced several 1/32 scale models of Ford tractors. One variation came complete with a front end loader.

A slightly newer Tootsietoy Ford variation was this all red model representing the NAA or Jubilee model. Like the other 8-N models, it was of the utility design which is low to the ground and having a wide front axle.

Ford (NAA Jubilee)   FOR-11

Another Ford NAA Jubilee model strongly resembling the Tootsietoy (FOR-11) model is this DCMT Lonestar model produced in Great Britain. It had the name Farm King on the sides of the hoods and came with a two wheel Estate trailer.

Ford (NAA Jubilee) Farm King   FOR-12

This rather uncommon plastic Hubley miniature made to a 1/25 scale is quite an accurate representation of a Ford 8-N. It is all gray.

Ford (8-N)   FOR-13

Ford H (960)   FOR-14

For many years the Hubley Company of the United States produced replicas of Ford tractors. Another unusual model is this 1/10 scale model of, probably the 960 Ford. On the front it had an "H" rather than any number. It came as part of a set having a variety of implements and was red and gray in color.

Ford 961 Powermaster   FOR-15a

Made to a slightly smaller 1/12 scale, this Hubley model represented the Ford 961 Powermaster tractor. It had working steering and a three point hitch. The cross drawbar could be removed and mounted implements such as a plow, scraper blade or post hole digger could be mounted. This particular variation had a wide front axle.

Ford 961 Powermaster   FOR-15b

This model is the Ford 961 Powermaster and the major difference is the row crop front end design. It, like FOR-15a, is red and gray.

The third variation of the Ford 961 model is this Select-O-Speed. On the real tractor, this was the model that was used to introduce a new type of transmission. On this Hubley miniature, the conventional gear shift located on the top of the transmission housing was replaced with a lever on the dash. The new transmission permitted shifting of gears without use of a clutch.

Ford (961) Select-O-Speed   FOR-15c

A slightly newer Ford model is this 4000. Although this particular miniature did not have the 4000 decal, it did have the general lines of that model. This one colored red and gray was sold through regular stores rather than through Ford Tractor dealers.

Ford (4000)   FOR-16a

This Ford 4000 carries not only the 4000 decal, but also some other differences. It has a wide front axle and has a new color pattern. The red and gray is now blue and gray. Like the other Hubley 1/12 models, this one has real steering and a three point hitch.

Ford 4000   FOR-16b

Ford 6000   FOR-17a

"The largest Ford tractor ever made," was the claim when the 6000 was introduced. This Hubley Ford miniature had not only real steering, but even a tilting steering wheel. On the real tractor, this feature made it easier for the operator to stand and stretch his legs while the tractor was still in operation. This first 6000 was red and gray.

Ford 6000   FOR-17b

A year later in 1964, Ford changed from the red and gray color scheme to the blue and gray. This change is reflected in this Hubley model which also has the three point hitch. The exhaust stacks on both Ford 6000's are chrome plated.

Ford Commander 6000   FOR-18a

More power for better farming was probably the idea behind this improved Ford 6000 tractor. It even had the name Commander added to its identification logo. On the scale model, the chromed exhaust is replaced by a plastic one and an air cleaner is added.

Ford Commander 6000   FOR-18b

The Commander 6000 tractor model was produced by Hubley for many years. After Hubley was made a part of Gabriel Industries, the plastic exhaust stack and air cleaner were deleted.

Ford 4000 with No. 21 Forklift   FOR-20

A battery powered Ford model in the 1/12 scale is this 4000 Industrial with a No. 21 rear mounted forklift. The remote control unit could be used to steer the tractor as well as make it go forward and backward. The fork lift is also battery powered in the miniature tractor.

Ford 4000 with Loader & Backhoe   FOR-21

Another Ford 4000 variation is this industrial tractor with a loader and backhoe. This Cragston model is battery powered and the attachments are functional as well. Backhoe is missing.

Ford 4000HD with Loader & Backhoe   FOR-22

Very similar to FOR-21, this miniature is numbered the Ford 4000HD. It too has the loader and backhoe.

Ford (4000)   FOR-23a & 23b

Lesney of Great Britain has produced many beautifully detailed die-cast metal models for years. These two miniature tractor models are no exceptions. The Ford miniatures are identical except for color. The all-blue model represent the farm tractor while the blue and yellow one is the industrial version. Lesney made a model of a Ford semi-tractor trailer with a load of three of these tractors.

Ford (4000)   FOR-24

This 1/56 scale model of a Ford tractor is quite similar in size to the Lesney Fords (FOR-23). The color is yellow with green trim. It has a separately-molded driver. This miniature was made in Spain by Gusival.

Ford 4000   FOR-25

In 1965 the Ertl Company released its first Ford miniature, this Ford 4000. Like the Hubley Fords before it, the Ford 4000 was made to the larger 1/12 scale. This tractor had a two piece sectional grill and a three point hitch.

Ford 4000   FOR-26a

In 1968 the Ford Motor Company restyled its tractor line slightly resulting in a one piece grill, rather than the sectional grill. Otherwise the tractors remained almost the same.

Ford 4400 Industrial   FOR-26b

The industrial version of the Ford 4000 is this yellow Ford 4400. Except for color, this tractor model is identical to the later 4000 (FOR-26a).

Ford 4600   FOR-27

The 1976 Ford tractor line is again restyled and this Ertl 1/12 miniature reflects this change in design. Notice the change from round to flat fenders.

Ford 5550 Industrial   FOR-28a

In 1972, Ertl released the Ford 5550 Industrial tractor with loader and backhoe. The tractor is a new design and not merely a modified farm tractor as is the Ford 4400 (FOR-26b). This tractor is constructed to the 1/12 scale.

Ford 8000   FOR-29a

The year 1968 finds the beginning of a new, larger Ertl Ford model, the 8000. This first variation has a three point hitch and the word "Ford" and number "8000" are quite small on the identifying decal. It is built to the larger 1/12 scale.

Ford 8000   FOR-29b

The decal is changed and the three point hitch is omitted on this 1970 version of the Ford 8000.

Ford 8600   FOR-29c

In 1973, Ford renumbered its tractor series. This Ertl miniature Ford is the 8600. In real life, it would represent an increase in horsepower as well as some other improvements.

Ford 9600 with Cab & Duals   FOR-29d

The Ford 9600 with a cab and dual wheels made to the 1/12 scale almost requires a life size garage to house it. This Ertl model is basically the same as the 8600 (FOR-29c) except for the cab and duals.

Ford 145 Hydro Lawn & Garden   FOR-30

Ford Motor Company also manufactures lawn and garden tractors. This 1/12 scale model 145 Hydro was made by Ertl. The Hydro refers to hydrostatic drive, a rather recent innovation that uses a hydraulic drive mechanism rather than the conventional gear drive.

Ford (4000)   FOR-31

This miniature Ford 4000 tractor was made by Gama of West Germany and came with a wagon. Made of die-cast metal and plastic, it also had a battery operated remote power unit. It is seven inches long, not including the wagon.

Ford (4000)   FOR-34

Careful examination of this 1/43 scale model Ford 4000 reveals unusual rear tire treads. rather than the usual bar type treads, it has button type, or turf, treads. These are popular on lawns since they do not cut up the surface as much as the conventional treads. This red, yellow and green miniature was made by Mini-Gama, also of West Germany.

While not specifically labeled Ford or 4000, this little tractor has that style. Measuring less than three inches in length, it is a solid cast model except for axles and wheels. It was made in New Zealand.

Very similar in design, but just about one and a half inches longer, this miniature is also made in New Zealand by Fun-Ho. The driver is cast in with the tractor. Both have pure white plastic tires.

Ford (4000) FOR-35
Ford (4000) FOR-36

Britains Limited, famous for its miniature soldiers, also made many farm models including this Ford 5000 Super Major. This particular model is a transitional model between the Fordson and the Ford lines made in Great Britain. It was available with a goose-neck Shawnee Puhl dump trailer. Notice the early style cab.

Ford 5000 Super Major FOR-38a

A slightly later Ford 5000 is shown here with a roomier, square type cab. All of the Britains' Ford 5000's had a lifting hitch on the rear for mounted equipment.

Ford 5000 with Later Cab FOR-38b

This Ford 5000 without a cab was made prior to the end of 1971. It was that year that a law in England went into effect requiring farm tractors to be equipped with a safety rollover protection system or a cab. This law did not affect tractors manufacture prior to 1971.

Ford 5000   FOR-38c

This Ford 5000, also made by Britains Limited, is different in several ways. It is built to a smaller 1/43 scale and, instead of being die-cast like the others, is a snap together plastic kit. It was made only a short time.

Ford 5000   FOR-39

A larger Ford tractor is represented in this 6600 model. It was released in 1976 and is the 1/32 scale like the other die-cast 5000 models by Britains.

Ford 6600   FOR-40

Another series of Ford tractors was manufactured by Corgi of Wales. Their line of toys is made to a smaller 1/43 scale and of die-cast metal. This Ford 5000 Super Major was first released by Corgi in 1966. It had a lifting hitch on the rear to attach mounted equipment, such as a plow.

Ford 5000 Super Major   FOR-41a

In 1970, Corgi added a rear trencher to its Ford 5000 Super Major resulting in the combination shown here. A trencher of this type would be used to dig ditches and other farm and construction digging jobs.

Ford 5000 Super Major with Rear Trencher   FOR-41b

Simply by redesigning the trencher unit and mounting it on the side of the tractor, another interesting variation is created. A trenching unit of this design would be quite useful for cleaning out ditches along a highway where it would not be possible to drive over the ditch. This is also a 1/43 Corgi miniature.

Ford 5000 Super Major with Side Trencher   FOR-41c

113

Ford 5000   FOR-42

The popular line of Ford tractors is manufactured in several countries. Miniature models are also manufactured in several countries. This one was made in red or blue color variations by Majorette of France. The scale is 1/55.

Ford (4000)   FOR-44

In the United States, a rather inexpensive line of plastic toys was made by Gay Toys. One of their creations this replica of a Ford 4000. It came in a variety of colors and was also available with a front end loader.

Ford (145) Lawn & Garden Tractor   FOR-45

A Gay Toy product was this Ford Lawn & Garden tractor. It probable represents the 145 LGT. This plastic model was made in the United States.

Ford 8600 with Cab   FOR-46

This eight and a half inch long model of a Ford 8600 was made by Processed Plastics Products Company, also of the United States. It came in a variety of colors and with some decal variations. The engine was made of "chromed" plastic.

Ford 4550 Industrial with Loader & Backhoe   FOR-47

This very well detailed die-cast miniature tractor is a Ford 4550 industrial loader and backhoe. It was first released in 1972 by the West German firm NZG.

Ford (9-N) with Plow   FOR-48

Information on this model is rather sketchy. However, it appears very similar to the cast iron Arcade Ford (9-N) (FOR-1). This 1/12 scale miniature is made of cast aluminum and has an attached two bottom plow complete with a lifting lever.

Ford (4000)   FOR-49

This rather crude model is representative of the Ford 4000. Made by Tomte in Norway, it has its driver molded in with the body of the tractor.

Ford 7700   FOR-50

Released in 1977, this large 1/12 Ertl model represents the Ford 7700. It is finished in blue with white trim. Notice the safety cab and the front weights.

Ford 9700   FOR-51

Also released in 1977 by Ertl, this model represents Ford's top of the line two wheel drive tractor the 9700. The miniature is identical to FOR-50 except for decals and dual rear wheels.

This miniature tractor resembling the Ford NAA or Golden Jubilee, made of plastic, is five and one half inches long. Ford Motor Company's 50th Anniversary was 1953. In that year the tractors had a type of commemorative seal emblem in the center over the top of the radiator. While the design lasted several years only the 1953 year bore the Golden Jubilee designation.

Ford (NAA) by Wyandotte   (FOR-55)

Henry Ford is credited with the first assembly line mass produced automobiles. He also is responsible for production of the first assembly line tractors, the Fordsons. After years of experimentation, he began production of the Fordson F in 1917. The Arcade Company began marketing miniature Fordson tractors about 1926. This one is less than four inches long.

Fordson (F)   FDN-1

Another slightly longer Fordson miniature by Arcade is shown here. Like most of the Arcade toys, these Fordsons came in a variety of colors. Later variations had rubber tires rather than steel wheels. This one is just less than five inches long.

Fordson (F)   FDN-2

117

Fordson (F)   FDN-5

This Arcade Fordson is quite similar to the other six inch size models, except it has solid cast wheels with rubber tires. The letters "W & K" are cast in each wheel. This style of wheel was used for road or other industrial use so the surface would not be damaged by regular tire lugs.

Fordson (F)   FDN-6

Another toy manufacturer that made a great many miniature Fordsons was Hubley. This Pennsylvania-based firm made a varity of sizes and colors just as Arcade did. This particular model is just under four inches long.

Fordson (F)   FDN-7

A later model of the Hubley three and a half inch Fordson is shown here. Like FOR-6, it has a cast-in driver and came in a variety of colors.

Fordson (F) with Loader   FDN-8

This Hubley Fordson F with operating front end loader was made in 1938. It is a rare item since it was just a year later that the Fordsons gave way to the more modern Ford 9-N's. Overall, this tractor and loader is nearly nine inches long. Since the Arcade and Hubley six inch Fordsons were quite similar and had separate drivers, the drivers could be interchanged. The Arcade Driver has a full brim-type hat while the Hubley had a cap-type hat.

Fordson (F)   FDN-9

This Hubley Fordson F is just under six inches in length. It came in a variety of colors, too.

Fordson (F)   FDN-13

This little Fordson tractor model is just under four inches long. Unusual features include nickle plated wheels and driver. This old cast iron miniature was made in Sweden by North & Judd.

Fordson (F)   FDN-14

Another unusual Fordson miniature is this one made by Dent. Made of cast iron, it is nearly six inches long. Although somewhat similar to the Arcade Fordson of the same size, it can be distinguished by the number of bands around the hood. This one has fewer bands than the Arcade.

Fordson (F)   FDN-15

This is a model of a 1934 Fordson tractor. It was first made in that year by Dinky of Great Britain. The scale is 1/43 and it is made of die-cast metal. Notice the steel lug type wheels and the fenders over them.

Fordson (F)   FDN-16

The resemblences between this Fordson F and the Dinky Fordson F (FDN-15) are more than a coincidence. This Varney Copy Cat is a reproduction of the one above. It was made in England in 1976.

Old Time Toys of Illinois reproduced one of the Arcade Fordsons around 1969. This model shown here was sand cast and made of aluminum rather than cast iron. It is six inches long.

Fordson (F)   FDN-17

In 1969, Ertl began making this 1/16 scale Fordson model. It is not reproduced from any particular old toy, but rather an original of Ertl's. The die-casting techniques produce a very nice, smooth model. The front axle is steerable.

Fordson (F)   FDN-18

This five and a half inch long tractor certainly has the Fordson lines. While not specifically labeled, it would appear that it was reproduced from an earlier toy. It is made in New Zealand by Fun-Ho and comes in a variety of wild colors.

Fordson (F)   FDN-19

Fordson Super Major   FDN-20

Fun-Ho made a rather complete line of small scale model automobiles and trucks. There are a few tractors produced including this Fordson Super Major in 187 scale. It was made around 1967, also in New Zealand.

Fordson (F)   FDN-21

Charles Souhrada, a model collector and craftsman from Iowa, added a bit of a fine touch to hsi Fordson tractor reproduction. Notice the fenders over the rear wheels. He also made models in the American color pattern, gray and red, and the English pattern, orange and blue. These variations were made in 1975. The matchplates were purchased by Pioneer Tractor in 1980.

Fordson (F) Farm   FDN-22a

A very tiny plastic kit was the basis for this 1/87 scale Fordson F farm type tractor. It was released in 1975 by Jordon Products.

A variation of the Jordon Products plastic kit is this Fordson F Industrial model. It is also 1/87 in scale.

Fordson (F) Industrial   FDN-22b

The vast majority of pictures in this book show scale model toys, but this one is not a childrens' toy, at least not when it is full. It is an Ezra Brooks Whiskey bottle. The nine and a quarter inch long bottle is made of glass. It represents the Fordson F tractor and was made as a salute to the TriState Gasoline Engine and Tractor Association of Indiana.

Fordson (F)   FDN-23

The Britains Limited Lilliput series included this tiny Fordson E-27-N tractor model. This 1/76 miniature was first made in 1953 and came with or without a driver.

Fordson (E-27-N)   FDN-28

Fordson (E-27-N)   FDN-29a & b

A tractor miniature very similar in design is this larger 1/32 scale Fordson E-27-N, also by Britains Limited. This 1948 die-cast model was available with steel lug wheels or rubber tires.

Fordson Super Major   FDN-31b
Fordson Power Major   FDN-30a

Very slight differences can be detected in this Fordson Super Major when compared with the Power Major. However, the headlights are now located in the grill rather than on the sides of the radiator like the Power Major. This 1/32 Britains Limited model was also available with or without the steel wheels.

A radical change in styling is noticable in the next series of Fordsons, particularly this Power Major model. Like the E-27-N, this one was available on steel or rubber. The headlights were mounted along the sides of the radiator.

Fordson Super Major Industrial   FDN-31c

This 1961 Fordson Super Major represents an industrial version. Basically the same as the farm model, it is painted yellow and is equipped with a cab.

Britains Limited made several variations of the Fordson 5000 Super Major. One was made with not cab while these show the first rounded-style cabs. Like the other Britains' Fordsons, except FDN-28, this one is also 1/32 scale. Notice the slightly different grills.

Fordson 5000 Super Major/Early Cab   FDN-32b

Chad Valley of England made three very well detailed Fordson model during the early 1950s. The first one is this front crank E-27-N made about 1952. This rather rare miniature had a unique ratchet mechanism which permitted the tractor to be pushed along by hand with out "springing" the clockwork mechanism. It was made of die-cast metal in the 1/16 scale.

Fordson (E-27-N)   FDN-34

The year 1954 found the Fordson restyled resulting in this Major model. This Chad Valley 1/16 miniature had a clockwork mechanism also. Other detail included a three point hitch and lifting hoods (bonnets) exposing the engine detail. Both the E-27-N (FDN-34) and this one had working steering.

Fordson Major   FDN-35

Fordson Dexta   FDN-36

The Fordson Dexta tractor miniature was made by Chad Valley in 1955. While a very nice model, it lacked much of the working details of the two previous models. It was designed for light duty farm work.

Fordson Major   FDN-39

This very well detailed 1/20 scale model Fordson Major was made by M. W. and marked inside the fender, Empire Made. Working detail on this die-cast metal model including operating steering.

Fordson Major   FDN-41

One of the regular Lesney Matchbox series models is this Fordson Major. It is die-cast metal and made to about a 1/62 scale. The miniature was first made in 1959 in Great Britain.

Lesney's King Size series included this 1/42 scale model of a Fordson Super Major tractor with a tandum trailer. This K-11 combination was first made in 1963.

Fordson Super Major   FDN-42

Corgi of Wales made several variations of the Fordson Power Major tractor. This first model was produced in 1961 and can be identified by the headlights on the sides of the radiator. It is made of die-cast metal and is 1/43 scale.

The second Corgi Fordson Power Major was released in 1961 also. While the front of the tractor was identical to FDN-43a, the rear had a set of crawler tracks, commonly called half-tracks, in place of rear wheels. The tracks on this miniature are gray rubber.

Fordson Power Major   FDN-43a
Fordson Power Major/Half Tracks   FDN-43b

The last Corgi 1/43 Fordson is this model with the half-tracks. Besides the repositioned head lights and exhaust stack, the color of the half tracks differed in that they were black.

The third Fordson Power Major by Corgi a year later had the headlights in the grill. The exhaust stack comes through the top of the hood rather than along the side as with the previous two. All of these Corgi Fordsons have a rear lift for attaching a mounted plow which was an available accessory.

Fordson Power Major/Half Tracks   FDN-44b
Fordson Power Major   FDN-44a

Fordson Major   FDN-45

In 1963 Politoys of Italy issued this miniature Fordson Major tractor. It is red and gray rather than the usual Fordson blue and orange. A four wheel wagon was a part of the two piece set that this 1/41 scale model tractor was sold with. It was made of plastic.

Fordson Super Major   FDN-46

This Minalux model of a Fordson Super Major tractor was made in France. The 1/43 plastic model was liberally adorned with chromed trim, including the wheels. It even had a lift mechanism on the rear. This one came from France.

(Fordson Super Major)   FDN-47

One of the very few miniature tractor models from Norway is this model appearing very much like a Fordson Major. Tomte marketed this 1/43 rubber-like model with a four wheel wagon with milk cans. A driver is molded in with the tractor.

Fordson (Dexta)   FDN-48

This 1/25 scale model Fordson Dexta was produced around 1957 by Crescent of Great Britain. Made of die-cast metal, it was available with a wagon or a plow.

(Fordson Dexta)   FDN-49

This rather strange appearing tractor with many Fordson Dexta features was made by Lucky of Hong Kong. It is over five inches long and made of plastic. The "stout" front end contains the gyro type motor. It is blue with chrome trim and orange wheels.

(Fordson Dexta)   FDN-50

This rather odd looking tractor model resembles a Fordson Dexta. Made in Hong Kong by MIC, it has a separate driver of plastic like the rest of it.

Fordson N   FDN-51

For the model maker, this 1/32 scale metal kit is a challange. Representing the early 1940s Fordson N Standard tractor, this kit was released in 1976 by Brown's Models of Great Britain.

Fordson (Dexta)   FDN-52

A larger version of a Fordson Dexta is this approximately 1/25 scale model Tomte. Notice the similarities to FDN-47. Both are made of a vinyllike plastic and come with four wheel wagons.

Fordson (F)   FDN-54

Famous for its early clockwork models, Bing of Germany produced some tin model tractors during the early 1900s. The eight inch long Fordson came in a couple of different variations including this agricultural tractor. Some models had the Fordson name imprinted on the top of the radiator while others didn't. The driver is missing from this model.

Another version of a Bing Fordson is this one having half-tracks instead of rear wheels. This may have been representative of some war time tractor since war vehicles commonly had half tracks for greater traction under adverse conditions. Like FDN-54, this model has the driver missing.

Fordson (F) with Halftracks   FDN-55

An interesting version of a cast iron Hubley Fordson is shown in this photo. It has the Fordson name cast in on both sides of the radiator and has a small crank cast into the front of the tractor. Most Fordsons had no electrical starters, and therefore needed a crank to get the engine running.

Fordson (F)   FDN-56

The W. Britains Company, now Britains Limited, made this tiny 1/76 scale plastic model with tin rear wheels before the later Britains metal model. It represents the Fordson E27N tractor.

Fordson (E27N) by W. Britains (FDN-57)

Fowler Big Lion Show Engine   FOW-1

Lesney of Great Britain produced a very colorful steam traction engine called the "Big Lion" Show Engine. The Model of Yesteryear was first released in 1958. It is die-cast to the 1/80 scale.

Frick 16 H.P.   FRI-1

Another steam traction engine is this 1/25 Frick. First made around 1964 by White's Hobby Shop, and later produced by Peterson's, and Irvin's, it was made of cast aluminum.

Graham Bradley   GB-1

The Graham Bradley tractor was short lived in the late 1940s. The rather streamlined design might have been just ahead of its time. This row crop rubber model was made by Aubrubber and is four inches long. There was a variety of David Bradley implements made to accompany this toy tractor.

Hanomag-Barrieros   HAN-1

This very tiny 1/86 scale model represents a Hanomag-Barrieros tractor. This miniature was made in 1964 by Auguplas-Minicars of Spain.

Hangmag Robust 900   HAN-4

This Hanomag Robust 900 farm tractor model was made by Siku of West Germany. It is green with red wheels and trim and made of die-cast metal to the 1/60 scale.

Huber Steam Traction Road Roller   HUB-1

A very old manufacturer of steam traction engines was the Huber Company. In 1929, the Hubley Company of Lancaster, Pennsylvania made a cast iron model of a Huber engine.

133

Huber Steam Traction Engine   HUB-2a

Cast aluminum reproductions of both types of Huber engines were made by first White, then Peterson and finally Irwin. Like the original cast iron model, these repros were made to a 1/23 scale.

Huber Steam Road Roller   HUB-4

This cast iron road roller is made of cast iron. Just over three inches in length, it has a wooden front roller and plated rear wheels. It was made by Hubley.

McCormick-Deering 10-20   IH-1a & b

Cyrus McCormick revolutionized harvesting with this reaper. The success of this machine lead to establishment of the giant McCormick-Deering Company. Following the early Mogul and Titan tractors, McCormick-Deering developed the famous 10-12. In 1925, the Arcade Company began making models of the 10-20. Many color, wheel style and other variations were sold for nearly fifteen years by Arcade. 1a has a movable pulley, whereas 1b has the pulley molded into the body.

During the 1920s, a new style of tractor was developed by McCormick-Deering. The Original Farmall served farmers who needed a smaller, more maneuverable tractor for row crop work. The first Arcade cast iron miniature Farmall has steel lug wheels, but later during the 1930s rubber tires were introduced on farm tractors, and of course, on the miniatures.

Farmall (F-20 or Original)   IH-2

The early crawler tractors were developed for farm use, and later adapted for industrial use. Shown here is an Arcade miniature McCormick-Deering Trac-Tractor crawler. This model had either sectional steel or rubber tracks. The driver was nickle plated.

McCormick-Deering (TD-40) Trac-Tractor Crawler   IH-3

A later, more modern McCormick-Deering Trac-Tractor crawler was introduced about 1940. Like the earlier model, it had a separately cast, nickle plated driver. At seven and a half inches in length, it was just a half inch shorter than the earlier model. Note the more stream lined design.

McCormick-Deering (TD-18) Trac-Tractor Crawler   IH-4

Farmall M IH-5

This cast iron Farmall M is just slightly over four inches long. An Arcade miniature, it has wooden wheels and a cast-in driver.

Farmall M IH-6

Another slightly larger Arcade model Farmall M is the one pictured here. The wheels are not the correct ones for this tractor.

Farmall M IH-7

Late in 1939, International Harvester introduced the Farmall M. Shortly after that, the Arcade Company released three different size models of the M. The largest one, seven inches long, was the most popular size. It is of row crop design and has a separate plated driver.

Farmall M Culti-Vision   IH-8

"Culti-Vision" is the term International used to describe the design of the new offset style Farmall A tractor in 1939. This design permitted better visability of row crops while being cultivated. This miniature is a cast iron model made by Arcade. The scale is different than the scale used for the Farmall M.

McCormick-Deering 10-20   IH-9

A rather unusual toy model of the McCormick-Deering 10-20 was made by Kilgore. This model was slightly smaller than the Arcade 10-20, being only about six inches in length. Like the Arcade model, it had a separately cast, plated driver.

McCormick-Deering 10-20   IH-10

Robert Gray of Iowa made a reproduction of the Arcade McCormick-Deering 10-20 (IH-1). Shown here is his model made of cast aluminum.

McCormick-Deering 10-20   IH-11

About the same time that Robert Gray was making his reproduction of the 10-20, Old Time Toys in Illinois was making a slightly different version of it. This model, first made around 1969, had slightly different color and rear wheels than Gray's.

Farmall (Regular)   IH-2 & IH-12

Old Time Toys or Pioneer Tractor also made a reproduction of Arcade's Farmall. The original cast iron model is on the left; works version on the right.

McCormick-Deering Trac-Tractor Crawler   IH-13

The McCormick-Deering Trac-Tractor crawler is recaptured in miniature by this wood 1/24 scale model kit, made in the United States by Mod-AC Mfg. Co.

Entering the era of plastic toys in the early 1950s, a company called Product Miniature introduced some tractor models as well as many car and truck models. The Farmall M row crop tractor was one of these early models. It was made to the popular 1/16 scale.

Farmall M   IH-14a

Product Miniature also had an unassembled plastic model kit representing the Farmall M. It was very simple to assemble. Here it is shown along with IH-62, a Farmall Cab Kit, not made by Product Miniature.

Farmall M   IH-14b

A very limited issue of the Farmall M in white plastic with red wheels and even stars is shown.

Farmall M   IH-14c

Farmall Super C   IH-15

In 1952, the Farmall C was replaced by the Super C. This medium size farm tractor was of row crop design. LaKone made a very well detailed plastic model in 1/16 scale. The seat even had a coiled spring, just as did the 1/1 Farmall Super C. The muffler is missing for this model.

Farmall 230   IH-16

An improved model replacing the Farmall Super C is the 230 model. This model is quite similar to the Super C (IH-15). And another model, the 200 which is not pictured.

International UD-24 Power Unit   IH-17

Stationary power units are used to power saw mills, irrigation pumps and many industrial operations. International made and sold many of these power units. This plastic model represents the UD-24 Power Unit and was made by Product Miniature. It also served as a cigarette dispenser.

International TD-24 Crawler   IH-18a

The International TD-24 crawler came in two variations by Product Miniature. This 1/16 scale model came as simply a crawler or as a crawler with bulldozer blade.

International TD-24 Bulldozer   IH-18b

Another variation of Product Miniature's International TD-24 crawler is this one with a bulldozer blade. It has a remote power unit which powers each of the tracks independently, making it possible to steer the crawler. Two speeds forward and two speeds in reverse along with functional healights results in "life like" action.

Farmall (M) Diesel   IH-19

Although not specifically identified as a Farmall, this tractor certainly has the lines of the Farmall M. It was manufactured during the middle 1950s by the Marx Company, came complete with a tool box full of tools and was available in a variety of colors. The 1/12 scale plastic model could be assembled and disassembled. Notice the word "Diesel" along the side of the radiator.

141

Photo Not Available

This Hubley miniature is not specifically marked with the Farmall name, but certainly has those lines. It is approximately 1/16 scale.

(Farmall) H   IH-20

(Farmall) (M)   IH-21

Another Hubley model having the Farmall lines but not the name is this slightly larger 1/12 scale model. Greater detail includes working steering and a springing seat.

(Farmall) (M)   IH-22

This four inch long rubber tractor with the Farmall line was made by Aubrubber. A driver having his head turned to the side was molded in with the tractor. This model came in a variety of colors.

(Farmall) (M)   IH-23

The Farmall M tractor was in production for close to twenty years and was often copied in miniature. Another example is this one made by Slik Toys. It is six and a half inches long.

(Farmall) (M)   IH-24

Very similar to the Slik Farmall M (IH-23), probably this Lincoln Specialities version was cast in the same molds. The wheels are slightly different. This one is painted gray and has the Lincoln decal across the hood.

(Farmall) (M)   IH-25

The first Ertl Farmal M style tractor did not bear the Farmall name either. This 1/16 scale model was one of Ertl's first toy creations in the 1940s. The driver was cast-in with the tractor. On this particular model the driver's head has been replaced with a different one.

(Farmall M)   IH-26

The second tractor resembling the Farmall M by Ertl is this slightly later one. It had no driver and had yellow, rather than red wheels. It is quite similar to the first Carter Tru-Scale Farmall M type tractor.

IH Cub Cadets   IH-27, 28, 29 and 30

During the 1960s, lawn and garden tractors began their surge of popularity. Shown here from left ot right are: 1966—122, 1968—125, 1970—126, 1972—129. These variations were available with mounted front end blades and trailers.

IH Cub Cadet 129 "Spirit of 76"   IH-30d

A limited issue of the 129 Cub Cadet was issued as a salute to the 1976 Bicentennial. This red, white and blue model was called the "Spirit of 76."

In 1976 I. H. redesigned its lawn and garden tractor line to provide less noise as well as other improvements. The covered sides reduced the engine noise and distinguishes this Cub Cadet from all the earlier models.

IH Cub (1650) Cadet   IH-31

This International 240 utility model was introduced during the latter 1950s. The Ertl model included a fast hitch and a steering wheel that worked the front axle.

International 240 Utility   IH-32a

Identical to Ertl's International 240 in all aspects except the decals, this 340 was made to the same 1/16 scale as the 240. The fast hitch was a two point hitch allowing an implement to become an integal part of the tractor.

International 340 Industrial Utility   IH-33

Farmall 400   IH-34

After many years of production, the Farmall M was finally replaced by first a Super M, then by the 300 and 400 series. The Ertl 400 was produced about 1954 and also had the fast hitch. This one has a mounted front-end loader.

International 404 Utility   IH-35

A successor to the International 340 is this International 404 utility. However, unlike the 340, it had the three point hitch instead of the fast hitch. It was made around 1960.

Farmall 404 Row Crop   IH-36a & b

A companion to the International 404 utility is this Farmall 404 row crop model. It was quite similar except for the front wheels. It did not have a three point hitch. The earlier variation had red wheels while the later one had white.

Farmall 450   IH-37

The Farmall 450 became the successor to the 400 in 1956. This Ertl 1/16 miniature was quite similar except the grill and decals. Like the 400, it had the fast hitch.

Farmall 460 & 560   IH-38a & 38b

This Ertl Farmall 460 was introduced about 1958. Compared to the 450, it was a completely redesigned tractor, the hood was consideably longer. It retained the fast hitch. Shown here also is the model 560 (IH-38b). It was this series of tractors in which I. H. introduced the six cylinder engine.

Farmall 560 with Cab   IH-38e
Farmall 560 with Duals   IH-38f

Another 560 variation came with white wheels and a cab. The cab was adapted from a later style tractor. Shown here is another variation with dual rear wheels.

147

International (2644) Industrial   IH-39

Two industrial variations replaced the 2504. Both were un-numbered but represented the 2644 model. Both tractors were row crop style, one having the narrow front axle and the other having a wide front axle. Both were modified 544 farm style tractors.

International 544 Row Crop   IH-39b
International 544 Row Crop   IH-39a

Three variations of the International 544 were sold in 1969 also. One of these variation simply had white rear wheels, another had dual rear wheels and third had a loader attached.

In 1969, Ertl released this International 544 row crop style tractor with a wide front axle. The wheels steered when the steering wheel turned. Notice the red wheels.

Flying Farmall (560)   IH-40

Ertl released three "Super Rod Pulling Tractors" in 1974. One was this modified Farmall 560, renamed the Flying Farmall.

Just a year later, the Farmall name was reduced in size and the International name took its place. This model is identical to IH-41a except for the decals.

In 1967 Ertl produced a smaller 1/32 scale miniature tractor. This Farmall 656 row crop model did not have working steering like the larger 1/16 models.

International 656   IH-41b
Farmall 656   IH-41a

Almost identical to the IH-42a, this International differed only in the front wheel design. It had the wide front axle.

A replacement for the International 656 is this Ertl un-numbered model. It has a slightly different design including the grill. It came out in 1974 and was made to the 1/32 scale.

International (666)   IH-42b
International (666)   IH-42a

In 1964 a new line of tractors was introduced by International. Their largest two wheel drive tractor was the Farmall 806. This Ertl replica came in two variations, the original 1964 model with round fenders and the 1965 model with flat fenders. Both featured working steering.

Farmall 806   IH-43

149

International 1056   IH-44b

A very short run Ertl IH model is the 1056 Hydro. It was made in 1971; wide front axle.

International 966 Hydro   IH-45a

In 1972, I. H. introduced the International 966 Hydro which had a hydraulically driven transmission, an automatic of sorts. The Ertl model had a wide front axle.

International 1066 Turbo   IH-45c

A replacement for the International 1026 could be this 1066 Turbo. However, the terms turbo and hydro should not be confused. Turbo refers to a super-charger or "blower" that forces more air into the engine resulting in more power. Hydro refers to a type of hydraulic transmission.

The model 1466 was introduced in 1972 by I. H. The Ertl model had a very well detailed grill compared to the simple decal type grills on earlier models. This one had a cab and dual rear wheels too.

A third size International 1466 is this 1/64 scale model made by Ertl. It had a wide front axle and a cab.

In 1974 Ertl released a plastic kit model of the IH 1466 in 1/25 scale. More information on this model can be found in the section on building and detailing kits by Ken Conklin.

International 1466   IH-45e   International 1466   IH-47
International 1466   IH-48

A new series of I. H. tractors was introduced in 1976. The International 886 model by Ertl came with a safety roll over frame. It was October of that year when a Federal O. S. H. A. law requiring farm tractors to have this protection went into effect.

International 886   IH-49a

A second variation of the casting used by Ertl to produce the 886 is this 1086 model. It had a cab enclosure over the safety frame.

International 1086   IH-49b

International 1586   IH-49c

The third variation is this 1586 International. It differed only in having both the cab and dual rear wheels. All three models were built to the popular 1/16 scale.

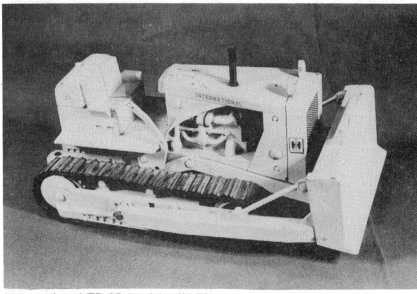

International TD-25 (early)   IH-50

International also makes industrial equipment. In the early 1960s, Ertl made a model of the International TD-25 bulldozer. It was industrial yellow and had headlights on the top of the radiator.

International TD-25 (late)   IH-51

Ten years later, Ertl made this restyled model of the International TD-25. It was considerably different and had headlights on the sides of the radiator. The blade lifting mechanism was different also.

A replacement model for the International 340 Industrial utility tractor is this model 2504. It was quite similar to the 340 but had a three point hitch instead of the fast hitch. Like the 340 industrial, it was yellow.

International 2504 Industrial Utility   IH-52

A tractor specifically designed for industrial use, not merely a "beefed up" farm tractor, is this 3414 International Industrial with loader and backhoe. Ertl first produced the 3414 in 1967, then the identical model with the 3444 decal in 1969.

International 3414 Industrial   IH-53a

The successor to the International 3444 is this 3400 series industrial wheel tractor with loader and backhoe. This very well detailed Ertl model was released in 1975. Detail even included tread plate for the drivers platform.

International (3400) Industrial   IH-54

IH Cub—Farmall   IH-59, 60, 61, 62

At least four different companies manufactured plastic 1/12 scale models of the Farmall Cub during the early 1950s. Alfinson, Atma, Design Fabricators and Saunders Swader all produced very similar products. The Farmall Cub was a very small tractor used primarily for cultivating or lawn mowing. In recent years, the smaller Cub Cadet has replaced the Cub in popularity.

Farmall (M)   IH-63

This little four inch long Farmall M style tractor was manufactured in Japan. It was made of tin and had a gyro motor. A very baby-like plastic driver was perched on the seat.

(Farmall M) with Loader   IH-64

This die-cast tractor model strongly resembling a Farmall M was made by Fun-Ho of New Zealand. It is almost a foot long including the front mounted loader. In place of the Farmall name, Fun-Ho used its own trade name. The model has a wide front axle.

Universal Cordeg of Hong Kong produced this 1/20 scale model of an International tractor in the style of the 240 - 340 series. There were two variations, an earlier one with white wheels and a later one with yellow wheels and a driver. Both were utility style tractors.

International (240) Utility   IH-65

Lesney, manufacturer of the famous Matchbox series made two variations fo the International B-250 Utility tractor. Both were made to the 1/37 scale and differed only in the wheel color, one having green wheels while the other had red wheels.

International B-250 Utility   IH-66

Another European company, Tekno of Denmark, manufactured model Interntional tractors. The earliest model, while not specifically numbered, was probably the model 414 Utility. It was made around 1966.

International (414) Utility   IH-67

International (574) Utility   IH-68

Another Tekno International model is this utility probably representing the 574. A later model than the IH-67, it was a bit more refined having a roll over protective frame and an interchangable front blade and brush. This tractor was first produced in 1971.

International 560   IH-69

Alps Toys of Japan made a tin plate model of an International 560. While probably more of a toy than a scale model, it did carry the International logo and 560 number. Unlike the regular International line, this model was tan instead of red. It even had smoking action.

International Hydraulic Excavator   IH-73

A relatively recent release is this Solido International hydraulic excavator. This 1/55 scale model was made in 1975 by Solido of France.

The cleated front tires on this model would indicate that it is a four wheel drive tractor. This IH 844 miniature is a recent addition by Eligor of France. Notice the front end weights and the roll over protection on this 1/43 scale model.

International 844 Four wheel Drive   IH-74

This Farmall F-30 is another one of Robert Gray's originals. It is made of Korloy and eight inches long.

Farmall F-30   IH-75

Robert Gray released this Korloy model of a 1939 McCormick W-9 in 1977. It represents the largest wheel tractor in the McCormick line at that time. This miniature is eight and one-half inches long.

McCormick W-9   IH-76

This little tin model has the IH Farmall logo, but is not very representative of any particular IH tractor. It has an attached loader.

IH Farmall   IH-77

This Farmall Cub model is similar to the plastic versions, but is made of metal. Here it is shown inside the round plastic container with IH emblem on top. Very little information is available on this model.

IH Farmall Cub   IH-80

This tiny two inch long plastic model is quite representative of the Farmall C which was made in the 1950s.

Farmall (C)   IH-81

The John Deere D tractor was the first to bear the John Deere name. Around 1930 a little toy manufacturer in Illinois called Vindex made a series of well detailed miniature farm models. This cast iron D proved to be a popular one and is a treasured prize with collectors today. The driver was cast separately and nickle plated.

John Deere (D)   JD-1

Small gasoline engines were needed on farms to power small machines. A portable engine such as this one readily served that purpose. This Vindex miniature was made about the same time as the D. The John Deere engine was also reproduced by Old Time Toys.

John Deere Gasoline Engine   JD-8 &JD-2

When Deere and Company introduced the row crop style of tractor, it was not long before, it became evident that a miniature was needed for the young, would be farmer. Since Vindex had ceased production, Arcade was contacted for the job. Like the D, the A and a separate plated driver. Arcade made a wagon to go along with this model.

John Deere (A)   JD-3

John Deere (D)   JD-4

In the early 1930s, a small company called Kansas Toy manufactured a line of lead toys which included this model of a John Deere D. Since this toy was not widely distributed, it is quite scarce today.

Froelich   JD-5

The Froelich tractor was the result of a very early attempt to produce a internal combustion engine tractor. Although it was not very successful, it did serve as an incentive for later efforts. This miniature was made by Charles Cox in very limited numbers. This model required one-hundred hours of time to hand-craft.

Waterloo Boy   JD-6

Another one of Cox's creations is this nine inch long scale model of the Waterloo Boy tractor. Deere and Company bought out the Waterloo Company, then began production of the D tractor. Cox made two variations of Waterloo Boy, one patterned after the N and one after the R. These hand-crafted models each required close to sixty hours of labor and were serial numbered.

Some reproductions of the Vindex John Deere D were made of cast aluminum in the late 1960s and early 70s. This one was made by Old Time Toys of Illinois.

John Deere (D)   JD-7

Although this model appears quite old, it is of relatively recent vintage. Robert Gray of Iowa created this "old time pioneer of power." It represents the John Deere A General Purpose tractor. Notice the lug type metal wheels.

John Deere (A General Purpose)   JD-9

Although not specifically marked, this small plastic tractor certainly has the lines of the John Deere MT tractor. It was made in the 1950s by Auburn. The driver was molded in and the Auburn name appeared on one side.

(John Deere MT)   JD-10

John Deere (A)   JD-11

A miniature tractor appearing very much like a John Deere A was made for a short time by Lincoln Specialities of Canada. It resembled the early Ertl Jonn Deere A (JD-21). One collector reported seeing this model in a variety store painted red rather than the traditional John Deere green and yellow.

John Deere Historical Set   JD-12 thru 19

In 1967, Ertl produced a set of historical models including the following; Froelich, 1914—Waterloo Boy, 1932—D, 1939—A, 1952—60, 1958—730, 1960—4010, and added later, 1972—4430. All these models were made to a small 1/64 scale and sold either as a set or individually.

John Deere D   JD-20

With the increased interest in old models, Ertl released this "old timer" in 1970. It is a John Deere D and is quite similar in size and weight to the original Vindex John Deere D (JD-1). It, however, does not have a driver.

This John Deere A tractor model was one of the original miniatures made by Mr. Ertl in 1945. This row crop style tractor had a molded-in driver with a flat top hat. Some of these tractors had wheels marked Arcade. Mr. Ertl had puchased the remaining stock of Arcade wheels when Arcade ceased production of toys.

John Deere (A)　JD-21

The original Ertl John Deere A tractor was slightly modified about 1947 to update the tractor. The original John Deere row crop tractors of the 1930s had no electrical starters and were started by turning the flywheel by hand. Later when electric starters were added, the flywheel was covered, making the tractor safer.

John Deere (A)　JD-22

Still other improvements in the John Deere A were made. This 1950 Ertl miniature was noticably different because the driver was missing. It was slightly larger than the earlier Ertl A's.

John Deere (A)　JD-23

John Deere (60)   JD-24

The John Deere 60 miniature by Ertl was a vastly improved toy. It not only had superior casting, but the front wheels could be steered by turning the steering wheel. The 1952 version of the Ertl 60 had a light on the rear of the driver's seat while the 1954 version had a three-point hitch to which implements could be attached.

John Deere 110 Lawn & Garden   JD-25

In 1965, Deere and Co. entered the lawn and garden tractor business. Their early series included this 110 model. Ertl made a miniature model that even had front wheel steering.

John Deere 140 Lawn and Garden   JD-26a

The John Deere 140 lawn and garden tractor had more horsepower than the 110. It was introduced in 1967. Like the 110, it had front wheels that could be steered. Its major feature was hydrostatic transmission.

In an attempt to attract more suburban customers, Deere and Company decided to produce the 140 in colors. This color key series included the following: *Ertl #571 Sunset orange, Ertl #572 Spruce blue, Ertl #573 April yellow, Ertl #574 Patio red*. The color key series was dropped less than two years after it was introduced in 1969.

John Deere 140 Color Key Set   JD-26b, c, d, e

In 1975, Ertl produced an un-numbered miniature John Deere lawn and garden tractor. It probably represented their 400 model tractor. In an effort to cut down on noise "pollution," this tractor had covers over the sides of the engine. Like the earlier 140 models, it was available with a blade and trailer.

John Deere (400) Lawn and Garden   JD-27

About 1958, Ertl introduced this scale model of the John Deere 430 Utility tractor. The wide axle front wheels could be steered. One variation came with a three point hitch while a later version sold through non-dealer outlets had no three point hitch.

John Deere (430) Utility   JD-28

John Deere (620)   JD-29a & b

The successor to the John Deere 60 in 1956 was the 620. It was quite similar to the 60 but had a yellow flash along and down the side. The Ertl miniature came with or without the three point hitch.

John Deere (630)   JD-30

Like the 620, this John Deere 630 model was available with or without a three point hitch. The original 1958 Ertl version had it. The styling was somewhat different than the 620. The metal exhaust stack had been replaced with a rubber one. One variation by Ertl had no exhaust stack. Some collectors refer to this model as a "730."

John Deere (2030) Utility   JD-31a & b

For small farm chores, the utility tractor is quite popular. John Deere's 2030 utility tractor fills the "chore tractor" role on many farms. This Ertl miniature introduced in 1973 even has a Slow Moving Vehicle bracket molded on the rear of the seat. The colorful SMV emblem is a warning to motorists that the vehicle ahead travels less than twenty-five miles an hour.

John Deere (2040) Utility   JD-32

In 1976, the 2030 was replaced by the 2040 utility. The front end styling is the most noticable difference between the two. Like the 2030, this 2040 was also available with mounted front end loader.

John Deere (3010 or 4010)   JD-33

The first miniature New Generation tractor was released in early 1961. It had a three point hitch and die-cast metal wheels. The engine of this 1/16 scale model tractor was a gasoline design.

John Deere (3020 or 4020)   JD-34

In 1964 the casting of this series of Ertl tractor was slightly changed. There were many variations, mostly wheel types. The engine was a diesel and a distinguishing feature was the presence of the fuel filters on the left side of the engine. Some variations had the three point hitch while others did not.

John Deere (3020 or 4020)   JD-35

A third major casting variation of this series was the one released in 1967. This one, like the previous one, was a diesel but had an alternator rather than a generator. Also, the two fuel filters were slightly longer. There were several wheel variations including one with a wide front axle. Another variation had the attached ROPS.

John Deere (4230)   JD-36

Generation II was introduced by Deere and Company in 1972. The Ertl Company introduced their model of the 4230 in that year also. This one had a wide front axle and their new Sound Gard cab. This model is their 1/16 scale die cast metal model.

John Deere (4230)   JD-37

In 1973, Ertl released a 1/32 scale model of the Generation II tractor. While this one had a cab like the 1/16 model, it had the narrow row crop type front axle.

Also in 1973 Ertl released a 125 scale model plastic kit which could be built into the 4430 John Deere. The detail in this kit was excellent and constructon was quite easy compared with many other plastic kit models. See the section on building kits.

John Deere 4430   JD-38

A truly fine example of die-casting is exhibited in this Ertl 1/16 scale model of the John Deere 5020. This "wheatland"style tractor has an oscillating front axle and steerable front wheels. Notice the shield around the operator's platform to protect him from dust, etc. The first miniature 5020 was released in 1969. A later one had no air cleaner stack.

John Deere 5020   JD-39

1972 was the year that this hefty four wheel drive John Deere 7520 was first marketed. Four wheel drive offered superior traction, especially in soft ground. This model steered by the articulated (bending) action between the front and rear halves. It was fitted with a cab.

John Deere (7520) Four Wheels Drive   JD-40

John Deere (8630) Four Wheel Drive   JD-41

The 7520 was replaced by a larger, more improved series of four wheel drive tractors in 1975. This miniature, probably representing the 8630, had not only four wheel drive, but also dual wheels all the way around. These dual wheels provide greater flotation and greater traction on soft ground. Also, the amount of soil compaction is greatly reduced.

John Deere (40) Crawler   JD-42a

Although Deere and Company made a model B crawler, it was not until they introduced the 40 crawler that Ertl made a scale model. this first model crawler could be fitted with an optional bulldozer blade which could be raised, lowered or angled left and right.

John Deere (40) Industrial Crawler   JD-42b

A year or so after the miniature John Deere 40 crawler was released in 1954, Ertl issued one painted yellow representing the industrial version. Like the other 40 crawler, it could be fitted with the optional bulldozer blade.

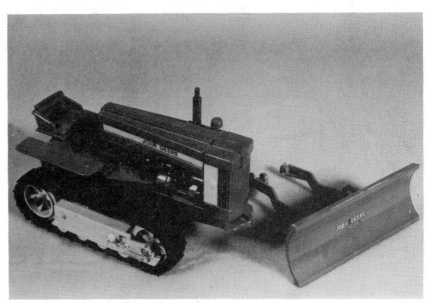

John Deere (420) Crawler   JD-42c

A third variation of Ertl's first crawler casting is this 420 crawler. This 1956 model differed only in the extra yellow trim along the sides.

John Deere (440) Industrial Crawler   JD-43

The replacement for the 420 crawler is this John Deere 440 industrial crawler. This 1959 version was yellow and had a metal embossed type grill. There was no blade for this one.

A companion model to the 440 crawler is this John Deere 1010 industrial wheel tractor. The original 1959 version had a three point hitch but a later version did not. Close examination reveals similarities to the John Deere 430 utility (JD-28). In fact, this industrial tractor was simply a "beefed up" version of the 430.

John Deere (440) Wheel Tractor-Industrial   JD-44

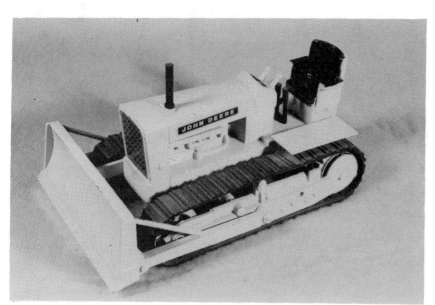

John Deere (1010) Industrial Crawler   JD-45

A 1963 John Deere industrial crawler was also numbered 1010. However, it was considerably different than the wheel tractor. This Ertl miniature was equipped with a blade. The grill was a paper decal rather than the embossed metal grill such as the 440 crawler had. The 1010 was a four cylinder engine, rather than the traditional two cylinder as in the 440.

Photo Not Available

The John Deere 500 crawler introduced by Ertl in 1965 had an attached bulldozer blade. Another version was released two years later with a winch on the rear.

John Deere (JD-450) Industrial Crawler   JD-46a

John Deere (JD-450) Industrial Crawler/ROPS   JD-46c

The 1973 version of the JD-500 crawler had both the winch and a ROPS on it.

John Deere (JD-310) Industrial   JD-47

This rather complicated model is a John Deere industrial tractor with a backhoe and loader. This style tractor is widely used for light construction work, especially home building, water and gas lines. Ertl marketed this 1/16 scale model in 1975. The loader and backhoe are operable.

John Deere JD-310 Industrial   JD-48

A 1/25 scale model of the John Deere JD-d350 in plastic kit form was also marketed in 1975; having the backhoe and front end loader.

Another John Deere construction model is this four wheel loader. The first version released in 1971 did not have the ROPS while the 1973 version did. This model is articulated. It is built to the smaller 1/25 scale.

John Deere Four Wheel Loader   JD-49

John Deere (570) Motor Grader   JD-50

Another 1971 Ertl John Deere release is this miniature motor grader, or as it is more commonly known, road grader. The introduction of this model by John Deere showed a new innovation, the articulated grader. This design permitted the grader to get into tight corners readily.

John Deere (690) Hydraulic Excavator   JD-60

The John Deere 690 hydraulic excavator. This miniature on crawler tracks represents a model used in heavy construction operation, by Rex of Germany.

John Deere (860) Scraper Pan   JD-52

Scraper pans have been used for many years on jobs requiring the movement of great amounts of dirt. This miniature John Deere 860 scraper pan has an elevating device making it a self loading pan. The first 1971 Ertl model had not ROPS but the 1973 version did.

In the forests, the loggers use a machine to skid logs out to be loaded and hauled away. This 1/16 scale model by Ertl is an articulated, four wheel drive log skidder. It came complete with a winch on the rear and a ROPS for protection of the operator. A blade on the front could be used to clear trails in the woods.

John Deere Log Skidder   JD-53

A little foundry in Iowa manufactures miniature farm implements and tractors that are distributed widely through variety stores. Although this particular line does not bear the John Deere name, the lines are unmistakably those of the 20 series. This red and silver tractor was also available with a brown cab.

(John Deere 3020)   JD-56

This 1963 version of the John Deere-Lanz was made in Great Britain by Lesney and marketed as one of the Matchbox series. There were two variations; one with black tires and the other with gray. The scale of this miniature is 1/16.

John Deere-Lanz 700   JD-57

John Deere-Lanz Utility   JD-59

This five inch long John Deere-Lanz utility tractor was made in West Germany by Rex.

John Deere Skid Loader   JD-61

A recent release by Ertl for Deere & Company is this four wheel skid loader. These loaders are used extensively on farms for loading and transporting items. The machine is steered by levers rather than a steering wheel.

Kohctpykto   KOH-1

This five inch long plastic model farm tractor was made in the USSR by Kohctpýkto about 1973. This may possibly be a model of a Belarus tractor since supposedly, there is only one company operated by the government making tractors in Russia. Information about this model is quite sketchy.

A relatively new brand of tractors being imported into the United States is the Kubota line made in Japan. This small 1/42 scale miniature was made in 1975 by Tomica of Japan. It is one of the "Pocket Cars" series.

Diapet of Japan made this miniature Kubota L-150 tractor. The well detailed blue and orange model came either singly or with one of the following implements; trailer, disk or rototiller. The 1/23 scale size of this model makes it approximately twice the size of KUB-1. Later a newer L-245 version was added.

Kubota   KUB-1
Kubota L-150   KUB-2c

A recent entry into the scale model tractor ranks is this Forma-Plast 1/43 Lamborghini. This Italian model features four-wheel drive and a safety cab which is removable. This model R 1056 is finished in a striking blue and white combination.

Lamborghini   R1056 Four-Wheel Drive   LAM-1

This early 1960s Mercury model represents a Landini R-4000 tractor. A brown tractor with blue hood and yellow wheels, it is 1/43 in scale. The hood tilts forward revealing the engine detail. The Landini Company became part of Massey-Ferguson Ltd.

Landini R-4000   LAI-1

Lanz Bulldog   LAZ-1

This very tiny 1/86 scale miniature represents a German Lanz Bulldog tractor. First made in 1959, this plastic miniature comes from Spain.

Lanz Utility   LAZ-4

This Rex miniature Lanz Bulldog tractor was manufactured in Germany. This blue tractor with red wheels is five inches long. It is made of plastic and is a companion to the John Deere-Lanz utility (JD-59).

Lanz Bulldog   LAZ-5

This very antique appearing model was actually first made in 1973. A German toy manufacturer, Wiking, made this Lanz Bulldog to a very tiny 1/87 scale. This plastic miniature is gray in color. See also John Deere.

Leyland 384   LEY-1a & b

BMC of Great Britain manufactures a line of farm tractors and markets them under the Leyland name. This well dataled 1/43 scale miniature is the 384 Leyland. Introduced in 1971 by Dinky, it was available in three colors; metallic red, metallic blue, or metallic orange. Wheels and exhaust stacks on both were white.

Massey-Ferguson 44   MF-1

Massey-Harris, famous for its combines and Ferguson famous for its three point hitch mounted implement system, were merged in 1954 to form what is now Massey-Ferguson. This Dinky miniature model 44 tractor represents the transitional model. The tractor is identical to MH-1 except for the identifying decals.

Massey-Ferguson 35   MF-7

This rather well detailed 1/32 scale Massey-Ferguson 35 was made in Denmark by Lion-Molberg. The hood tips forward to reveal the engine detail.

From far off India comes this 1/25 scale model Massey-Ferguson 35. The detail in this Morgan Milton Ltd. model is amazingly precise. The headlights are jeweled for realism.

Massey-Ferguson 35   MF-8

Mercury of Italy manufactured the Massey-Ferguson 35 utility tractor shown here. Several implements were available with this 1/43 scale model. It was first made around 1961.

Massey-Ferguson 35   MF-9

From Columbia, South America we find a miniature tractor quite similar to the Lion Molberg (MF-7) model. The hood also tilts on this Chico Toys 1/32 model. However, the color of this one is red over black with metallic blue fenders rather than all red. It does not bear the Massey-Ferguson name or number 35.

(Massey-Ferguson 35)   MF-11

In the industrial line, Corgi of Wales manufactured this Massey-Ferguson 50-B in at least two variations. The first variation was the tractor alone in 1973 while just a year later a front end loader was added.

Massey-Ferguson 50-B   MF-12a & b

A Massey-Ferguson 65 tractor was made in at least three variations. The little utility was available separately or with either a front end bucket or fork. The engine and transmission on all three variations was tan rather than the usual gray color. The rest of the tractor was red.

Massey-Ferguson 65   MF-13a, b, & c.

A slightly later replacement for the Massey-Ferguson 65 is this 165 model. Like the 65, it was built to the standard Corgi 1/43 scale. It was available with a front end loader or a plow on the rear.

Massey-Ferguson 165   MF-14b & c

Massey-Ferguson 165/Saw Trimmer   MF-14d

A unique variation of the Massey-Ferguson 165 by Corgi is this one that came with a saw trimming attachment. This style tractor and trimmer was used to trim branches hanging over roadways. The operator was protected by a grid attached to the tractor.

Massey-Ferguson 165 Industrial   MF-15

Another industrial version of the Massey-Ferguson tractor is this tiny 1/78 scale 165 with front end blade and cab. It was manufactured by Corgi Jr. about 1969.

Massey-Ferguson 65   MF-16

One of the very few tractor miniatures made in Ireland is this Triang Spot-On Massey-Ferguson 65. This die-cast metal model is made to the popular European 1/43 scale.

For some reason, unknown to the authors, one Massey-Ferguson miniature tractor has the letter X after the number. This MF 65X was made and marketed under two different names, Mini-Mac and Jue, both of Brazil, South America. The scale of this well detailed model is 1/43.

Massey-Ferguson 65X   MF-17

This nice little die-cast Massey-Ferguson 275 was made in Brazil. The current manufacturer is Minimac but the model may be in a Jue box.

Massey-Ferguson 275 by Minimac   MF-18b

Jue of South America also made a Massey-Ferguson 3366 Industrial crawler. It, too, is built to the 1/43 scale and was made in 1972.

Massey-Ferguson 3366 Crawler/Blade   MF-19

From the Union of South Africa comes this rather unique 1/38 scale model of the Massey-Ferguson 135 Diesel tractor. This little utility tractor, made about 1969, was available with a trailer.

Massey-Ferguson 135 Diesel   MF-20

A larger scale 1/20 companion model to MF-20 is this miniature Massey-Ferguson 175 Diesel. The detail on it is excellent including the working steering and the Goodyear tires. This model, also made about 1969, is quite rare in the United States.

Massey-Ferguson 175 Diesel   MF-21

A 1976 release of the Massey-Ferguson miniature by Britains Limited is this 595 model. Although it is also the 1/32 scale, it is considerably larger than the 135 model. The cab is much blockier in appearance than the cab on the 135 (MF-22a).

Britains Limited of England issued this Massey-Ferguson 135 utility with fiberglass cab in 1969. The 1/32 scale model is a combination of die-cast metal and plastic. The tractor was also available without a cab.

Massey-Ferguson 595   MF-23
Massey-Ferguson 135 Utility   MF-22a

A slightly different version of the Massey-Ferguson 135 utility is this Britains industrial model. It is basically the same model as MF-22a except it is yellow and has a front end loader.

Massey-Ferguson 135 Industrial Utility   MF-22b

Lesney, manufacturer of the Matchbox models, first made this Massey-Ferguson 165 with cab in 1970. The 1/43 scale miniature was made in England.

Massey-Ferguson 165   MF-24

Bearing a strong resemblence to the Corgi Massey-Ferguson 165 (MF-14), this miniature came from Spain. It was made around 1970 by Joal and was available with or without a front end loader. The words 'Massey-Ferguson' appear on only one side of the hood while the words 'Fabricacion Ebro' appear on the other side.

Massey-Ferguson 165   MF-25a & b

Massey-Ferguson 165   MF-26

This Massey-Ferguson 165 is a 1/20 scale model in plastic kit form. Since it is a snap together kit, it is quite simple to assemble. It has a battery powered electric motor.

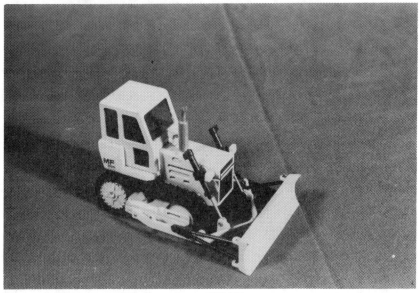

Massey-Ferguson 300 Crawler   MF-27

NZG of West Germany a well know model manufacturer, produced this nicely detailed miniature Massey-Ferguson 300 industrial crawler in 1974. It comes with an adjustable bulldozer blade and a cab with tinted windows.

Massey-Ferguson 450-S Hydraulic Excavator   MF-28

Another NZG industrial miniature is this Massey-Ferguson 450-S hydraulic excavator. Like the 300 crawler it is 1/50 scale and made of die-cast metal. The three hydraulic cylinders are all adjustable.

Ertl's first Massey-Ferguson is this 175 Diesel model introduced in 1965. This 1/16 scale model has realistic steering.

Massey-Ferguson 175   MF-29a

An industrial version of a Massey-Ferguson tractor is this 1/16 Ertl 3165. It is basically the 175 (MF-29a) painted yellow instead of red and with a front end loader installed. It is a very limited run tractor made around 1967.

Massey-Ferguson 3165 Industrial Loader   MF-29b

Ten years later in 1975, another Ertl Massey-Ferguson tractor, similar in size but quite different in style replaced the 175. This MF 275 features a roll over protection system (ROPS).

Massey-Ferguson 275   MF-30

Massey-Ferguson 1080   MF-31a

The castings used to produce the Massey-Ferguson 175 (MF-29a) provided a base for several other MF models by Ertl. This miniature 1080 made in 1970, had a protective cab.

Massey-Ferguson 1150 Six   MF-31c

Still another error in decaling shows up in this Massey-Ferguson 1150 six cylinder engine tractor by Ertl. This one should have a V-8 engine.

Massey-Ferguson 1150 V-8   MF31d

This Ertl 1970 miniature Massey-Ferguson 1150 correctly has the V-8 engine. In addition to the cab, this rather husky model has dual rear wheels.

In 1973, Massey-Ferguson introduced its 1105 model and Ertl quickly followed with a miniature. Two variations were produced, a red wheeled one in 1973 and gray wheeled one in 1975. Both had cabs.

Massey-Ferguson 1105   MF-32

In a very small 1/64 scale, Ertl produced good detail in this Massey-Ferguson 1155 model. There were two wheel size variations produced by Ertl.

Massey-Ferguson 1155/Cab   MF-33

Another 1/16 scale model Massey-Ferguson 1155 by Ertl was produced with two wheel color variations, one red and the other gray. This model has a V-8 engine and a cab.

Massey-Ferguson 1155 V-8/Cab   MF-34

Massey-Ferguson 1155   MF-35

Still another Ertl Massey-Ferguson 1155 model is this 1/25 plastic kit. More information can be found in the section on building and detailing kits.

Massey-Ferguson 1155 "Spirit of America"   MF-36

In celebration of the 1976 Bicentennial, Ertl reworked their MF 1155 plastic kit (MF-35) to produce this "Spirit of America" tractor. When completely done as per the instructions, this one would have the patriotic colors; red, white and blue.

Massey-Ferguson 590 & 595   MF37a & b

In 1977 the Ertl Company released two Massey-Ferguson models made for the foreign markets. The 590 and 595 models shown here have different grills and safety cabs than the American models. The castings are identical but the cab color and identification decals are slightly different. Both are 1/16 scale.

190

Massey-Ferguson 165   MF-38

From Argentina comes this very well detailed scale model Massey-Ferguson 165 tractor. The three-point-hitch has movable lower links.

Massey-Harris 44   MH-1

The Massey-Harris 44 model tractor was undoubtedly the most copied tractor as far as miniatures go. This Dinky model was produced in two distinctively different variations. The first one made in 1948 had metal wheels and tires while the later 1954 variation had rubber tires on metal rims. The later one also had a painted driver. The 1/43 scale model was available with some miniature implements.

This 1959 model 55 Massey-Harris-Ferguson utility tractor was blue in color. It was made to a tiny 1/80 scale and frequently sold for use in model train layouts.

Massey-Harris-Ferguson 55 Utility   MH-2

From Scotland we find a rather crude Massey-Ferguson 44 tractor. The scale is a tiny 1/87. It was made by BJW Wardie in 1950.

Massey-Harris (44)　MH-3

Several companies produced 1/87 scale models of the Massey-Harris 44 tractor. Shown in this grouping are the following; AHI—Hong Kong, Fun-Ho—New Zealand, Lesney—England and others.

Massey-Harris 44's　MH-4, 5, 8 and others

Although this rather crude miniature does not bear the Massey-Harris name or number 44, it has those lines. It was made by Fun-Ho of New Zealand and is three inches long.

(Massey-Harris 44)　MH-6

192

Still another Fun-Ho model resembling the Massey-Harris 44 is this one. It is six and one-half inches in length and has a wide front axle arrangement. Shown beside it is a Fun-Ho International (IH-64).

(Massey-Harris 44)   MH-7

The original Lesney model was this 1/15 scale Moko Number 1 Massey-Harris 745D, first made in 1951. It has excellent detail including realistic steering. Close examination of this photograph reveals the tire treads which are backwards. Since this model was made for a very limited time, it is quite rare today.

Massey-Harris 745D   MH-9

Raphael-Lipkin of Great Britain marketed this miniature in their Pippin line of toys. Although it does not bear the Massey-Harris name or number 745, it could not be patterned after any other tractor. It is blue with red wheels and approximately 1/20 scale.

(Massey-Harris 745)   MH-10a

Massey-Harris 745   MH-10b

Official Massey-Harris red and yellow colors and logo make this model much more realistic. It is identical to MH-10a except for the items mentioned above.

Massey-Harris 745D   MH-14

Another Massey-Harris 745D model was made by PMI in the Union of South Africa. This red tractor with yellow wheels is made to a 1/38 scale and is quite rare in the United States today.

Massey-Harris 44 Standard   MH-15

This Massey-Harris 44 standard tractor was made around 1950 by Lincoln Specialities of Canada. The two unusual features of this miniature tractor are the fenders that extend over the rear tires and the "screw-in" air cleaner and exhaust stacks. The 1/20 scale castings used for this model are rather crude but it is a unique Massey-Harris 44 miniature.

Lincoln Specialities of Canada made at least three variations of the conventional Massey-Harris 44 tractor. The variations are tires: one has tires marked Dominion Royal, another one Goodyear and still a third with wooden rims and plain rubber tires. It was also available with a front end loader.

Massey-Harris 44   MH-16

A row crop tractor is one with the wheels under the radiator. Slik Toys made two variations of a Massey-Harris 44 row crop. One was of pot metal while the other was thinner diecast type of casting. The bottom is closed on the alter one. The driver is cast separately on both.

Massey-Harris 44 Row Crop   MH-17

A rather crude casting was used to produce this 1/16 scale miniature Massey-Harris 44 row crop tractor. It was made during the early 1950s by The King Company and had a separately cast driver in two variations.

Massey-Harris 44 Row Crop   MH-18

Massey-Harris 44 Row Crop   MH-20

If there is an absolutely "Super" miniature scale model Massey-Harris tractor, it has to be this one by Ruehl Products of Wisconsin. This miniature MH 44 was cast in separate pieces and could be assembled and disassembled. The steering was functional as was lift on the rear. Ruehl Products made a variety of implements to accompany this tractor including a mounted plow and a front end loader.

(Massey-Harris 44)   MH-21

From France comes this unusual little Massey-Harris 44 tractor and trailer. It is made of die-cast metal by Gitanes and was used for a cigarette promotion.

Massey-Harris Challenger   MH-22

The antique style tractor shown here is another of Robert Gray's creations. It represents a Massey-Harris Challenger tractor. Notice the "lug" wheels on this model which is approximately 1/12 scale.

Massey-Harris tractors were popular during the 1950s. This well-detailed miniature made by Lincoln Micro Models is six inches long. It has functional steering.

Massey-Harris (745) by Lincoln Micro Models   MH-23

This rather stout model represents a Massey-Harris 55. It has a clockwork windup mechanism and is steerable. It was made by Plasticum.

Massey-Harris (55)   MH-24

Mercedes-Benz, the West Germany automobile manufacturer, also makes a line of agricultural tractors including a MB-Trac four-wheel-drive model. This well detailed 1/90 scale model was made in 1974 by Wiking, a West German toy manufacturer.

Mercedes-Benz MB-Trac Four Wheel Drive   MB-1

Mercedes-Benz Unimog   MB-2

At first glance, this would appear to be simply a pick-up truck. It is, infact, a model of a dual purpose vehicle. It can be used as a light duty tractor since it has four wheel drive and a lifting hitch on the rear. This machine is a Mercedes-Benz Unimog. The miniature is a 1/32 scale model by Britains Limited.

Mercedes-Benz MB TRAC 1300   MB-3

This very well detailed miniature comes from Gescha of West Germany. It represents the MB TRAC 1300 four-wheel-drive tractor. The cab doors open and close for added realism.

Mercedes-Benz MB Trac Four Wheel Drive   MB-4

A recent addition to the line of miniature Mercedes-Benz tractors is this MB-Trac four-wheel-drive tractor. This colorful tractor was made by Gama of Germany.

During World War II, the materials shortage practically eliminated any type of toy manufacturing. Some company managed to produce this Minneapolis-Moline Standard-style tractor out of wood. Although the detail is quite crude, the scale is approximately 1/12.

Minneapolis-Moline Standard (U)   MM-1

Another World War II era Minneapolis-Moline model tractor is this one made by Werner Wood and Plastic Company of South St. Paul. It is approximately 1/12 in scale. The front wheels of this row crop style tractor can be turned by the little lever on top.

Minneapolis-Moline Row Crop (Z)   MM-2

A little 1/32 rubber miniature Minneapolis-Moline tractor was made during the 1950s by Arcor. This row crop model came in a variety of colors and had a molded in driver.

Minneapolis-Moline (U)   MM-3b

Minneapolis-Moline (Z)   MM-4

Another Arcor model Minneapolis-Moline tractor is this 1/16 scale Z. It came in a variety of colors and had a driver looking to the side.

Minneapolis-Moline UB Row Crop   MM-5

Slik Toys of the United States made several Minneapolis-Moline miniatures during the 1950s. This well detailed 1/16 model represents the UB row crop tractor. It has functional steering.

Minneapolis-Moline (R) Row Crop   MM-6

This 1/32 scale model of a Minneapolis-Moline row crop R tractor was made around 1956 by Slik Toys. It has the letters MM cast on the sides and a driver cast-in also. Lincoln Specialities of Canada marketed a tractor almost identical to this one (MM-9).

The Minneapolis-Moline Company introduced a very streamlined, modernistic tractor in the 1950s. Slik made a 1/32 replica of this tractor. It had a wide front axle. This model probably represented the 4 or 5 Star tractor. A slightly later Minneapolis-Moline model was the 445. Slik Toys also made a model of this one in a 1/32 scale. The grill is the major difference between the two miniatures.

Minneapolis-Moline 445   MM-8
Minneapolis-Moline 4 Star   MM-7

An early 1950s model of the Minneapolis-Moline Z is this one made by Slik. Notice the flat hat on the driver's head on this 1/16 scale model.

Minneapolis-Moline (Z)   MM-10

It was not until 1963 that Ertl made another miniature Minneapolis-Moline tractor model. This 1/25 scale row crop tractor was yellow with a bronze or brown bottom and plastic wheels.

Minneapolis-Moline Row Crop   MM-11

Minneapolis-Moline LPG Row Crop   MM-12

This Ertl Minneapolis-Moline row crop tractor has a unique feature, the pressurized LPG (Liquidified Petroleum Gas) fuel tank. Except for the fuel tank, this model is quite similar to MM-11 above.

Minneapolis-Moline LPG Row Crop   MM-13

This third Ertl variation of the Minneapolis-Moline row crop als has the LPG fuel tank. It differs in that it has working steering and rubber tires instead of the plastic ones on the two previous models. It too, is a 1/25 scale model.

Minneapolis-Moline G-1000   MM-14

A very husky model is this 1/16 model of the Minneapolis-Moline G 1000 Vista. This tractor was designed for the larg   eat fields of the West. The first variation   tl in 1967 had yellow wheels while the later 1972 variation had white wheels and no G-1000 Vista decal.

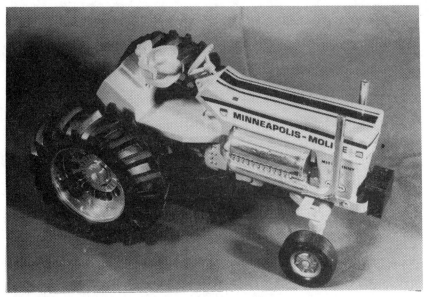

In 1974, Ertl produced a Minneapolis-Moline modified G-1000 "Super Rod" pulling tractor. This model was named "MIGHTY MINNIE."

Minneapolis-Moline Mighty Minnie   MM-15

The last Ertl made Minneapolis-Moline is this G-1355 tractor. It had dual rear wheels and a ROPS. Like the G-1000 model it was made to the 1/16 scale.

Minneapolis-Moline G-1355   MM-16

A 1973 variation of the Muir-Hill industrial tractor by Dinky comes equipped with a backhoe as well as the loader. It is 1/43 scale.

Muir-Hill Industrial Tractor/Loader & Backhoe   MUH-1b

Muir-Hill Industrial Four Wheel Drive   MUH-2

This rather stout-appearing tractor is a Muir-Hill industrial four wheel drive tractor. It was made by Lesney and came with a detachable front blade and a tandum trailer. This yellow model with red wheels is over four inches in length.

Norm   NOR-1

This tiny 1/90 plastic scale model represents a German Norm tractor. It was made in West Germany and has excellent detail for such a small tractor. This Wiking miniature was available in a variety of colors.

Nuffield   NUF-1

A truly excellent miniature Nuffield tractor is this 1/16 scale model by Densil skinner of Great Britain. This rare 1954 model was cast in separate pieces with great detail.

Another British toy manufacturer, Raphael Lipkin, made this Nuffield model about 1963. This 1/15 plastic model had only one headlight and was available with a dump trailer.

BMC Nuffield   NUF-2

Although it does not have Nuffield decals, this Minic No. 2 tractor strongly resembles a Nuffield. It was made around 1954 and has a clockwork mechanism. A most unusual feature of this tractor is the holes in the rear tires that permit the wind-up key to be inserted. The driver is molded separately on this 1/16 scale plastic and metal mode. It even has a smoking mechanism.

(Nuffield) No. 2 Minic   NUF-3

The first cast iron miniature Oliver tractors were made by the Arcade Company in 1936. This five and a quarter inch long model represents the row crop style Oliver 60. The red tractor has the driver cast-in with the rest of the model.

Oliver (60)   OL-1

Oliver 70   OL-2

This Arcade cast iron Oliver 70 row crop tractor was available either painted red or green. Both variations had a separately cast nickle-plated driver.

Oliver 70 Orchard Tractor   OL-3

In 1938, the Hubley Company of Lancaster, Pennsylvania began manufacturing a miniature Oliver 70 orchard tractor. A unique feature of this tractor was the fenders that extended over and around the rear wheels, preventing tree branches from being damaged by the wheels. This five inch long cast iron tractor had a separately cast driver.

Oliver 70   OL-4

After Arcade ceased production of toys, Slik Toys began manufacturing the Oliver 70 row crop tractor, not in cast iron, but in cast aluminum. Note the similarities between this one and OL-2.

Oliver 77   OL-5a

This miniature Oliver 77 tractor was first manufactured by Slik Toys in 1948. The 1/16 scale model had a driver with a helmet type hat.

Oliver 77 Row Crop   OL-5b

The 1950 Oliver 77 Row Crop model by Slik Toys was identical to the 1948 77 except for the decals.

The first Slik Toys Oliver miniature with working steering was this 77 Row Crop-Diesel Power in 1952. This is the last Oliver model to have the "side curtains" covering the sides of the engine.

Oliver 77 Row Crop-Diesel Power   OL-6

Oliver Super 77   OL-7

Another Slik Toys Oliver miniature with working steering is this Super 77. The side curtains on this 1954 model are missing. Like the earlier Slik Toys Olivers, this one is 1/16 in scale.

Oliver Super 55   OL-8

The Oliver Super 55 utility tractor model by Slik Toys was the only one in their line to be made in the 1/12 scale. This 1955 model had a wide front axle, but the steering was not functional. It did, however, have a working three point hitch and a two bottom plow to attach to it.

(Oliver 880)   OL-9

This 1/32 scale Slik Toys tractor model resembles the Oliver 880 model. The steering was not functional. It was widely distributed through variety stores under the Slik Toys name.

Oliver 880   OL-10

The 1/16 scale Oliver 880 model was one of Slik Toys last Oliver miniatures. Made around 1958, this model did not have working steering like most of the other Olivers by Slik Toys. It was a rather short run tractor and, consequently, is difficult to find today.

Oliver OC-6 Crawler   OL-11

The Oliver Corporation made light weight, wide track crawlers for many years. These were used for row crop work, especially by potato growers who liked the crawler since it did not compact the soil as much as many wheel tractors. This very well detailed miniature in 1/16 scale was made by Slik Toys. It was painted yellow rather than the usual Oliver green.

Oliver 70 Row Crop   OL-12

The Oliver 70 was recreated in miniature by this 1/25 scale model made of rubber by Arcor. The row crop tractor had the driver molded in.

This very scarce Oliver model is the Lincoln Specialities 77 Standard tractor. It was made in the early 1950s in Canada. Although the casting is quite crude, it is an interesting Oliver variation.

Oliver 77 Standard   OL-13

This dazzling bright Oliver 70 orchard tractor is a reproduction of the Hubley model (OL-3). It was made in a variety of colors by Fun-Ho of New Zealand. The wheels are a very clean white color.

Oliver 70 Orchard Tractor   OL-14

Robert Gray of Iowa created this Hart Parr 28-44 miniature in 1971. It represents the forerunner of the Oliver line from the 1930s. Mr. Gray made this tractor to approximately the 1/12 scale in either cast aluminum or Korloy.

Hart-Parr 28-44   OL-15

Oliver 70 Row Crop   OL-16a

Mr. Gray also made two Oliver 70 variations. The first one is this 70 row crop. These were available with either rubber or steel wheels. He first made both Oliver 70's in 1976.

Oliver 1800   OL-17a & b

In 1963, the Ertl Company began manufacturing miniature Oliver tractors. The 1800 tractor had working steering and was made with three decal variations representing the Series A, Series B and Series C.

Oliver 1800 Four Wheel Drive   OL-17c & d

The Oliver 1800 was also made with cleted front wheels representing a four wheel drive tractor. This 1/16 Ertl model was first marketed in 1963.

Oliver 1850   OL-17e, f & g

Oliver's next model was the 1850. It was made in miniature in both row crop and four wheel drive models. The tractor is the same, only the decals are different. One row crop variation came without fenders.

White Oliver 1855   OL-17h, i & j

The name 'White' was added to Oliver upon the acquisition by White Motor Company around 1970. Ertl continued using basically the same casting, changing only the decals and front wheel design. These Oliver 1855s were available as a row crop, wide front axle or four wheel drive variations.

Oliver 1855/ROPS & Duals   OL-17k

The final Oliver model by Ertl is this 1855 with a wide front axle, dual rear wheels and a ROPS. Note the similarity between this 1855 and the Minneapolis-Moline G-1355 (MM-16). After these two models, White Motor Company dropped both the Oliver and Minneapolis-Moline names, changed the tractor style and began marketing their line under simply, the White trademark.

Tootsietoy, now a part of the Strombecker organization, began marketing a 1/43 scale model strongly resembling the Oliver series of tractors in 1970. This little green and white tractor came with or without a tandum manure spreader.

(Oliver 1955)   OL-18

The Owatonna Maunfacturing Company in Minnesota had the Ertl Company make a limited number of these miniature Mustang skid steer loaders. On a farm the real skid steer loader finds many uses including handling of feed or manure.

The name basic casting was used by Ertl as the one used for the John Deere skid steer loader (JD-54).

Owatonna Mustang Skid Steer Loader   OW-1

This seven and a half inch long tin model comes from Germany and is a model of a Perplex tractor. Made by Arnold, it is equipped with a battery powered electric motor and has realistic steering. The model number 7300 appears on the sides of the tractor seats.

Perflex 7300   PER-1

This unique miniature is a plastic scale model of a PGS Pigiessi 420 Diesel four wheel drive garden tractor. Articulated in the middle, it has a lifting hood, and was manufactured in 1976 by Protar Micro Modelli Provini of Italy.

PGS Pigiessi 420 Diesel Four Wheel Drive Garden Tractor   PGS-1

This tractor, just under three inches in length, is made by Gama of West Germany. The style is that of the Porsche tractor. It is made of a combination of tin and plastic and was available with a wagon. A clockwork mechanism powered it.

(Porsche)   POR-1

Siku of West Germany made this miniature Porsche Diesel T in several color variations. Like the other models in the Siku line, this one is made of die-cast metal. The scale is 1/60.

Porsche Diesel T   POR-2

214

This tiny 1/90 scale model represents an older style Porsche tractor. It has excellent detail like the other Wiking models. First made in 1958, there have been several color variations made over the years of production.

Porsche   POR-3

This scale model tractor does not have the Porsche name, but certainly must represent one. It is seven inches long, made of plastic and die-cast metal, and has a friction gyro type motor. It bears the T-N trademark and was made in Japan.

(Porsche) TB-20   POR-4

Very little information is available on this model. However, it is over a foot long and made of plastic. The model pictured here has the seat and fenders missing.

Porsche Diesel   POR-5

Renault (E-30)   REN-1

This early style Renault tractor model was made by CIJ of France. It is heavy die-cast metal and 1/32 scale.

Renault E-30   REN-2

In 1959 the old style Renault was replaced by this more streamlined E-30 model. Like the earlier model, it was painted orange.

Renault E-30   REN-3

The third Renault E-30 variation is this one which has a different grill and came in either red or orange. All three have wide front axle arrangements.

A larger 1/16 pressed steel model of the Renault is shown here. This one is an earlier version and had a clockwork mechanism. It was made by CIJ Europarc.

Renault (E-30)   REN-4a

A slightly later variation of the Renault E-30 is this one in red rather than orange. It has an electric motor powered by batteries rather than the clockwork. It is also 1/16 scale and made by CIJ Europarc.

Renault (E-30)   REN-4b

This little 1/43 plastic miniature Renault R-86 was made in France by Norev. It was available in a variety of colors and had a separately molded driver. It even had some chrome plated plastic trim.

Renault R-86   REN-6

217

Renault 652 Industrial   REN-7

All the previous Renault models shown represent agricultural tractors while this one represents an industrial tractor. It is a 652 with a front loader. This French miniature is battery operated and steerable from the remote unit. It has a removable cab and is yellow in color.

Rumley Oil Pull   RUM-1

The third, and perhaps, the smoothest and best detailed Rumley Oil Pull is this slightly smaller one by Irvin's Hobby Shop of Ohio. It is just over six inches in length and has a rubber band operating flywheel and belt pulley. It also has a canopy over the driver's platform.

Rumley Oil Pull   RUM-2

The second recreation of the Oil Pull is this one by Alvin Ebersol of Pennsylvania. Like the first one, it was made to the 1/16 scale but had much smoother castings. It was made in 1975.

The Rumley Oil Pull tractor was a popular one during the 1930s, but it was not until the 1970s that anyone decided to recreate this tractor in miniature. The first Oil Pull was made in 1972 by Old Time Toys of Illinois and was consecutively serial numbered. It was made to approximately the 1/16 scale out of sand cast aluminum.

Rumley Oil Pull   RUM-3

SAME, pronounced Saw-Me, is an Italian make of tractor. This tiny 1/80 miniature represents the Leone model and was made by Politoys of Italy. Not particularly well detailed, it falls in the same catagory as the Lesney Mod type tractor models.

SAME Leone 70   SAM-1

This 1/15 scale model SAME Centauro four wheel drive tractor has very good detail. It was made in 1966 by Dugu of Italy, the same company that manufactures a very nice variety of auto models, particularly antique type. It is a combination of plastic and die-cast metal and has operating steering and three point hitch lift.

SAME Centauro Four Wheel Drive   SAM-2

SAME Leone 70 Four Wheel Drive   SAM-3

This 1976 model of a SAME represents the Leone 70 four wheel drive tractor. It is made of plastic and is approximately 1/12 scale. This orange and blue miniature was made in Italy also.

SAME Buffalo 130 Four Wheel Drive   SAM-4

This 1977 model is a SAME Buffalo 130 four-wheel-drive tractor. Since SAME and Lamborghini are now manufactured by the same organization in Italy, it is understandable that it is similar in design to the Lamborghini previously shown. Both of the miniatures are manufactured by FormaPlast to a 1/43 scale. This blue and orange model has removable cab. It differs from the Lamborghini in that it has an air cleaner on the hood.

Sheppard Diesel   SHE-1

The Sheppard Company of Hanover, Pennsylvania manufactured diesel tractors for only a few years around 1949-50. This row crop model resembled the Allis-Chalmers and because of the similarity of colors, was often mistaken for Allis-Chalmers. There was no connection between the two. The model shown here was made by the Sheppard Company and was about 1/12 scale.

The Steiger Tractor Company of North Dakota began manufacturing tractors in 1958. The two Steiger Brothers decided to build a tractor suitable for their farm needs, and since it was successful, began building for other farmers. This model is a cast model of the Cougar II four wheel drive and was made on a very limited basis in 1975.

Steiger Cougar II Four Wheel Drive   STE-1

In 1976 the Steiger tractor line was restyled and a limited number of these cast Bearcat III models were made. Note the dual wheels all the way around and the articulating center between the front and rear sections of the tractor. Another variation with red, white and blue trim was made to commemorate the '76 Bicentennial. This one is labeled The Panther III.

Steiger Bearcat III Four Wheel Drive   STE-2a

Reportedly the largest internal combustion tractor ever made, the Twin City 60-90 was manufactured in 1918. It wasn't until Robert Gray of Iowa released his version of the Twin City that a miniature was available. His model was made of Korloy, a material somewhat like cast iron. This heft model was scaled to approximately 1/16.

Twin-City (60-90)   TC-1

Pictured here are two very scarce items, a cast iron model of a Vindex Wallis tractor and a cast iron Wallis bear. The tractor probably represents a 20-30 Wallis and was made by Vindex. It is approximately 1/20 scale.

Wallis (20-30)   WAL-1

This Weatherhill Hydraulic Shovel miniature was made by Lesney of Great Britain. This industrial model is three and a half inches long, including the loader. It is yellow in color.

Weatherhill Hydraulic Shovel   WH-1

The White line of farm equipment has evolved from three other lines, Oliver, Minneapolis-Moline and Cockshutt of Canada. The 1/16 scale model is manufactured by a new toy maker, Dyersville Die-Casting selling under the name Scale Models. Shown here is the 2-135 with cab. The 2-155 will be identical except for decals and dual rear wheels.

White 2-135   WH-1a

222

Zetor 5511   ZET-1

The Zetor is a popular tractor in Czechoslovakia. This small 1/80 scale orange tractor was made by Corgi Jr. of Great Britain and Hong Kong. It represents the Zetor 5511 tractor and comes with a cab.

Zetor Super Diesel   ZET-2

An earlier style Zetor Super Diesel is shown here. This three and a half inch long model was made in Czechoslovakia by U. S. U. D. It is made of yellow and white plastic and has a friction type gyro motor. Detail is rather crude.

MISC-1, Dole tin, 8 in., D

MISC-2, Animated Toy "Baby", 3½ in., USA

MISC-3, Bing, 7½ in., D

MISC-4, Unknown tin, 4¼ in., D or F

MISC-5, Marx "American Tractor", 8¼ in., USA

MISC-6, Unknown (military?), 6 in.

MISC-7, Gama, 7¼ in., D

MISC-8, Unknown (B), 6½ in., J

MISC-9, Gescha crawler, 7 in., D

MISC-10, Betaltin plate, 3½ in.

MISC-11, Unknown, 5½ in.

MISC-12, Unknown tin, 3½ in.

MISC-13, Unknown tin, 6½ in., J

MISC-14, TCO crawler-loader, 7½ in., D

MISC-15, Minic crawler, 3¼ in., GB

MISC-16, Minic tractor, 3¼ in., GB

MISC-17, Mettoy crawler and tractor, 5½ in., GB

MISC-18, Mettoy tractor, 9½ in., GB

MISC-19, LBZ crawler, 6 in., D

MISC-20, K "new" tractor, 5ft. 3½ in., J

MISC-21, Joustra, 12 in., F

MISC-22, CKO crawler, 3½ in., D

MISC-23, Cortland, 7 in., USA

MISC-24, Cortland, 5½ in., USA

MISC-25, Marx, 14 in., USA

MISC-26, Arnold, 7 in., F

MISC-27, Unknown wood, 4 in.

MISC-28, Unknown wood, 10½ in.

MISC-29, Chad Valley wood, 7 in., GB

MISC-30, Unknown cast iron crawler-roller, 3½ in.

MISC-31, Hubley "Monarch" crawler, 3 in., USA

MISC-32, Hubley tractor, 4 in., USA

MISC-33, Arcade tractors, 2½ & 3 in., USA

MISC-34, Unknown cast iron crawlers, 3 in.

MISC-35, Unknown crawlers, 3 in.

MISC-36, AR steam tractor, 2½ in., F

MISC-37, Unknown crawlers, 2½ in.

MISC-38, Charbens tractors with reapers, 3½ & 3½ in., GB

MISC-39, Unknown slush mold, 2 in.

MISC-40, Unknown slush mold, 2 in.

MISC-41, Tootsietoys, 3 in., USA

MISC-42, Tootsietoys, 3½ in., USA

MISC-43, Gama crawlers & tractors, 3 in., D

MISC-44, Gama tractor & crawler, 3½ & 4 in., D

MISC-45, Banner plastic & unknown slush mold, 2½ in.

MISC-46, Unknown crawler, 6½ in.

MISC-47, Unknown tractor, 1 in.

MISC-48, Charbens tractor, 3½ in., GB

MISC-49, Charbens tractor, 4 in., GB

MISC-50, Mettoy tractors, 3 & 2½ in., GB

MISC-51, Lansing tractor with loader, 11 in., USA

MISC-52, Dolecek "Dol-trac", 11½ in., USA

MISC-53, Gama tractors, 4½ in., D

MISC-54, Unknown tin, 5½ in.,

MISC-55, Unknown lead, 1½ in.,

MISC-56, Hubley tractor with cast iron driver, 5½ in., USA

MISC-57, Hubley tractor, 4½ in., USA

MISC-58, Tru-Scale (Farmall M), 1/16 scale, USA

MISC-59, Lee Toys tractor/trailer, 3 & 3 in., USA

MISC-60, Lee Toys tractors, 6¼ in., USA

MISC-61, Slik Toy 9890 tractor, 8 in., USA

MISC-62, Unknown plastic, 8 in.

MISC-63, Tudor Rose tractor, 5¼ in., GB

MISC-64, DBCM "Big" tractor/wagon, 12 & 12 in., D

MISC-65, Gay Toys tractor, 7½ in., USA

MISC-66, Unknown tractor, 2 in.

MISC-67, Unknown plastic (battery), 5½ in.

MISC-68, Gama tractor, 12 in., D

MISC-69, Tootsietoy tractor, 2 in., USA

MISC-70, Tootsietoy tractor, 3½ in., USA

MISC-71, Tomy-Matic 340, 9 in., J

MISC-72, Buddy-L, 3½ in., USA

MISC-73, Nasta (slow wheels), 3 in., USA

MISC-74, Fun-Ho crawlers, 9 in., NZ

MISC-75, Fun-Ho crawlers, 6 in., NZ

MISC-76, Fun-Ho tractor, 4 in., NZ

MISC-77, Fun-Ho tractor, 2 in., NZ

MISC-78, Lesney Mod tractors, 2 & 4 in., GB

MISC-79, Plastic unknown, 9 in.

MISC-80, Avon glass bottle, 6 in., USA

MISC-81, Aubrubber, 4 in., USA

MISC-82, Aubrubber, 6 in., USA

MISC-83, Tomica baggage & airport tractors, 1/50 & 1/119, J

MISC-84, Marx Donald Duck, 3½ in., HK

MISC-85, Sun Rubber "Mickey's" tractor, 4 in., USA

MISC-86, Barr Ohio tractor, 4 in., USA

MISC-87, Brio crawler/wagon, 4½ in., S

MISC-88, Urtrac crawler, 2 in., E-G

MISC-89, Paya, 12 in., E

MISC-90, Caterpillar on the World, 6 in., USA

MISC-91, Unknown WWII composition, USA
MISC-92, Unknown wood, USA

MISC-93, Unknown cast iron crawler/roller, 3¾ in., USA

MISC-94, Wooden Toys, Jackson, MI, 12 in., USA

MISC-95, GS, 5 in., USA

MISC-96, Multiple Products, 5½ in., USA

MISC-97, Steho, vinyl-like plastic (length given for tractor only), 6 in., D

MISC-98, Plasto, 9½ in., Fin

MISC-99, Hubley (composition/cast iron plated driver's head-No. 125), 5 in., USA

MISC-100, Crescent caterpillar (No. 1822), 4 in., GB

MISC-101, Crescent tractor (possibly a Fordson E-27-N), 4½ in., GB

MISC-102, KDN tractor with clockwork & working gear shift, 6 in.

MISC-103, TM tractor/implements, 5½ in., J

MISC-104, Unknown tin clockwork crawler/log wagon (length given for crawler only), 2½ in., D

MISC-105, Unknown slush mold row crop tractor, 2¾ in.

MISC-106, Fun-Ho group of three row crop tractors, 3¾, 3 & 2 in., NZ

MISC-107, Plastic remote control tractor.

MISC-108, Plastic and pressed steel lawn and garden tractor, 4-3/8 in., Russia

MISC-109, CKO tin tractor and wagon made by DCGM, nuber 389 with driver and friction drive, 3¾ in.

Machinery Models

5

Tractors and other power units would be of little value without a proper selection of implements for particular jobs. For example, a one-hundred horsepower tractor cannot turn soil without a plow or other similar implement.

This section will show just some of the many miniature implements that were manufactured to accompany the miniature tractors. Some model manufacturers marketed sets which included a tractor with one or more implements. Other manufacturers marketed these individually so that the buyer could make up his own "set."

Case spreader—Vindex

Case hay loader—Vindex

This tractor and group of implements was made by Solido of France. In addition to the heavy die-cast Beauce tractor with keywind clockwork, the set includes two different wagons, a three-gang lawn or field roller, a sickle-bar mower, culipacker, single roller and an adjustable three-bottom plow.

IMP-1

This little Tekno Ferguson tractor set includes a three-bottom plow, spring-tooth harrow, wagon and a rear-mounted carrier complete with milk churns (cans).

IMP-2

Oliver implements

IMP-3

IMP-4

During the 1950s, the Oliver Corporation had quite a nice variety of implements made by The Slik Company.

IMP-5

During the 1950s, the Minneapolis-Moline had quite a nice variety of implements made by The Slik Company.

IMP-6

Minneapolis-Moline had a variety of miniatures, also made by Slik. All the models shown except the disk and plow are 1/32 scale.

IMP-7

This rather interesting tiny plastic set was made in Hong Kong. The tractor resembles an Allis-Chalmers or Sheppard Diesel. Notice the pile of pumpkins, the "shock" of corn and various bales. The implement with the teeth or tines in the lower right is a dump hay rake.

IMP-8

Complete with a box that converts to a barn, this lithographed steel set was made by Marx. The implement in the lower left is a corn planter. The wire on it represents a row marker.

IMP-9

Pictured here are some John Deere miniatures made by Ertl in the early 1950s. The tractor in the fore-ground is a John Deere A hitched to the early manure spreader. The tractor with the well detailed loader is the model 60.

IMP-10

Another 1950s John Deere grouping is this model 60 tractor with a mounted two row corn picker and flair wagon. The end gate of the wagon can be raised or lowered as well as swung out for unloading.

IMP-11

The 1960s tractor is a John Deere 3010 and is hitched to an earlier baler. The wagon bed is a creation made by C. E. Burkholder. The wagon "running gear" is identical to the one above.

IMP-12

This interesting grouping is a part of Robert Condray's collection. The miniature "fuel" barrel is really a bank. The two tractors are modifications made by Bob. The hand truck has a sack commemorating the Kansas Centennial 1961. The Buddy Lee doll has a hand made John Deere uniform.

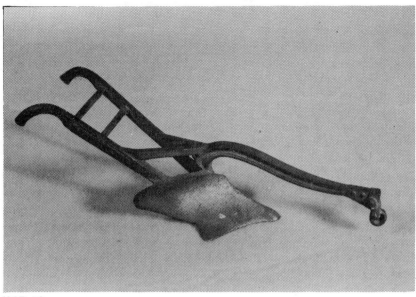

IMP-13

The plow shown here is a model of a John Deere horse drawn plow. The plow miniature was available in either cast iron or pot metal. These plows were donated to Future Farmers of America chapters by Deere & Company for use as the symbol of the vice-president's office.

IMP-14

This Hubley Ford tractor featured a three point hitch to which a variety of implements could be mounted. Shown here on the tractor is a post hole digger. On real tractors it was powered by the power take off and raised and lowered by the hydraulic system. On the miniature, the auger can be turned by the crank on top. The three bottom plow and back scraper blade were available with the tractor. The "Dearborn Equipment" plow accompanied a Product Miniature Ford tractor and bears a strong resemblence to the Hubley plow.

IMP-15

The Ertl Company made this tilt-bed truck in several variations. The crank on top can be used to pull the tractor up on the truck bed. Both the truck and tractor represent International models.

IMP-16

This grouping of two and four wheel trailers includes dumps, tanks, horse, cattle and even one with a clockwork used to power a Britains tractor. Most of these were made in Great Britain, France and Germany. Notice the log trailer.

IMP-17

This selection of four wheel wagons includes some made in Europe as well as in the United States.

IMP-18

This four wheel wagon was made in the early 1950s by Advanced Products for the Cockshutt Company. The die-cast model features real "auto type" steering.

The Case wagon in the rear is made by Ertl while the one beside it is a Carter Tru-Scale. The Massey-Harris wagon in front center is a very well detailed Ruehl Products miniature made in the 1950s. The other two plastic wagons are recent 1/25 Ertl kits.

IMP-19

The Ertl Company made a variety of gravity grain wagons including this one with the M & W logo on the side.

IMP-20

Another Ertl gravity box is this one with the Huskee trademark. These wagons had a crank wheel on the unloading side for raising the slide door. The wagon running gear features "auto" steering.

IMP-21

IMP-22

Product Miniature made plastic wagons for International Harvester in the early 1950s. Shown here are two flair wagon variations having slightly different identification decals.

IMP-23

The cast iron spreader in the foreground is an Arcade. It has the words 'McCormick-Deering' cast into the sides. The other spreaders are Internationals and careful examination of the decals reveals the transition of the name McCormick-Deering to International.

IMP-24

Although not much space has been devoted to horse drawn farm equipment in this book, there were many fine miniatures made by a variety of companies. These McCormick-Deering spreaders and wagon were made by Arcade around 1930.

IMP-25

This group of spreaders represents small scale models. The top one is made by Slik. The rear right one is a Tootsietoy. The one on the left is made of rubber by Alcor while the well detailed Massey-Harris is made by Dinky of England.

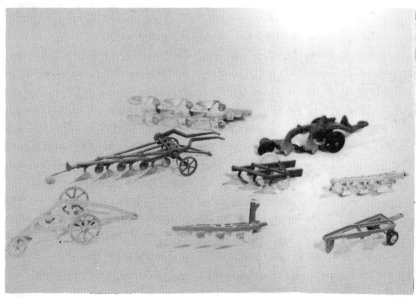

IMP-26

These Case implements include a plastic spreader made by Monarch Plastic to accompany the Case DC tractor. The wagon and plow are metal models probably made by Carter Tru-Scale.

IMP-27

Included here is a "two way" or roll over plow that is used to turn all furrows in the same direction, thus eliminating the back and dead furrows on larger fields. The three middle plows and the roll over plow are all Britains Ltd. The top right one is a rubber Arcor. The lower left trailing plow was made by A. R. France. The bottom hydraulic three point hitch plow is a Corgi while the last one is a Tootsietoy.

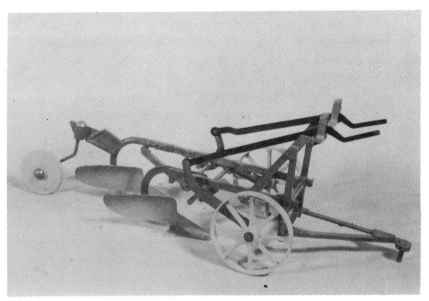

IMP-28

This 1/16 scale plow (plough) made by Mettoy of Great Britain has excellent detail. The individual levers operate either the furrow wheel or the landside wheel. The tail wheel pivots allowing the plow to turn easily. Notice the long moldboards which are quite common on plows made in Great Britain.

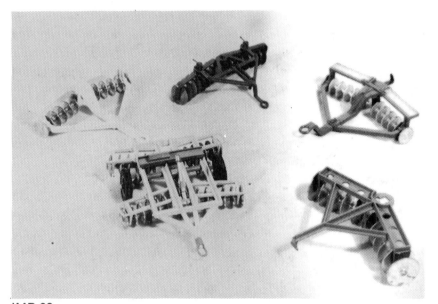

IMP-29

This 1/16 scale plow (plough) made by Mettoy of Great Britain has excellent detail. The individual levers operate either the furrow wheel or the landside wheel. The tail wheel pivots allowing the plow to turn easily. Notice the long moldboards which are quite common on plows made in Great Britain.

IMP-30

Here are two Allis-Chalmers single disks and a two bottom trailing plow. These were made to the same scale as the American Precision Allis-Chalmers model C tractor.

From New Zealand comes a line of toys called Fun-Ho. This line, although rather crude, features rather unique models of implements. Shown here are the following; a two bottom trailing plow, a disk harrow, a spike tooth harrow or smoothing drag and a land roller. This group is approximately 1/16 scale.

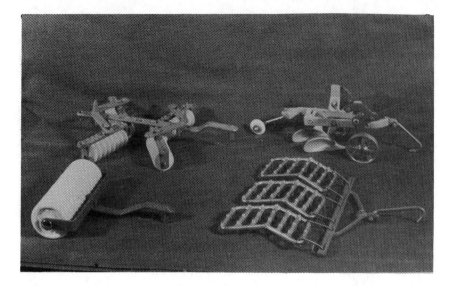

IMP-31

In 1975 the International and World Plowing competition was held in Ontario, Canada. To commemorate this event, Jon Hall made up this model horse drawn plow mounted on a base.

IMP-32

Here is a variety of horse drawn implements made by Britains Limited years ago. The one on the left is a dump hay rake. The center one is a single bottom plow while the one on the right is a land roller.

IMP-33

253

IMP-34

The Arcade Company made a variety of cast iron toys during the 1920-30s. Many implements were made to accompany the Allis-Chalmers, Fordson, McCormick-Deering and other tractors of that era. Shown here are both the single and tandem, or double, disks. The center implement is a slip scoop, or not so complimentarily referred to as a man killer. If the cutting edge caught on a rock, the man on the handles could easily be airborne in a hurry. The top left plow is an Oliver while the other one is a McCormick-Deering. The rear center implement is a dump rake.

IMP-35

While it can be debated if this is a farm implement or a household appliance, it was made by several companies including McCormick-Deering. This Arcade miniature represents a cream separator. Centrifugal force caused a separation of the lighter cream from the heavier milk, each coming out a separate spout. The cream would then be churned into butter.

IMP-36

All the implements shown here, except the top left wagon, are Arcades. That wagon is a Hubley. These represent smaller scale implements and include the following; corn planter, spike tooth harrow, one-row corn binder, sickle bar mowing machine, dump rake, scraper-dump trailer, side tipping trailer and two high sided wagons.

Probably the most "romantic" farm implement is the thresher. It was this implement that brought about the neighboring cooperative spirit at harvest time. Shown here are two size variations of the Arcade McCormick-Deering separators (threshers). There are many color variations of these Arcade miniatures. Shown in the foreground is a McCormick-Deering plow, also made by Arcade.

IMP-37

Here are four variations of John Deere flair type wagons. The one in the lower left is the earliest, having solid rubber tires-wheels. All but the top left one have removable wagon boxes.

IMP-38

A well detailed 1/32 scale New Holland baler complete with a thrower and a blae wagon was made in the 1960s by Advanced Products Company. The bale thrower has a rubber band mechanism that throws the bales into the wagon. Advanced Products Company also made a larger 1/16 scale model baler for New Holland.

IMP-39

IMP-40

Here are two variations of the John Deere pull type combines made in the 1950s. One features a belt conveyer while the other has an auger mechanism.

IMP-41

Massey-Harris, long famous for its combines, had several model companies make miniatures for them. All of these pictured here have working features. Beginning in the front, the smallest one is made by Lesney (Matchbox), then Corgi, Pippin by Raphael Lipkin, The King Company, Ruehl products and finally the large Massey-Ferguson by Ertl.

IMP-42

In addition to the self propelled combine miniature by Ruehl shown above, there were at least two variations of their pull type Clipper combine. The Ruehl Products models had excellent detail and came with a parts sheet so extra parts could be ordered.

IMP-43

From Rex of Germany comes this plastic miniature combine representing a John Deere-Lanz. This rather fragil model has good detail.

IMP-44

Allis-Chalmers, famous for its Gleaner combines, had some miniatures made by The Ertl Company. At least one variation had interchangable corn and grain heads. The corn head is used to both pick and shell corn. The plastic barge wagon in the back was made to accompany the Allis-Chalmers WD-45 tractor model.

IMP-45

Claas of West Germany has manufactured combines for many years. Shown here are three miniatures. The one in the foreground is a Lesney. It is number 65 in their regular series. The next one is also a Lesney, but one of the King Size series. The largest one is a rather recent one by Gama.

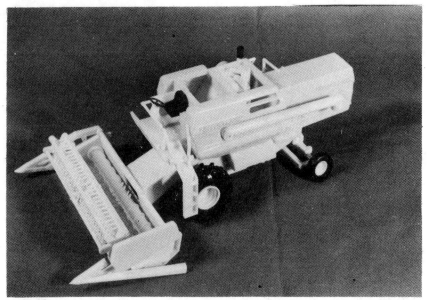

IMP-46

The New Holland Company has manufacturing plants in Europe including Belgium. This miniature came from Belguim and represents their combine manufactured there. It is made of plastic and is nine and a half inches long.

IMP-47

Here are two slightly different variations of the Ertl John Deere self propelled combines. The major difference is the drive mechanism for the reel.

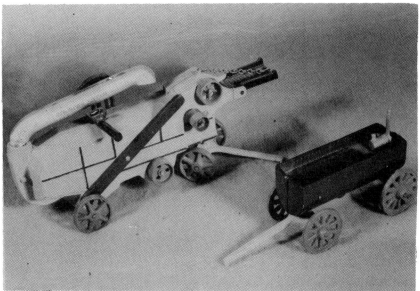

IMP-48

Robert Gray of Iowa created these original models of old time implements. The thresher represents a Red River Special. The other implement is a water wagon which was used to supply water needed by the steam traction engines used to power the separator.

IMP-49

Shown here with a Vindex Case L tractor are two other implements made by Vindex. Both the three bottom plow and the manure spreader are cast iron Case models.

IMP-50

This is an example of a trailer plow. Notice that it has three wheels. The furrow wheel in front, landside wheel (almost hidden) and the tail wheel behind the moldboards are the names of the three wheels. This miniature is an Ertl Eska.

IMP-51

A semi-mounted plow is one which is supported by the hydraulic system on the rear of the tractor. This is an Ertl seven bottom plow made for International.

IMP-53

This combine is the latest in the Ertl series of Allis-Chalmers Gleaner combines. It has greater detail than the earlier models.

IMP-54

The 1978 Britains Ltd. New Holland 376 baler with bale sledge (sled) that accumulates bales for group dropping in the field. This 1/32 scale model has a compartment inside the baler with a rubber band mechanism that "distributed" bales as the baler moves along.

IMP-55

This 10-1/2 inch long plastic New Holland baler is made in Europe.

IMP-56

Fahr is the name of a West German farm machinery manufacturer. This miniature represents the Fahr M1102 self propelled combine. It is made of red plastic with yellow trim and is 8-1/4 inches long.

IMP-57

The 1978 Claas self propelled three row forage harvester miniature is made by GAMA of West Germany. It is 6-1/4 inches long.

Directory

6

This chapter was prepared to give the reader a concise summary of available information on individual models. The information contained here is correct to the best of the author's knowledge and information.

A summary of the information contained and/or terms in each column follows:

Pictures—an asterisk here indicates that a picture appears elsewhere in the book.

Code No.—an arbitrary letter-number system to identify models.

Model—Some miniatures have identifying model numbers or letters on them and this is shown in this column. Eg. Allis Chalmers HD-5. In cases where the model number or letter is not on the miniature, the probable model identification appears in parenthesis. Eg. Allis-Chalmers (WD-45)

Scale or Size—Scale refers to the relative size in comparison with the real machine. For example, a 1/1 machine scale would be actual size, while a 1/16 scale would be sixteen times smaller than the real machine, a 1/25 scale would be twenty-five times smaller than the real machine. Where a scale is not given, the actual size of the miniature is given in inches.

Type of Material:

    C. A.—cast aluminum

    C. I.—cast iron

    D.—diecast: a broad term used to describe models which have metal forced under pressure into dies which give the proper form or shape.

    D. in Lucite—diecast metal model in clear lucite plastic

    Glass

    Kor—Korloy: a heavy metal having the approximate weight of cast iron.

    L—Lead

    M. S.—Machined steel: hand made model as opposed to a production line model.

    P—plastic

    P. K.—plastic kit

    Pot—pot metal: a broad term describing a variety of alloys used in molding toy models.

R—rubber

S. S.—stamped steel/*T*—tin: These two terms are frequently used interchangably, although this is not particularly correct.

W—wood

W. K.—wood kit

Z.—Zymac: a type of pot metal.

Manufacturer and Country—see Chapter II—a list of farm toy manufacturers.

Stock Number—this is the manufacturer's number identifying his product. This number should not be confused with the model number. In many cases, the stock number was not available.

Year—this is the actual year of manufacture of the miniature, not the real machine. In many cases, the years are the same. This year is the first year of manufacture. Keep in mind that some miniatures were manufactured for many years, even after production on the real machine ceased. In a few cases, old dies were brought out and miniatures were made years after the first production schedule ceased.

Remarks—brief definitions of terms used follows:

Air cleaner stack—an extension of the air cleaner extending up through or beside the hood.

Antique—refers to very old style tractors, not necessarily following the one-hundred year old technical definition of antique.

Articulated—a machine that bends in the middle, usually for the purpose of steering.

Backhoe—an attachment for the rear of a tractor or crawler that is used to dig trenches, etc. It is sometimes referred to as a trencher.

Battery operated or battery powered—a miniature have a miniature battery-powered electric motor that operates a part or parts of the model.

Blade—refers to a device on the front or rear of a tractor or crawler that is used to push or pull dirt, snow, manure, etc.

Bulldozer—a crawler with a blade.

Cab—an enclosure over the driver's platform that protects the driver from the elements. Many of the new cabs are equipped with a heater, air conditioner, radio, tape player and other options.

Canopy—a simple overhead protection, not enclosing the driver's platform but simply covering the top of it.

Cast-in driver—on miniatures the driver is sometimes cast with the parts of the tractor.

Cast-in name—on some cast iron or aluminum models, the name appears in raised or recessed markings on the casting.

Cigarette dispenser—a model so made as to serve as a holder and dispenser of cigarettes.

Cigarette lighter—a model with a lighter mechanism built in.

Cleated front wheels—front tires having treads, usually indicating that it is a four-wheel-drive tractor.

Clockwork—a keywind mechanism that powers the miniature. A few models have a ratcheting mechanism rather than a keywind.

Crawler—a type of tractor fitted with tracks, usually steel on the real tractors and rubber on the miniatures, that greatly increases traction.

Crawler-loader—a crawler with a front end hydraylic loader.

Cultivision—a term used by International Harvester to describe the offset design of some of their small tractors. This design is particularly good for cultivating row crops such as corn or cotton.

Custom made—a one of a kind or a few of a kind not made on an assembly line.

Decal—the paper or cellophane-like strip bearing the tractor indentification name and model number.

Disk—an implement having many cutting wheel-like blades used to break up the soil after tillage.

Duals or dual rear wheels—two wheels on each rear axle providing greater traction and flotation on soft ground. A few four wheel drive tractors have duals on both front and rear axles.

Earth mover—a machine used to move dirt from one location to another. Some simply are a trailer with a loading and unloading mechanism while others have power units as an integral unit.

Electric—usually refers to a small battery powered electric motor but a few models have a transformer and use regular household current to power them.

Embossed—having a stamped-out design such as on the grill of some models.

Exhaust stack—the pipe, usually having a muffler, extending up through or along side the hood that carries exhaust away from the tractor.

Fast hitch—a term used by International Harvester to describe a hitching system for their tractors and implements. It was most popular during the 1950s.

Flywheel—a heavy wheel at the end of the crankshaft that makes the engine run smoothly.

Four-wheel-drive (4WD)—a term used to describe a tractor that has power to both the rear and front wheels. The front tires will have cleats also.

Four wheel skid loader—a relatively new implement used on farms for loading, scraping, etc. Both wheels on one side can be stopped while the other wheels keep moving to steer it, hence the name, skid loader.

Four wheel steer—all four sheels are used to steer; permitting manuvering in close places or on steep hillsides.

Friction motor—a gyro type of motor used to power some miniatures.

Grill—the protective mesh-like screen that protects the radiator.

Gyro motor—a type of impulse motor used to power some miniatures.

Half tracks—a tractor having metal or rubber tracks attached to the rear wheels and an extra set of wheels, called boogie or idler wheels. These permitted better traction and were popular before four wheel drive tractors became so popular.

Hood—the covering over the engine.

Hydraulic—a pump powered by the engine that raised or lowers mounted implements by means of hydraulic cylinders.

Hydro (hydrostatic)—a term used to describe a hydraulically operated transmission now found on certain tractors.

Industrial—tractors or equipment used mostly for non-farm construction purposes. There are usually identified by the yellow color.

Integral—a tractor and an implement hitched so as to act as a single unit. For example, a tractor with a three-point-hitch mounted plow.

Lawn & garden tractor (LGT)—a small tractor used for mowing lawns and light garden work as well as a host of other chores.

Loader—a bucket-like device on the front of a tractor used to scoop up and load materials such as dirt, manure, etc.

Metal wheels—on miniatures the tires and wheels are sometimes cast or molded as a single unit. This also can refer to the material from which the wheel is made.

Mislabeled—the incorrect name or model number on miniature.

Molded-in driver—a driver molded into the tractor unit of either a plastic or rubber miniature.

Mod-type—a miniature that is not realistic in appearance but rather a modernistic creation.

Original—someone's own creation, usually of an old tractor or implement.

Paperweight—a solid cast model not having a great amount of detail designed primarily as a desk piece.

Plastic wheels—the wheels of a miniature being made of plastic rather than metal.

Plated—a material having an extra coating or cover of another shiny material. For example, many of the old cast iron drivers had a plating of nickle and some of the new plastic models have a chrome-like coating.

Radiator—the cooling mechanism of a tractor.

Remote control—the device attached to some miniatures that permits steering, etc. and is usually battery powered.

Reproduction—a copy of an original model.

Roll-over-protection-system (ROPS)—a frame like attachment on a tractor designed to protect the operator in the event the tractor tips over. As of October 1976, all tractors over twenty horsepower manufactured in the United States are required to have type of ROPS or safety cab. Orchard or other low profile tractors are exempt from this federal order. Great Britain has had a similar law since 1971.

Roto-tiller—an implement that breaks up the soil.

Row crop—a farm tractor havng two closely-spaced front wheels used for cultivation and other chores involving row crops.

Rubber tracks—on miniatures in the crawler category, most of the tracks are rubber rather than metal like the real ones.

Rubber wheels-tires—on miniatures, some of the wheels ad tires are molded as single pieces.

Safety frame—a type of ROPS.

Separate driver—many of the older cast iron tractors had drivers which were cast separately from the tractors. In most cases these were chrome or nickle plated.

Slow moving vehicle sign (SMV)—safety emblem for tractors.

Sound Gard Cab—a trademark name given to the safety cab by Deere & Company.

Standard—refers to a style of tractor having a fixed tread or axle spacing. This type of tractor is usually larger than row-crop type tractors.

Steam traction engine—an old style tractor powered by steam.

Steering or steerable—a miniature that has working steering.

Super Rod—a term used to describe The Ertl Company's versions of pulling tractors.

Three-point-hitch—an integral hitching system on most modern tractors for rear, or in some cases front-mounted implements.

Trailer—a two or four wheel implement used for hauling various items.

There are many different types of trailers.

Trencher—a type of backhoe.

Turf tires—special treaded tires used on lawns to prevent damage to the grass.

Turbo (Turbocharger)—a blower on diesel engines that provides more air to the engine for greater combustion and thus, more power.

Utility—a type of tractor designed for many different uses on a farm.

V-blade—a blade shaped like a V that pushes dirt or snow off to both sides.

Weight—ballast for greater traction or balance on the front, sides, rear or on the wheels of a tractor.

Wheatland—a standard style of tractor used mainly on the great plains.

Wide front end (WFE)—front wheels spaced the same or nearly the same distance apart as the rear wheels. This style of tractor is usually more stable than a row-crop.

Winch—a device on the rear or front of a tractor or crawler used to pull items such as logs. It can also be used to pull a stuck tractor out of the mud.

Wood wheels—some of the old cast iron miniatures had wooden wheels-tires rather than rubber or cast iron.

Code No.	Model	Scale or Size	Type of Material	Manufacturer	Stock No.	Year	Country	Remarks
ALLCHIN								
*ALL-1	7-32	1/80	D	Lesney	Y-1	1955	GB	Represents a 1925 steam traction engine
*ALL-2	7-32	1/76	D	ABS-Models	R-00(9)	1976	GB	Metal kit—similar to ALL-1, canopy optional
ALLIS—CHALMERS								
*AC-2	(A)	1/12	C.A. or K	Robert Gray		1971	USA	Old style 'standard' model from the 1920s—30s
*AC-3	(U)	3''	C.I.	Arcade		1934	USA	'Standard' with cast-in driver; represents a 1929 model
*AC-4	(U)	5''	C.I.	Arcade		1934	USA	'Standard' with cast-in driver and cast-in name
*AC-5	(WC)	6''	C.I.	Arcade		1940	USA	Row crop with cast-in driver and cast-in name; AC introduced the WC in 1934
*AC-6	(WC)	7''	C.I.	Arcade	3740	1940	USA	Row crop with separate driver (Plated) and decal name
*AC-7	(WC)	1/16	C.I.	Dent		1940	USA	Row crop with separate driver (Painted) and cast-in name
*AC-8	(WC)	1/16	P	Auburn Rubber		1950	USA	Row crop with molded-in driver; red and silver
*AC-9	(C)	1/12	D	American Precision		1950	USA	Row crop
*AC-10	(WD-45)	1/16	P	Strombecker, Kelton, Kaysun Plastics	KC-3	1952	USA	Row crop
*AC-11a	(D-Series)	1/25	P	Strombecker, Kelton, Kaysun Plastics	D61-149 KC-1	1960	USA	WFE—assembled
*AC-11b	(D-Series)	1/25	PK	Strombecker, Kelton, Kayson Plastics	D61-149 KD-100	1960	USA	WFE—kit
*AC-12	HD-5	1/16	P	Product Miniature		1955	USA	Crawler with Baker blade
*AC-13	HD-5	1/20	Pot				USA	Crawler with Baker blade; over head cable left; paperweight
*AC-14	HD-5	1/20	Pot				USA	Crawler with Baker blade; hydraulic side lifts; paperweight
AC-15	(WC)	6''	D	Ertl		1945	USA	Row crop with cast-in driver, similar to Arcade (AC-5)
*AC-16a	(D-17 Ser. I)	1/16	D	Ertl	104	1960	USA	WFE—steerable; orange wheels, black grill & decal trim; headlights

Code No.	Model	Scale or Size	Type of Material	Manufacturer	Stock No.	Year	Country	Remarks
*AC-16b	(D-17 Ser. II)	1/16	D	Ertl	104	1961	USA	WFE—steerable; beige wheels, light grill & decal trim; headlights
*AC-16c	(D-17 Ser. III)	1/16	D	Ertl	104	1964	USA	WFE—steerable; beige wheels; long decals; no headlights
*AC-17a	B-110	1/16	D	Ertl	197	1967	USA	Lawn & garden tractor
*AC-17b	B-112	1/16	D	Ertl	AC-197	1969	USA	Lawn & garden tractor with blade, mower & trailer
*AC-18	(LGT)	1/16	D	Ertl	151	1972	USA	Lawn & garden tractor with blade & trailer
*AC-19a	190	1/16	D	Ertl	192	1965	USA	WFE with metal wheels, bar grill.
AC-19b	190	1/16	D	Ertl	192	1966	USA	WFE with plastic wheels, bar grill.
*AC-20	190XT	1/16	D	Ertl	192	1969	USA	WFE—no bars on grill
*AC-21	190XT—Ser. III Landhandler	1/16	D	Ertl	AC-188	1971	USA	WFE—large tires; ROPS
*AC-22	Big Ace	1/16	D & P	Ertl	2703	1972	USA	WFE—modified 190 super rod pulling tractor
*AC-23	200	1/16	D	Ertl	AC-152	1972	USA	WFE—Black trim; has air cleaner & exhaust stacks
*AC-24a	7030	1/16	D	Ertl	1202	1974	USA	WFE
AC-24b	7040	1/16	D	Ertl	1201	1975	USA	WFE
*AC-24c	7050	1/16	D	Ertl	1200	1973	USA	WFE—cab, wide rear tires
AC-24d	7060	1/16	D	Ertl	1200	1975	USA	WFE—cab; no air cleaner stack, wide rear tires
*AC-25a	12-G	1/25	D	Ertl	AC-198	1967	USA	Industrial crawler—loader
*AC-25b	Fiat-Allis 12-G-B	1/25	D	Ertl	198	1975	USA	Industrial crawler—loader
*AC-26	HD-16	4''	P	Lionel			USA	Crawler with blade
*AC-27	Scraper Pan	7 1/2	P	Lionel			USA	Earth mover
AC-28	Crawler	1/80	D	Mercury	517	1961	I	Crawler with blade
*AC-29	260 Scraper Pan	1/74	D	Lesney	K-6	1961	GB	Earth mover—articulated
*AC-30	D-Series	12''	P	Empire				Row crop—molded-in driver
AC-31	7045	1/64	D	Ertl	1623	1978	USA	WFE—cab
AC-32a	7045	1/16	D	Ertl	1201	1978	USA	WFE—black transmission & engine
AC-32b	7060	1/16	D	Ertl	1208	1978	USA	WFE—cab

Code No.	Model	Scale or Size	Type of Material	Manufacturer	Stock No.	Year	Country	Remarks
								(Restyled)—black transmission & engine
AC-33	WC	1/12	CA & D	Scale Models		1978	USA	Row crop model with "Steel Lug Type" wheels. It represents a 1934 model. Only 2000 were made.
AVERY								
*AV-1	Avery	4 1/2''	C.I.	Hubley		1920	USA	Rounded radiator—name on side
*AV-2	Avery	4 1/2''	C.I.	Arcade		1929	USA	Flat radiator
*AV-3	Avery	4 1/2''	C.A.	Peterson, White, Irvin		1964	USA	Preproduction of Hubley (AV-1)
AV-4	Avery Under-mount	9''	C.A.	Irvin		1978	USA	Called 'Undermount' because the engine is mounted under the steam boiler.
B.M. Volvo								
BMV-1	800	1/66	D	Husky	34	1967	GB	WFE
*BMV-2	800	1/66	D	Corgi Jr.			GB-HK	WFE—almost identical to BMV-1
*BMV-3	800	4 3/4''	P			1975		WFE—cab
BATES								
*BAT-1	40 Steel Mule	1/16	C.I.	Vindex	4	1930	USA	Solid cast with wheels under tracks; crawler; has separately cast driver.
BEAUCE & FLANDRE								
*BEA-1	Wheel tractor	1/32	D	Solido	85	1948	F	Has 'Solido' name cast on sides of hood; clockwork; usually came with implements
*FLA-1	Crawler tractor	1/32	D	Solido	87	1948	F	Has 'Solido' name cast on sides of hood; clockwork; same body casting—Also came as a kit which could be made into a wheel or crawler tractor.
BELARUS (BYALARUS)								
*BEL-1	420-4WD	1/16	P	Miniluxe (?)		1975	F	Model of a Russian tractor—excellent detail; front wheels steer; has cab
BLAW-KNOX								
*BK-1	Crawler	1/43	D	Dinky	561	1948	GB	Rubber tracks
*BK-2	Bulldozer	1/43	P	Dinky	961	1964	GB	Crawler with blade; rubber tracks
*BK-3	Crawler	1/43	D	Moko-Lesney		1951	GB	Rubber tracks
BUFFALO-PITTS								
*BP-1	Steam traction engine	8 3/4''	Kor	Robert Gray		1974	USA	Model of an antique tractor; available with a thresher & water wagon

Code No.	Model	Scale or Size	Type of Material	Manufacturer	Stock No.	Year	Country	Remarks
BUKH								
*BUK-1	D-30 Diesel	1/30	D	Chico Toys	17	1976	CO	WFE
CASE								
*CAS-1	(L)	1/16	C.I.	Vindex	36	1930	USA	Standard style tractor; separate plated driver; very rare; CASE introduced the 'L' in 1929
*CAS-2	(L)	1/16	C.A.	Old Time Toys, Pioneer Tractor Works		1968	USA	Reproduction of CAS-1
*CAS-3a	(SC)	1/16	P	Monarch Plastic		1950	USA	Row crop; orange; the first CASE SC was introduced in 1939
*CAS-3b	(SC)	1/16	P	Monarch Plastic		1951	USA	Row crop with fenders; orange
*CAS-4	(800) Casomatic	1/16	P	JoHan		1956	USA	Row crop; beige & orange
CAS-5a	930 C.K.	1/16	D	Ertl	204	1963	USA	Standard or wheatland style; round orange fenders; 930 or 1030 decals; wheels steer
*CAS-5b	1030 C.K.	1/16	D	Ertl	204	1963	USA	Same as CAS-5a
*CAS-6	1030 C.K.	1/16	D	Ertl	204	1967	USA	Standard or wheatland style; flat beige fenders; wheels steer
CAS-7a	1070 A.K.	1/16	D	Ertl	200	1969	USA	WFE—cab
*CAS-7b	1070 A.K.	1/16	D	Ertl	210	1969	USA	WFE—cab; dual rear wheels
*CAS-7c	1070 A.K. Demonstrator	1/16	D	Ertl	210	1970	USA	WFE—cab; dual wheels; black trim with beige cab
*CAS-7d	1070 A.K.—451 Cubes Demonstrator	1/16	D	Ertl	210	1971	USA	WFE—cab; Dual wheels; black & gold trim—"Black Knight"
*CAS-8a	1270 A.K.—451 Cubes	1/16	D	Ertl	215	1972	USA	WFE—CAS-8 Series is a larger casting
CAS-8b	1270 A.K.—451 Cubes	1/16	D	Ertl	216	1972	USA	WFE—cab
*CAS-8c	1370 A.K.—504 Turbo	1/16	D	Ertl	216	1972	USA	WFE—cab
*CAS-8d	(1370 A.K.)	1/16	D	Ertl	216	1974	USA	WFE; power/red & white
*CAS-8e	(1370 A.K.)	1/16	D	Ertl	262	1974	USA	WFE—cab; power/red & white
*CAS-8f	(1570 A.K.)—Spirit of 76	1/16	D	Ertl	217	1976	USA	WFE—cab; Red, white & blue with stars, stripes
*CAS-9	Steam Traction Engine	1/25	C.A.	White, Peterson or Irvin		1945	USA	Antique steam tractor with driver & canopy; available

Code No.	Model	Scale or Size	Type of Material	Manufacturer	Stock No.	Year	Country	Remarks
								with thresher & water wagon; Irvin's models have the Irwin name stamped on the casting
*CAS-9b	Steam Roller	1/25	C.A.	Irvin		1976	USA	A variation of the steam traction engine
*CAS-10	Case-David Brown-995	1/43	D	Dinky	305	1975	GB	WFE—cab; three point hitch; power; red & white
*CAS-11	Case-David Brown-1412	1/25	D	N.Z.G.	156	1976	D	WFE; ROPS; three point hitch; power; red & white; weights on front end.
*CAS-12	(1412)	1/25	D	N.Z.G.	159	1976	D	Same as CAS-11—Except without weights & ROPS
*CAS-13	(2670) Traction King 4WD	1/40	D	N.Z.G.	149-154	1976	D	4WD; four wheel steering; cab; three point hitch
*CAS-14	580 C—C.K.	1/40	D	N.Z.G.		1976	D	Industrial backhoe and loader, Case yellow (orange) with black cab
*CAS-15	(2670) Traction King—4WD	1 1/4''	D**			1976	USA	Paperweight prism—3 3/8'' overall—**In Lucite
*CAS-16	Bulldozer	1/82	D	Lesney	16d	1969	GB	Crawler with cab & blade, red & white
*CAS-17	Bulldozer	3 1/2''	D	Lesney	K-17		GB	Crawler with cab & blade, red & yellow
*CAS-18	580 C.K.	1/16	P	Tomy	20531	1967	HK	Industrial backhoe & loader
*CAS-19	580 B—C.K.	1/16	D	Gescha	600	1973	D	Industrial backhoe & loader, two color variations
*CAS-20	Bulldozer	1/16	P	Tomy (?)		1967	HK	Industrial crawler with blade, battery powered—blade raises & lowers
*CAS-21a	Case-David Brown 1412	1/32	D	Corgi	34	1977	GB	WFE—cab & tipper trailer
*CAS-21b	Case-David Brown 1412	1/32	D	Corgi	1112	1977	GB	WFE—cab; has mounted J-F combine harvester
*CAS-22	C.C.	1/16	C.A.	Earl Jurgensen		1977	USA	1929 Row crop model—very limited
CAS-23		1/64	D	Ertl	1624	1978	USA	WFE—cab
*CAS-24	850 B Crawler	1/35	D	N.Z.G.	176	1978	D	Crawler with angle/tilt dozer & ROPS
CAS-25a	2390	1/16	D	Ertl		1979	USA	WFE-small rear wheels/cab; also, collectors serieslimited edition, serial numbered.

Code No.	Model	Scale or Size	Type of Material	Manufacturer	Stock No.	Year	Country	Remarks
CAS-25b	2590	1/16	D	Ertl		1979	USA	WFE—large rear wheels/cab; also, collectors series limited edition, serial numbered.

CLARK MELROE BOBCAT

Code No.	Model	Scale or Size	Type of Material	Manufacturer	Stock No.	Year	Country	Remarks
*CL-1a	M-700	1/24	D	Gescha	401	1975	D	Four wheel skid steer loader; black; ROPS
*CL-1b	M-700	1/24	D	Gescha		1977	D	Four wheel skid steer loader; white; ROPS
*CL-2	533 Hydrostatic	1/24	D	Gama	9420	1978	D	Four wheel skid steer loader; black; ROPS
CL-3	1399 Hydro-static	1/24	P & SS	Tonka	837087	1979	USA	Four wheel skid steer loader; black; ROPS

CLETRAC

Code No.	Model	Scale or Size	Type of Material	Manufacturer	Stock No.	Year	Country	Remarks
*CLE-1	Crawler		D	Ronson Lighter Co.		1920s	USA	Cigarette lighter

COCKSHUTT

Code No.	Model	Scale or Size	Type of Material	Manufacturer	Stock No.	Year	Country	Remarks
*COC-1	30	1/16	D	Advanced Products			USA	Row crop; red & yellow
*COC-2	(540)	1/16	D	Advanced Products			USA	WFE; tan; three point hitch
COC-3	30	1/16	POT	Lincoln Toys			CDN	Row crop; red & yellow
*COC-4	30	1/16	D	Lincoln Toys			CDN	WFE; red & yellow
*COC-5a	1850	1/16	D	Ertl		1968	USA	Row crop; tan & red
*COC-5b	1850	1/16	D	Ertl		1968	USA	Row crop; red & white
*COC-6	30	1/16	P	Product Miniature		c.1954	USA	WFE—excellent detail; all plastic with die-cast front axle

COLORADO

Code No.	Model	Scale or Size	Type of Material	Manufacturer	Stock No.	Year	Country	Remarks
*COL-1	Crawler	5"	D	Quarilu		1975	F	Clockwork with V-Blade

CO-OP

Code No.	Model	Scale or Size	Type of Material	Manufacturer	Stock No.	Year	Country	Remarks
*CO-1	(E-3)	1/16	POT	Advanced Products		1950	USA	Row crop; orange; predecessor to Cockshutt 30—A 1949 model; two variations

DAVID BROWN

Code No.	Model	Scale or Size	Type of Material	Manufacturer	Stock No.	Year	Country	Remarks
*DB-1	(25-D)	1/16	D	Densil Skinner		1954	GB	WFE; steerable; excellent detail
*DB-2	990	1/43	D	Dinky	305	1964	GB	WFE—cab; three point hitch; red & yellow
*DB-3	990	1/43	D	Dinky	305	1966	GB	WFE—cab; three poin hitch; brown & white (see also CASE)
*DB-4	Cropmaster	1/16	P			c.1950	GB	WFE—Similar to DB-1 except it is plastic and has shields around drivers platform; has double seat.

Code No.	Model	Scale or Size	Type of Material	Manufacturer	Stock No.	Year	Country	Remarks
*DB-5	Vakia	1/72	PK	Airfix		1978	GB	Aircraft tow tractor (part of airplane kit #682)—The real tractors were sold to farmers after WW II. Fitted with front pulley to power to power threashing machines, etc.

DEUTZ

Code No.	Model	Scale or Size	Type of Material	Manufacturer	Stock No.	Year	Country	Remarks
DE-1	Deutz		D	Mini-Auto	297		D	WFE
*DE-2	60 B.S.	1/90	D	Schuco	752	1962	D	
DE-3a	Crawler	1/90	D	Schuco	753	1962	D	
DE-3b	Bulldozer	1/90	D	Schuco	754	1962	D	Crawler with blade
*DE-4	DM-55	1/25	P.K.	Trol	5113	1964	BR	WFE—rare
*DE-5a	06 Series	1/30	D	Ziss R.W. Modelle		1970	D	WFE; dark green, gray with orange seat
*DE-5b	06 Series	1/30	D	Ziss R.W. Modelle		1975	D	WFE; light green, brown with red seat
DE-6	Deutz	1/22	P	Arthur Hammer	2452	1972	D	
DE-7	Deutz	1/25	P	Cursor			D	
*DE-8a	Deutz	1/29	D	Gama	424	1976	D	WFE—4WD
DE-8b	Deutz	1/29	D	Gama	426	1978	D	With 4WD & roll over guard
*DE-9a	Intrac 2005	5 1/2''	D	Gama	420	1976	D	4WD; front & rear three point hitches
*DE-9b	Intrac 2005	5 1/2''	D	Gama	420	1976	D	With dump
*DE-9c	Intrac 2005	5 1/2'' +	D	Gama	4225	1976	D	With dump trailer
*DE-9d	Intrac 2005	5 1/2''	D	Gama	421	1976	D	With sprayer tank
*DE-10	Deutz	1/90	P	Wiking			D	WFE; with driver—good detail
*DE-11	Deutz	1/90	P	Wiking	383		D	WFE; with driver—good detail
*DE-12	Gama-Deutz	1/19	D	Gama	432	1977	D	4WD; front weights—no cab
DE-13	DX110	1/32	D & P	Britains	9526	1978	GB	4WD with cab
DE-14	D6206	1/20	D	Hausser	4425	1978	D	Light green with red wheels operating rear lift

DUTRA

Code No.	Model	Scale or Size	Type of Material	Manufacturer	Stock No.	Year	Country	Remarks
*DU-1	D-4K-B	9''	Tin			1965	H	4WD; tin or stamped steel; clockwork drive

EICHER

Code No.	Model	Scale or Size	Type of Material	Manufacturer	Stock No.	Year	Country	Remarks
*EI-1	4WD	1/20	D & P	M.S.	1775		D	WFE; hood raises; green & red color

Code No.	Model	Scale or Size	Type of Material	Manufacturer	Stock No.	Year	Country	Remarks
ESCORT								
ES-1	335	1/25	D	Morgan Milton LTD		1977	IN	WFE—orange and white
FAHR								
FA-1	Fahr	1/25	P	Cursor			D	
FA-2	Fahr	1/90	P	Wiking	38	1956	D	WFE—color variations
FA-3	Fahr	1/60	D	Siku	V-48		D	
FAIRBANKS-MOORSE								
*FMO-1	Z-Engine	3 1/2''	C.I.	Arcade		1930	USA	Small portable engine used to power small implements; no wheels
*FMO-2	Z-Engine	3 1/2''	C.A.	Old Time Toys, Pioneer Tractor Works, Irvin Models		1968	USA	Reproduction of FMO-1
FENDT								
FEN-1	Fendt	1/25	P	Cursor			D	
FEN-2	F-250-G.T.	1/25	P	Cursor			D	Geratrager—dump bed in front
*FEN-3	F-250-G.T.	1/43	D	Cursor	570		D	Geratrager—dump bed in front
*FEN-4	4WD	1/43	D	Cursor	067		D	WFE—name 'Veith' on tires
FEN-5	Favorite 45	1/43	D	Cursor	967	1970	D	Turbomatic—4WD w/cab
*FEN-6	Favoris	1/43	D	Cursor			D	Same as FEN-5
FERGUSON								
*FER-1	(30)	3''	D	Benbros			GB	WFE; available with log trailer
*FER-2	(30)	3 1/2''	D	Moko-Lesney		1951	GB	WFE
*FER-3	(30)	1/16	D	Chad-Valley		1955	GB	WFE; green with red wheels; hood hinged in front; rare
*FER-4	(30)	1/13	P	Topping Models		1954	USA	WFE; gray; available with three point hitch disk plow
*FER-5	(30)	1/12	POT	Advanced Products		1948	USA	WFE; gray; three point hitch
*FER-6	(30)	1/43	D	Tekno	460	1954	DK	WFE; red; hood hinged in front
FER-7	(TE-20)	5 1/2''	D	Mettoy-Castoys			GB	WFE; red & blue; steers
*FER-8	30	1/20	P.K.	Airfix		c.1950	GB	WFE; three point hitch; red color
FER-9	30	1/25	P	Allemagne-Plasty	8	1955	D	WFE
*FER-10	(30)	4 1/2''	D	Fun-Ho	402		NZ	WFE; blue, silver & yellow

Code No.	Model	Scale or Size	Type of Material	Manufacturer	Stock No.	Year	Country	Remarks
*FER-11	(35)	6 1/2	D	Fun-Ho	520		NZ	WFE; red & silver
FER-12	(35)	1/32	D	Micro-Models	4337	1955	NZ	WFE
FER-13	30	1/16	P	Nova		1951	F	Promotional model

FIAT

Code No.	Model	Scale or Size	Type of Material	Manufacturer	Stock No.	Year	Country	Remarks
*FIA-1	Fiat Concorde 700-S	1/43	D	Buby	Promo	1971	RA	WFE
*FIA-2	550	1/36	D	Dugu	2	1966	I	WFE
FIA-3a	Fiat	1/43	D	Mini-Gama	914	1961	D	WFE; orange & white
FIA-3b	Fiat	1/43	D	Mini-Gama	914	1961	D	930 with blade
FIA-3c	Fiat	1/43	D	Mini-Gama	914	1961	D	934 with trailer
*FIA-3d	Fiat	1/43	D	Mini-Gama	914	1961	D	940 with loader
*FIA-4a	550	1/36	D	Ziss R.W. Modelle		1970	D	WFE
*FIA-4b	600	1/36	D	Ziss R.W. Modelle		1973	D	WFE
*FIA-5a	780	1/43	D	Forma-Plast Mattel & Yaxon	055	1976	I	WFE
*FIA-5b	880 DT—4WD	1/43	D	Forma-Plast Mattel & Yaxon	056	1976	I	WFE—4WD
*FIA-6a	40 CA	1/60	D	Siku	V-238	1964	D	Crawler with bucket
*FIA-6b	40 CA	1/60	D	Siku	V-239	1964	D	Crawler with blade
*FIA-7a	FL-10 Crawler	1/24	D	Mini-Auto	6032	1973	D	Crawler loader—excellent detail
FIA-7b	Fiat-Allis—FL-10	1/24	D	Mini-Auto		1975	D	Crawler loader (see also Allis- Chalmers)
FIA-8	640	1/36	D & P	Oldcars	51	1978	I	WFE—replaces FIA-2 Fiat 550 made by Dugu in 1966
FIA-9	Fiat-Allis 41-B	1/50	D	Gescha		1979	D	Crawler with Dozer Blade & Ripper/cab
FIA-10	(880)-4WD	132	D & P	Britains	9528	1979	GB	4WD/cab; orange
FIA-11a	780	1/12	P	Forma-Plast		1978	I	WFE
FIA-11b	880DT-4WD	1/12	P	Forma-Plast		1978	I	4WD
FIA-12	780	1/87	P	Mercury	810	1979	I	WFE with ROPS

FIELD MARSHALL

Code No.	Model	Scale or Size	Type of Material	Manufacturer	Stock No.	Year	Country	Remarks
*FM-1a	Single Cylinder	1/43	D	Dinky	27N	1952	GB	WFE; metal tires; driver; color variations
*FM-1b	Single Cylinder	1/43	D	Dinky	301	1954	GB	WFE; rubber tires; painted driver

FORD

Code No.	Model	Scale or Size	Type of Material	Manufacturer	Stock No.	Year	Country	Remarks
*FOR-1	(9N)	6 1/2''	C.I.	Arcade		1940	USA	WFE—Cast-in driver; available with or without

Code No.	Model	Scale or Size	Type of Material	Manufacturer	Stock No.	Year	Country	Remarks
								three-point hitch plow. The Ford-Ferguson was introduced in 1939
*FOR-2	(9N)	1/12	C.I.	Arcade		1941	USA	WFE—cast-in driver; available with earth mover #7300
*FOR-3	(9N)	3 1/4"	C.I.	Arcade		1940	USA	Row crop—cast-in driver (Ford never made a row crop 9N)
*FOR-4	(8N)	1/12	P	Product Miniature		1952	USA	WFE—three point hitch; The ford 8N was introduced in 1947
*FOR-5a	NAA Jubilee	1/12	P	Product Miniature		1953	USA	WFE—three point hitch; 50th Anniversary Model
*FOR-5b	600	1/12	P	Product Miniature		1955	USA	WFE—three point hitch; lights on sides
*FOR-6	900	1/12	P	Product Miniature		1955	USA	Row crop—three point hitch
FOR-7	(8N)	1/12	P	AMT-Aluminum Model Toys		1950	USA	WFE—clockwork
FOR-8	(8N)	1/12	P	M.P.C.		1952	USA	WFE—clockwork—long body
*FOR-9	(8N)	5"	C.A.	Quiralu		1957	F	WFE—separate cast diriver; variety of colors & implements
*FOR-10a	(8N)	1/32	D	Tootsietoy	290		USA	WFE; red; has loader
*FOR-10b	(8N)	1/32	D	Tootsietoy			USA	WFE; red & silver'
*FOR-11	(NAA Jubilee)	1/32	D	Tootsietoy			USA	WFE; red
*FOR-12	(NAA Jubilee Roadmaster)	1/32	D	DCMT Lonestar	1258		GB	'Farm King' name on hood; WFE; has trailer similar to FOR-11; red
*FOR-13	(8N)	1/25	P	Hubley	309		USA	WFE; gray
*FOR-14	(960) H	1/10	D	Hubley	90		USA	Row crop with implements; red & gray
*FOR-15a	961 Powermaster	1/12	D	Hubley	507	1961	USA	WFE; three point hitch; red & gray
*FOR-15b	961 Powermaster	1/12	D	Hubley	507	1961	USA	Row crop; three point hitch; red & gray
*FOR-15c	961 Select-O-Speed	1/12	D	Hubley	508	1962	USA	Row crop; three point hitch; red & gray
*FOR-16a	(4000)	1/12	D	Hubley	1508		USA	Row crop; three point hitch; red & gray; no decals
*FOR-16b	4000	1/12	D	Hubley	1508	1965	USA	WFE; three point hitch; blue & gray; Ford vertically cast into grill

Code No.	Model	Scale or Size	Type of Material	Manufacturer	Stock No.	Year	Country	Remarks
*FOR-17a	6000	1/12	D	Hubley	509	1963	USA	Row crop; chromed exhaust; red & gray
*FOR-17b	6000	1/12	D	Hubley	509	1964	USA	Row crop; chromed exhaust; blue & gray
*FOR-18a	Commander 6000	1/12	D	Hubley	1509	1963	USA	Row crop; plastic exhaust & air cleaner; blue & gray
*FOR-18b	Commander 6000	1/12	D	Hubley-Gabriel	26157	1975	USA	Row crop; no exhaust & air cleaner; blue & gray
FOR-19	1841 Industrial	1/12	T	Cragston	90010		J	WFE; loader & remote control
*FOR-20	4000	1/12	T	Cragston			J	WFE; no. 21 forklift (rear) & remote control
*FOR-21	4000	1/12	T	Cragston			J	WFE; red; loader & backhoe; remote control
*FOR-22	4000 H.D.	1/12	T	Cragston			J	WFE; loader & backhoe; remote control
*FOR-23a	(4000)	1/56	D	Lesney	39	1967	GB	WFE; blue
*FOR-23b	(4000)	1/56	D	Lesney	39	1967	GB	WFE; blue & yellow (Industrial version)
*FOR-24	(4000)	1/56	D	Gusival	250		E	WFE; driver; green & yellow; similar to FOR-23b
*FOR-25	4000	1/12	D	Ertl	805	1965	USA	WFE; three point hitch; two piece sectional grill
*FOR-26a	4000	1/12	D	Ertl	805	1968	USA	WFE; three point hitch; one piece grill
*FOR-26b	4400 Industrial	1/12	D	Ertl	805	1972	USA	WFE; three point hitch; one piece grill; yellow
*FOR-27	4600	1/12	D	Ertl	A-805	1976	USA	WFE; flat fenders
*FOR-28a	5550 Industrial	1/12	D	Ertl	820	1972	USA	WFE; backhoe & loader; yellow
FOR-28b	7500 Industrial	1/12	D	Ertl	820	1975	USA	WFE; backhoe & loader; yellow
*FOR-29a	8000	1/12	D	Ertl	800	1968	USA	WFE; three point hitch; small '8000' on side decals
*FOR-29b	8000	1/12	D	Ertl	800	1970	USA	WFE; no three point hitch, on some models; large '8000' on side decals
*FOR-29c	8600	1/12	D	Ertl	A-800	1973	USA	WFE; no three point hitch
*FOR-29d	9600	1/12	D	Ertl	A-821	1974	USA	WFE—cab; no three point hitch; dual rear wheels
*FOR-30	145 Hydro	1/12	D	Ertl	808	1972	USA	Lawn & garden tractor/trailer

Code No.	Model	Scale or Size	Type of Material	Manufacturer	Stock No.	Year	Country	Remarks
*FOR-31	(4000)	7''	D & P	Gama	1856 1866		D	WFE; remote control; with wagon
FOR-32	(4000)	4 1/2''	D	Gama	9141		D	WFE; with clockwork; red, yellow & green
FOR-33	(4000)	4 1/4''	D & T	Gama			D	WFE; clockwork
*FOR-34	(4000)	1/43	D	Mini-Gama			D	WFE; turf tires; red, yellow & green
*FOR-35	(4000)	2 1/4''	D	Fun-Ho			NZ	WFE; cast-in driver
*FOR-36	(4000)	3 3/4''	D	Fun-Ho	103		NZ	WFE; cast-in driver
FOR-37	5000 Super Major	1/32	D	Britains	9630		GB	WFE; with Shawnee Puhl Gooseneck dump trailer
*FOR-38a	5000	1/32	D	Britains	9527	1971	GB	WFE; rounded cab
*FOR-38b	5000	1/32	D	Britains	9527	1973	GB	WFE; square cab
*FOR-38c	5000	1/32	D	Britains	9527		GB	WFE; no cab; with mule dozer on some
*FOR-39	5000	1/43	P.K.	Britains	1101		GB	WFE; snap together kit
*FOR-40	6600	1/32	D	Britains	9524	1970	GB	WFE; square cab
*FOR-41a	5000 Super Major	1/43	D	Corgi	67	1966	GB	WFE
*FOR-41b	5000 Super Major	1/43	D	Corgi	72	1970	GB	WFE; rear trencher
*FOR-41c	5000 Super Major	1/43	D	Corgi	74	1970	GB	WFE; side trencher
*FOR-42	5000	1/55	D	Majorette	255	1972	F	WFE; red or blue; available with log trailer, wagon, etc.
FOR-43	(4000)	1/61	D	Tiny Car		1968	BR	WFE
*FOR-44	(4000)		P	Gay Toys		1975	USA	WFE; variety of colors; with or without loader
*FOR-45	(145)		P	Gay Toys	615	1975	USA	Lawn & garden tractor; variety of colors
*FOR-46	8600	8 1/2''	P	Processed Plastic Products		1976	USA	WFE; variety of colors & decals; chromed engine
*FOR-47	4550 Industrial	1/35	D	N.Z.G.	130	1972	D	WFE; backhoe & loader
*FOR-48	(9N)	1/12	C.A.	Arcade (?)			USA	WFE; with driver & mounted plow
*FOR-49	(4000)	1/43	P	Tomte		1976	N	WFE
*FOR-50	7700	1/12	D	Ertl	819	1977	USA	WFE—cab
*FOR-51	9700	1/12	D	Ertl	817	1977	USA	WFE—cab & dual wheels
FOR-52		1/64	D	Ertl	1621	1978	USA	WFE—cab
FOR-53	3600	1/25	D	Morgan Milton LTD		1977	IN	WFE

Code No.	Model	Scale or Size	Type of Material	Manufacturer	Stock No.	Year	Country	Remarks
FOR-54	2N	1/12	KOR	Pioneers of Power		1978	USA	WFE; driver & "Steel" wheels; modified copy of FOR-1 (Arcade)
*FOR-55	(NAA Jubilee)	5 1/2"	P	Wyandotte			USA	WFE

FORDSON

Code No.	Model	Scale or Size	Type of Material	Manufacturer	Stock No.	Year	Country	Remarks
*FDN-1	(F)	3 7/8"	C.I.	Arcade	273X	1926	USA	WFE; variety of colors; cast-in driver; steel or rubber tires; The first Fordson F was made in 1917.
*FDN-2	(F)	4 3/4"	C.I.	Arcade	274X	1926	USA	WFE; variety of colors; cast-in driver; steel or rubber tires
FDN-3	(F)	5 3/4"	C.I.	Arcade	280X	1932	USA	WFE; variety of colors; cast-in driver; steel or rubber tires
FDN-4	(F)	6"	C.I.	Arcade	275X	1932	USA	WFE; variety of colors; plated driver; smooth or Lug steel wheels
*FDN-5	(F)	6"	C.I.	Arcade			USA	WFE; W & K solid wheels & rubber tires; plated driver
*FDN-6	(F)	3 3/4"	C.I.	Hubley		1928	USA	WFE; variety of colors; steel wheels; cast-in driver
*FDN-7	(F)	3 1/2"	C.I.	Hubley	336	1938	USA	WFE; variety of colors; rubber tires; cast-in driver
*FDN-8	(F)	8 1/2"	C.I.	Hubley	727	1938	USA	WFE; steel or rubber tires; with loader; plated driver
*FDN-9	(F)	5 1/2"	C.I.	Hubley			USA	WFE
FDN-10	(F)	4"	C.I.	Kilgore			USA	WFE; steel wheels; cast-in driver
FDN-11	(F)	5 1/8"	C.I.	Kilgore			USA	WFE; steel wheels; cast-in driver
FDN-12	(F)		C.I.	Kenton			USA	WFE; steel wheels; cast-in driver
*FDN-13	(F)	3 1/2"	C.I.	North & Judd			S	WFE; plated separate driver
*FDN-14	(F)	5 3/4"	C.I.	Dent			USA	WFE; fewer hood bands; plated driver
*FDN-15	(F)	1/43	D	Dinky	22E	1934	GB	WFE; steel wheels; fenders
*FDN-16	(F)	1/43	D	Varney-Copy Cat	1	1976	GB	Copy of FDN-15
*FDN-17	(F)	6"	C.A.	Old Time Toys, Pioneer Tractor Works		1969	USA	WFE; reproduction of FDN-4
*FDN-18	(F)	1/16	D	Ertl	850	1969	USA	WFE; steel wheels; no driver; steers
*FDN-19	(F)	5 1/2"	D	Fun-Ho	104-B		NZ	WFE; cast-in driver; steel wheels

Code No.	Model	Scale or Size	Type of Material	Manufacturer	Stock No.	Year	Country	Remarks
*FDN-20	Super Major	1/87	D	Fun-Ho	16	1967	NZ	WFE
*FDN-21	(F)	1/16	Kor	Charles Souhrada		1975	USA	WFE; American or English color versions; painted driver; fenders
*FDN-22a	(F) Farm	1/87	P.K.	Jordon Products	C-218	1975	USA	WFE; cleated wheels
*FDN-22b	(F) Industrial	1/87	P.K.	Jordon Products	C-219	1975	USA	WFE; smooth, solid wheels
*FDN-23	(F)	9 1/4''	Glass	Ezra Brooks		1972	USA	WFE; glass whiskey bottle
FDN-24	(F)	3 3/4''	C.I.	A.C. Williams			USA	WFE; cast-in driver; plated wheels
FDN-25	(F)	4 3/4''	C.I.	A.C. Williams			USA	WFE; cast-in driver; plated wheels
FDN-26	(F)	5 3/4''	C.I.	A.C. Williams			USA	WFE; cast-in driver; plated wheels
FDN-27	(F) Roller	4 1/2''	C.I.	A.C. Williams			USA	Roller front
*FDN-28	(E27N)	1/76	D	Britains	LV-604	1953	GB	WFE; with or without driver
*FDN-29a	(E27N)	1/32	D	Britains	127F	1948	GB	WFE; lug wheels
*FDN-29b	(E27N)	1/32	D	Britains	128F	1948	GB	WFE; rubber tires
*FDN-30a	Power Major	1/32	D	Britains	171F	1959	GB	WFE; steel wheels; lights on side of radiator
FDN-30b	Power Major	1/32	D	Britains	172F 9525	1959	GB	WFE; rubber tires; lights on side
FDN-31a	Super Major	1/32	D	Britains	171F	1961	GB	WFE; steel wheels; lights in grill
*FDN-31b	Super Major	1/32	D	Britains	172F 9525	1961	GB	WFE; rubber tires; lights in grill
*FDN-31c	Industrial Major	1/32	D	Britains		1961	GB	WFE—cab; rubber tires; yellow
FDN-32a	5000 Super Major	1/32	D	Britains	9527	1965	GB	WFE
*FDN-32b	5000 Super Major	1/32	D	Britains	9527	1971	GB	WFE; rounded cab
FDN-33	5000	1/32	D	Britains	9527	1973	GB	WFE; square cab
*FDN-34	(E27N)	1/16	D	Chad Valley		1952	GB	WFE; rare; front crank clockwork; steers
*FDN-35	Major	1/16	D	Chad Valley		1954	GB	WFE; clockwork; hoods lift; steers
*FDN-36	Dexta	1/16	D	Chad Valley		1955	GB	WFE
FDN-37	Major	1/43	D	Clifford	CS-1	1968	HK	WFE; replica of FDN-40 Taiseiya
FDN-38	Major	1/20	D	Clifford		1968	HK	WFE
*FDN-39	Major	1/20	D	M.W.-Empire Made	5101	1962	HK	WFE; steers

Code No.	Model	Scale or Size	Type of Material	Manufacturer	Stock No.	Year	Country	Remarks
FDN-40	Major	1/43	D	Taiseiya, Cherryca Phoenix, Micropet or Replica	501	1965	J	WFE
*FDN-41	Power Major	1/62	D	Lesney	72A	1959	GB	WFE
*FDN-42	Super Major	1/42	D	Lesney	K-11	1963	GB	WFE; with tandum trailer
*FDN-43a	Power Major	1/43	D	Corgi	55	1961	GB	WFE; lights on side of radiator
*FDN-43b	Power Major	1/43	D	Corgi	55	1961	GB	WFE; lights on side of radiator; half tracks
*FDN-44a	Power Major	1/43	D	Corgi	55—60	1962	GB	WFE; lights in grill
*FDN-44b	Power Major	1/43	D	Corgi	54	1962	GB	WFE; lights in grill; half tracks
*FDN-45	Major	1/41	P	Politoys	65	1963	I	WFE; red & gray; with wagon
*FDN-46	Super Major	1/43	P	Minaluxe		1967	F	WFE; blue & silver
*FDN-47	Super Major	1/43	P	Tomte		1975	N	WFE; molded-in driver; with wagon
*FDN-48	(Dexta)	1/25	D	Crescent	1805	1957	GB	WFE
*FDN-49	(Dexta)	5 1/4"	P	Lucky	184		HK	WFE; gyro-motor
*FDN-50	(Dexta)		P	MIC	D-6		HK	WFE; battery operated; orange; with driver
*FDN-51	N Standard	1/32	D-Kit	Brown's Models		1976	GB	WFE; model of 1944 English version of Fordson 1941-1945; good detail
*FDN-52	(Dexta)	1/25	P	Tomte		1977	N	WFE; variety of colors
FDN-53	F/Loader	1/16	C.I.	Arcade			USA	Rare; similar to FDN-8; rear crank operate loader
*FDN-54	F	8"	Tin	Bing		c.1920	D	WFE; clockwork
*FDN-55	F with Halftracks	8"	Tin	Bing		c.1920	D	WFE; clockwork
*FDN-56	F	5 1/2"	C.I.	Hubley			USA	WFE; with crank & driver; Fordson name cast on sides of radiator. Also reproduced.
*FDN-57	E27N	1/76 00 & HO	P	Britains	LV-604		GB	WFE; driver

FOWLER

*FOW-1	Big Lion	1/80	D	Lesney	Y-9	1958	GB	Show engine—steam traction engine

FRICK

*FRI-1	16 H.P.	1/25	C.A.	White, Peterson or Irvin		1964	USA	Steam traction engine

GRAHAM-BRADLEY

*GB-1	Graham-Bradley	4"	R	Aubrubber			USA	Row crop; David Bradley implements; model of a

Code No.	Model	Scale or Size	Type of Material	Manufacturer	Stock No.	Year	Country	Remarks
								1937 tractor; sold by Sears, Roebuck Co.

GUIDART

Code No.	Model	Scale or Size	Type of Material	Manufacturer	Stock No.	Year	Country	Remarks
GUI-1	Guidart	1/25	P	Cursor			D	

HANOMAG (Now Part of Massey-Ferguson Ltd).

Code No.	Model	Scale or Size	Type of Material	Manufacturer	Stock No.	Year	Country	Remarks
*HAN-1	Hanomag-Barrieros	1/86	P	Auguplas-Minicars	98	1964	E	WFE; red with blue wheels
HAN-2	Hanomag	1/25	P	Cursor			D	
HAN-3	55 CV	1/60	D	Siku	165		D	
*HAN-4	Robust 900	1/60	D	Siku	V-329 182	1973	D	WFE
HAN-5	K12C	1/43	D	Cursor	1269	1971	D	Crawler-loader (Industrial)

HOLDER

Code No.	Model	Scale or Size	Type of Material	Manufacturer	Stock No.	Year	Country	Remarks
HO-1	Cultitrac A55	1/30	D	Cursor	1076	1978	D	4WD; articulated garden tractor

HUBER

Code No.	Model	Scale or Size	Type of Material	Manufacturer	Stock No.	Year	Country	Remarks
*HUB-1	Steam Roller	1/25	C.I.	Hubley		1929	USA	Antique
*HUB-2a	Steam Traction Engine	1/25	C.A.	White, Peterson or Irvin		1964	USA	Modified reproduction of HUB-1
HUB-2b	Steam Roller	1/25	C.A.	White, Peterson or Irvin		1964	USA	Reproduction of HUB-1
HUB-3	Huber Warco 10-D Grader	1/40	D	Jue	HO-002/1		BR	Road grader
*HUB-4	Steam Roller	3 1/4''	C.I.	Hubley		1929	USA	Antique

McCORMICK-DEERING—I.H.

Code No.	Model	Scale or Size	Type of Material	Manufacturer	Stock No.	Year	Country	Remarks
*IH-1a	(10-20)	1/16	C.I.	Arcade	276-X	1925	USA	Standard with plated driver—red or gray; steel lug; white rubber, black rubber or W & K solid with rubber wheels
*IH-1b	(10-20)	1/16	C.I.	Arcade	276-O	1925	USA	Same as IH-1a except has belt pulley; the 10-20 was introduced in 1922
*IH-2a	Regular Farmall	1/16	C.I.	Arcade	279-X	1926	USA	Row crop with painted driver; red or gray; steel lug or rubber wheels
IH-2b	Regular Farmall	1/16	C.I.	Arcade	279-O	1926	USA	Same as IH-2a except has belt pulley; the Farmall was introduced in 1924
*IH-3	Trac-Tractor (TD-40) Crawler	1/16	C.I.	Arcade	277	1936	USA	Crawler with plated driver—A 1932 model; steel tracks or rubber tracks
*IH-4	Trac-Tractor (TD-18) Crawler	1/16	C.I.	Arcade		1941	USA	Crawler with plated driver; rubber tracks; a 1939 model
*IH-5	M	4 1/4''	C.I.	Arcade	7321	1942	USA	Row crop with cast-in driver; wood wheels

Code No.	Model	Scale or Size	Type of Material	Manufacturer	Stock No.	Year	Country	Remarks
*IH-6	M	5 1/4"	C.I.	Arcade	2329	1941	USA	Row crop with cast-in driver; rubber wheels
*IH-7	M	7"	C.I.	Arcade	7070	1940	USA	Row crop with separate plated driver; rubber wheels
*IH-8	A	1/12	C.I.	Arcade	7050	1941	USA	WFE—separate plated driver; offset "Culti-vision" design; introduced in 1939
*IH-9	(10-20)	1/20	C.I.	Kilgore			USA	Standard—separate plated driver
*IH-10	(10-20)	1/16	C.A. or Kor	Robert Gray		1970	USA	Reproduction of IH-1
*IH-11	(10-20)	1/16	C.A.	Old Time Toys, Pioneer Tractor Works		1969	USA	Reproduction of IH-1
*IH-12	Regular Farmall	1/16	C.A.	Old Time Toys, Pioneer Tractor Works		1969	USA	Reproduction of IH-2
*IH-13	Trac-Tractor Crawler	1/24	Wood Kit	Mod-AC Mfg.	146-I		USA	
*IH-14a	(M)	1/16	P	Product Miniature	2853	1950	USA	Row crop
*IH-14b	(M)	1/16	P.K.	Product Miniature	2853	1950	USA	Row crop
*IH-14c	(M)	1/16	P	Product Miniature	2853	1951	USA	Row crop—special issue; white with red wheels & blue stars
*IH-15	Super C	1/16	P	Lakone Co.		1952	USA	Row crop—IH-15, IH-16a & IH-16b are very similar except decals & trim
IH-16a	200	1/16	P	Lakone Co.		1953	USA	
*IH-16b	230	1/16	P	Lakone Co.		1954	USA	
*IH-17	UD-24 Power Unit	1/16	P	Product Miniature		1950	USA	Used to power sawmills, etc; model is actually a cigarette dispenser
*IH-18a	TD-24 Crawler	1/16	P	Product Miniature		1952	USA	Crawler—the IH TD-24 crawler is a 1947 model
*IH-18b	TD-24 Crawler	1/16	P	Product Miniature		1952	USA	Crawler with blade; remote electric motor & lights
*IH-19	(M) Diesel (Fixall)	1/12	P.K.	Marx		1954	USA	Row crop—has driver and set of tools
IH-20	(H)	1/16	D	Hubley			USA	Row crop—cast-in driver
*IH-21	(M)	1/12	D	Hubley			USA	Row crop—front wheels steer

Code No.	Model	Scale or Size	Type of Material	Manufacturer	Stock No.	Year	Country	Remarks
*IH-22	(M)	4''	R	Aubrubber			USA	Row crop with driver—variety of colors
*IH-23	(M)	6 1/2''	D	Slik-Toys	8924		USA	Row crop
*IH-24	(M)	6 1/2''	D	Lincoln Specialities	9824		CDN	Row crop— similar to IH-23
*IH-25	(M)	1/16	D	Ertl		1945	USA	Row crop—driver cast-in and has flat top hat.
*IH-26	(M)	1/16	D	Ertl		1950	USA	Row crop—yellow wheels; no driver
*IH-27a	Cub Cadet 122	1/16	D	Ertl	432	1966	USA	Lawn & garden tractor
IH-27b	Cub Cadet 122	1/16	D	Ertl	433	1966	USA	Lawn & garden tractor with blade
IH-28a	Cub Cadet 125	1/16	D	Ertl	432	1968	USA	Lawn & garden tractor
*IH-28b	Cub Cadet 125	1/16	D	Ertl	433	1968	USA	Lawn & graden tractor with blade
*IH-29a	Cub Cadet 126	1/16	D	Ertl	432	1970	USA	Lawn & garden tractor
IH-29b	Cub Cadet 126	1/16	D	Ertl	433	1970	USA	Lawn & garden tractor with blade
IH-30a	Cub Cadet 129	1/16	D	Ertl	432	1972	USA	Lawn & garden tractor
*IH-30b	Cub Cadet 129	1/16	D	Ertl	473	1972	USA	Lawn & garden tractor with blade
IH-30c	Cub Cadet 129	1/16	D	Ertl	474	1972	USA	Lawn & garden tractor with blade & trailer
*IH-30d	Cub Cadet 129	1/16	D	Ertl	473	1976	USA	Lawn & garden tractor; red, white & blue; special issue—Spirit of 76
*IH-31a	Cub Cadet	1/16	D	Ertl	435	1976	USA	Lawn & garden tractor; covered engine
IH-31b	Cub Cadet	1/16	D	Ertl	436	1976	USA	Lawn & garden tractor with blade & trailer; covered engine
*IH-32a	240	1/16	D	Ertl		1959	USA	WFE—utility with fast hitch
IH-32b	340	1/16	D	Ertl		1959	USA	WFE—utility with fast hitch
*IH-33	340 Industrial	1/16	D	Ertl		1959	USA	WFE—yellow; different grill; utility with fast hitch
*IH-34	400	1/16	D	Ertl		1954	USA	Row crop with fast hitch
*IH-35	404	1/16	D	Ertl		1961	USA	WFE—utility with three point hitch
*IH-36a	404	1/16	D	Ertl	437	1964	USA	Row crop with red wheels

Code No.	Model	Scale or Size	Type of Material	Manufacturer	Stock No.	Year	Country	Remarks
*IH-36b	404	1/16	D	Ertl	437	1967	USA	Row crop with white wheels
*IH-37	450	1/16	D	Ertl		1956	USA	Row crop with fast hitch
*IH-38a	460	1/16	D	Ertl		1958	USA	Row crop with fast hitch
*IH-38b	560	1/16	D	Ertl	408	1957	USA	Row crop with fast hitch
IH-38c	560	1/16	D	Ertl	408	1964	USA	Row crop
IH-38d	560	1/16	D	Ertl	408	1967	USA	Row crop with white wheels
*IH-38e	560	1/16	D	Ertl	460	1967	USA	Row crop with white dual wheels
*IH-38f	560	1/16	D	Ertl	409	1968	USA	Row crop with cab and white wheels
IH-38g	(560)	1/16	D	Ertl	408	1972	USA	Row crop—no 560 decals or exhaust
IH-38h	560	1/16	D	Ertl		1978	USA	A limited number of these 560s were recast and dated 1/ll/78 for the first National Farm Toy Show held in Dyersville, Iowa. It differs from the original 560 in that it has a wide front axle & different wheels. Only 500 were produced.
IH-38i	560	1/16	D	Ertl		1979	USA	500 more were recast and dated 3/1/79 as a second commemerative issue. These had dual rear wheels as well as the wide front axle.
*IH-39a	544	1/16	D	Ertl	414	1969	USA	WFE—red wheels
*IH-39b	(544)	1/16	D	Ertl	415	1969	USA	Row crop
IH-39c	(544)	1/16	D	Ertl	417	1969	USA	Row crop with white dual rear wheels
IH-39d	(544)	1/16	D	Ertl	418	1969	USA	Row crop with white wheels; loader
IH-39e	(2644) Industrial	1/16	D	Ertl	421	1970	USA	Row crop with loader—yellow
IH-39f	(2644) Industrial	1/16	D	Ertl	416	1969	USA	WFE—yellow
*IH-40	Flying Farmall	1/16	D	Ertl	5855	1974	USA	Row crop—modified 560; super rod pulling tractor
*IH-41a	Farmall 656	1/32	D	Ertl	40	1967	USA	Row crop
*IH-41b	International 656	1/32	D	Ertl	40	1968	USA	Row crop
*IH-42a	(666)	1/32	D	Ertl	405	1974	USA	Row crop

Code No.	Model	Scale or Size	Type of Material	Manufacturer	Stock No.	Year	Country	Remarks
*IH-42b	(666)	1/32	D	Ertl	405	1976	USA	WFE
*IH-43a	806	1/16	D	Ertl	435	1964	USA	WFE—round fenders
*IH-43b	806	1/16	D	Ertl	435	1965	USA	WFE—flat fenders
*IH-44a	856	1/16	D	Ertl	419	1968	USA	WFE
*IH-44b	1026 Hydro	1/16	D	Ertl	401	1971	USA	WFE
*IH-44c	1256 Turbo	1/16	D	Ertl	420	1968	USA	WFE with cab & duals
*IH-44d	1456 Turbo	1/16	D	Ertl	420	1971	USA	WFE with cab & duals
*IH-45a	966 Hydro	1/16	D	Ertl	401	1972	USA	WFE
IH-45b	966	1/16	D	Ertl	403	1975	USA	WFE with cab & duals
*IH-45c	1066 Turbo	1/16	D	Ertl	402	1972	USA	WFE with ROPS
IH-45d	1066 Turbo	1/16	D	Ertl	411	1975	USA	WFE with cab
*IH-45e	1466	1/16	D	Ertl	403	1972	USA	WFE with cab & duals
IH-46	1206 Turbo	1/16	D	Ertl	436	1966	USA	WFE with white wheels & trim
*IH-47	1466	1/25	P.K.	Ertl	8003	1974	USA	WFE with cab
*IH-48	1466	1/64	D	Ertl	1355	1974	USA	WFE with cab
*IH-49a	886	1/16	D	Ertl	461	1976	USA	WFE with safety frame
*IH-49b	1086	1/16	D	Ertl	462	1976	USA	WFE with cab
*IH-49c	1586	1/16	D	Ertl	463	1976	USA	WFE with cab & duals
*IH-50	TD-25 Bulldozer	1/25	D	Ertl	427	1961	USA	Crawler with blade—yellow; lights on top of radiator
*IH-51	TD-25 Bulldozer	1/25	D	Ertl	452	1971	USA	Crawler with blade—yellow; lights on side of radiator
*IH-52	2504 Industrial	1/16	D	Ertl	434	1963	USA	WFE—yellow; utility with three point hitch
*IH-53a	3414 Industrial	1/16	D	Ertl	428	1967	USA	WFE—with backhoe & loader; yellow
IH-53b	3444 Industrial	1/16	D	Ertl	428	1969	USA	WFE—with backhoe & loader; yellow
*IH-54	(3400) Industrial	1/16	D	Ertl	472	1975	USA	WFE—with backhoe & loader; yellow
IH-55	Hough Payloader	1/25	D	Ertl	426	1968	USA	Four-wheel loader—yellow
IH-56	IH Payhauler	1/16	D	Ertl	419	1960	USA	Steers—hydraulic dump truck—yellow
IH-57a	180 Payhauler	1/25	D	Ertl	425	1968	USA	Hydraulic dump truck—yellow; duals

Code No.	Model	Scale or Size	Type of Material	Manufacturer	Stock No.	Year	Country	Remarks
IH-57b	180 Payhauler	1/25	D	Ertl	425	1968	USA	Hydraulic dump truck—yellow; duals; white cab
IH-58	350 Payhauler	1/25	P.K.	Ertl	8013	1974	USA	Dump truck—yellow; duals
*IH-59	Cub	1/12	P.K.	Alfinson		c.1950	USA	WFE—offset "Culti-vision" style; The IH cub was introduced in 1947
IH-60	Cub	1/12	P.K.	ATMA		c.1950	BR	WFE—offset "Culti-vision" style
*IH-61	Cub	1/12	P.K.	Design Fabricators		c.1950	USA	WFE—offset "Culti-vision" style
*IH-62	Cub	1/12	P.K.	Saunders-Swader		c.1950	USA	WFE—offset "Culti-vision" style
*IH-63	(M)	4"	Tin				J	Row crop with driver—gyro engine
*IH-64	(M)	11 1/2"	D	Fun-Ho	531		USA	WFE—loader; green & silver
IH-65a	(240)	1/20	T & P	Universal-Cordeg	5101		HK	WFE—utility; white wheels
*IH-65b	(240)	1/20	T & P	Universal-Cordeg	5102		HK	WFE—utility; yellow wheels; driver
*IH-66a	B-250	1/37	D	Lesney	K-4	1960	GB	WFE—utility with green wheels
*IH-66b	B-250	1/37	D	Lesney	K-4	1961	GB	WFE—utility with red wheels
*IH-67	(414)	1/32	D	Tekno	465	1966	DK	Utility
*IH-68	(574)	1/32	D	Tekno	466-467	1971	DK	WFE—utility with ROPS, blade & brush
*IH-69	560	1/16	Tin	Alps Toys	5855	1973	J	WFE—smoking tractor; tan & red
IH-70a	TD-25 Crawler	1/80	D	Mini-Dinky	94	1969	HK	Crawler with blade
IH-70b	TD-25 Crawler	1/80	D	Mini-Dinky		1969	HK	Crawler
IH-70c	TD-25 Crawler	1/80	D	Mini-Dinky	85	1969	HK	Crawler with Drott loader
IH-71	Hough Payloader	1/80	D	Mini-Dinky		1969	HK	Four-wheel loader; white
IH-72	TD-25 Crawler	1/80	D	Mercury Lil-Toy	101		USA	Crawler
*IH-73	Hydraulic Excavator	1/55	D	Solido	365	1975	F	Crawler shovel
*IH-74	844—4WD	1/43	D	Eligor	3003	1976	F	WFE with cab & front weights
*IH-75	Farmall F-30	8"	Kor	Robert Gray		1976	USA	Row crop—antique type
*IH-76	McCormick W-9	8 1/2"	Kor	Robert Gray		1977	USA	1939 model—standard; WFE

Code No.	Model	Scale or Size	Type of Material	Manufacturer	Stock No.	Year	Country	Remarks
*IH-77	Farmall	6 1/2''	Tin				J	Tin model has loader which moves up & down when pushed along.
IH-78	560 Pay loader	4 3/4''	D	Tomy	4519	1976	J	Articulated industrial loader
IH-79	1086	1/64	D	Ertl	1620	1978	USA & HK	WFE—cab
*IH-80	Cub	1/12	D				USA	WFE—metal; offset Culti-vision
*IH-80	Farmall (C)	2''	P					Row crop
*IH-81	Farmall (C)	8''	P			c.1950		
IH-82	3588 2 + 2 4WD	1/16	D & P	Ertl	464	1979	USA	New design, row crop 4WD with articulated steering & control center on rear section. Also, a "First Edition" model was supplied to each dealer as part of promotional display.
IH-83	Farmall M	1/16	CA & D	Scale Models		1979	USA	Row crop model with "Steel Lug Type" wheels. It represents a 1939 model. Only 2000 were made.

JOHN DEERE

Code No.	Model	Scale or Size	Type of Material	Manufacturer	Stock No.	Year	Country	Remarks
*JD-1	(D)	1/16	C.I.	Vindex		1930	USA	Standard—plated driver; rare; the JD-D was introduced in 1923
*JD-2	Gasoline Engine	1/16	C.I.	Vindex	79	1930	USA	Portable engine
*JD-3	(A)	1/16	C.I.	Arcade		1941	USA	Row crop—plated driver; the A was introduced in 1938
*JD-4	(D)	5''	Lead	Kansas Toy		1932	USa	Standard—rare
*JD-5	Froelich	8''	M.S.	Charles Cox	Serial No.	1973	USA	Custom made 1892 model—Predecessor of John Deere
*JD-6a	Waterloo Boy (N)	9''	M.S.	Charles Cox	Serial No.	1974	USA	Custom made 1914 model
JD-6b	Waterloo Boy (R)	9''	M.S.	Charles Cox	Serial No.	1974	USA	Custom made 1914 model
*JD-7	(D)	1/16	C.A.	Old Time Toys, Pioneer Tractor Works		1969	USA	Reproduction of JD-1
*JD-8	Gasoline Engine	1/16	C.A.	Old Time Toys, Pioneer Tractor Works		1969	USA	Reproduction of JD-2
*JD-9	(A) General Purpose	1/12	C.A. or Kor	Robert Gray		1971	USA	Row crop—steel shape wheels; the A-GP was introduced in 1934

Code No.	Model	Scale or Size	Type of Material	Manufacturer	Stock No.	Year	Country	Remarks
*JD-10	(MT)	1/20	P	Auburn			USA	Row crop—molded-in driver; Auburn name on one side
JD-11	(A)	1/16	D	Lincoln Specialities	923	c.1950	CDN	Row crop—molded-in driver
*JD-12	Froelich	1/64	D	Ertl	1301	1967	USA	1892 model
*JD-13	Waterloo Boy	1/64	D	Ertl	1302	1967	USA	1914 model
*JD-14	D	1/64	D	Ertl	1303	1967	USA	1932 model
*JD-15	A	1/64	D	Ertl	1304	1967	USA	1939 model—row crop
*JD-16	60	1/64	D	Ertl	1305	1967	USA	1952 model—row crop
*JD-17	730	1/64	D	Ertl	1306	1967	USA	1958 model—row crop
*JD-18	4010	1/64	D	Ertl	1307	1967	USA	1960 model—row crop
*JD-19	4430	1/64	D	Ertl	1308	1972	USA	1972 model—WFE with cab
*JD-20	(D)	1/16	D	Ertl	500	1970	USA	1932 model—standard; no driver
*JD-21	(A)	1/16	D	Ertl		1945	USA	Row crop—molded-in driver with flat top hat; open flywheel
*JD-22	(A)	1/16	D	Ertl		1947	USA	Row crop—molded-in driver with flat top hat; closed flywheel
*JD-23	(A)	1/16	D	Ertl		1950	USA	Row crop—no driver
*JD-24a	(60)	1/16	D	Ertl		1952	USA	Row crop—front wheels steer; light on rear of seat
JD-24b	(60)	1/16	D	Ertl		1954	USA	Row crop—front wheels steer; three point hitch; no light on seat
*JD-25	110	1/16	D	Ertl	538	1965	USA	Lawn & garden tractor
*JD-26a	140	1/16	D	Ertl	550	1967	USA	Lawn & garden tractor
*JD-26b	140	1/16	D	Ertl	571	1969	USA	Lawn & garden tractor; JD 26b-e Color Key Set, Sunset Orange #571
*JD-26c	140	1/16	D	Ertl	572	1969	USA	Lawn & garden tractor; Spruce Blue #572
*JD-26d	140	1/16	D	Ertl	573	1969	USA	Lawn & garden tractor; April Yellow #573
*JD-26e	140	1/16	D	Ertl	574	1969	USA	Lawn & garden tractor; Patio Red #574
JD-26f	140	1/16	D	Ertl	515	1974	USA	L.G.T. with blade & trailer
*JD-27a	(400)	1/16	D	Ertl	591	1975	USA	L.G.T.

Code No.	Model	Scale or Size	Type of Material	Manufacturer	Stock No.	Year	Country	Remarks
JD-27b	(400)	1/16	D	Ertl	515	1975	USA	L.G.T. with blade & trailer
*JD-28a	(430)	1/16	D	Ertl	20	1958	USA	WFE—utility with three point hitch
JD-28b	(430)	1/16	D	Ertl	20	1962	USA	WFE—utility; no three point hitch
*JD-29a	(620)	1/16	D	Ertl		1956	USA	Row crop—no three point hitch
*JD-29b	(620)	1/16	D	Ertl		1956	USA	Row crop—with three point hitch
*JD-30a	(630)	1/16	D	Ertl	10	1958	USA	Row crop—with three point hitch
JD-30b	(630)	1/16	D	Ertl	10	1959	USA	Row crop—no three point hitch; also without muffler or with muffler
*JD-31a	(2030)	1/16	D	Ertl	584	1973	USA	WFE—utility
*JD-31b	(2030)	1/16	D	Ertl	592	1975	USA	WFE—utility with loader
*JD-32a	(2040)	1/16	D	Ertl	516	1976	USA	WFE—utility
JD-32b	(2040)	1/16	D	Ertl	517	1976	USA	WFE—utility with loader
*JD-33	1961 (3010-4010)	1/16	D	Ertl	530	1961	USA	Gasoline engine with generator; three point hitch; upside down u-shaped grip; three levers on top left side of dash; one lever on top right side—All four wheels die cast metal—rear 3/4'' rims; front 5/16'' rims
*JD-34	1964 (3020-4020)	1/16	D	Ertl	530	1964	USA	Diesel engine with generator—two fuel filters 3/16'' long on left side of engine; three levers on top left side: One lever top right, one lever left side, one lever right side
JD-34a	1964 (3020-4020)				530			Three point hitch—die cast rear rims—3/4'', plastic front rims—5/16''
JD-34b	1964 (3020-4020)				530			Three point hitch—plastic rear rims—3/4'', plastic front rims—5/16''
JD-34c	1964 (3020-4020)				530			Die cast rear rims—3/4'', plastic front rims—5/16''
JD-34d	1964 (3020-4020)				530			Die cast rear rims—3/4'', die cast front rims—5/16''
JD-34e	1964 (3020-4020)				530			Plastic rear rims—3/4'', plastic front rims—5/16''

Code No.	Model	Scale or Size	Type of Material	Manufacturer	Stock No.	Year	Country	Remarks
JD-34f	1964 (3020-4020)				541			Die cast rear rims—1 1/16", plastic front rims—1/2"
JD-34g	1964 (3020-4020)				541			Plastic rear rims—1 1/16", plastic front rims—1/2"
JD-34h	1964 (3020-4020)				547			WFE; plastic rear rims—I 1/16", plastic front rims—1/2"
*JD-35	1969 (3020-4020)	1/16	D	Ertl		1960	USA	Diesel engine with alternator; two fuel filters 5/16" on left side; one lever top left side one lever top right side; no levers on either side
JD-35a	1969 (3020-4020)				530	1965	USA	Plastic rear rims 3/4"; plastic front rims 5/16"
JD-35b	1969 (3020-4020)				541	1965	USA	Plastic rear rims 1 1/16"; plastic front rims 1/2"
JD-35c	1969 (3020-4020)				547	1967	USA	WFE; plastic rear rims—1 1/16"; plastic front rims—1/2"
JD-35d	1969 (3020-4020)				553	1968	USA	WFE; plastic rear rims—1 1/16"; plastic front rims—1/2"; Attached ROPS
*JD-36	(4230)	1/16	D	Ertl	512	1972	USA	WFE—sound gard cab
*JD-37	(4230)	1/32	D	Ertl	66	1973	USA	Row crop—sound gard cab
*JD-38	4430	1/25	P.K.	Ertl	8005	1973	USA	WFE—sound gard cab
*JD-39a	5020	1/16	D	Ertl	555	1969	USA	WFE—standard or wheatland style, has air cleaner
JD-39b	5020	1/16	D	Ertl	555	1975	USA	WFE—standard or wheatland style, no air cleaner
*JD-40	(7520)	1/16	D	Ertl	510	1972	USA	4WD—articulated, cab
*JD-41	(8630)	1/16	D	Ertl	597	1975	USA	4WD—duals, articulated, cab
*JD-42a	(40) Crawler	1/16	D	Ertl		1954	USA	Green—blade optional
*JD-42b	(40) Industrial Crawler	1/16	D	Ertl		1955	USA	Yellow—blade optional
*JD-42c	(420) Crawler	1/16	D	Ertl		1956	USA	Green with yellow strip, blade optional
*JD-43	(440) Industrial Crawler	1/16	D	Ertl		1959	USA	Yellow—no blade; embossed metal grill
*JD-44a	(1010) Industrial Tractor	1/16	D	Ertl		1959	USA	WFE—yellow, with three point hitch

Code No.	Model	Scale or Size	Type of Material	Manufacturer	Stock No.	Year	Country	Remarks
JD-44b	(1010) Industrial Tractor	1/16	D	Ertl		1962	USA	WFE—yellow, no three point hitch
*JD-45	(1010) Industrial Crawler	1/16	D	Ertl	526	1963	USA	Yellow, with blade
JD-46a	(JD-500) Industrial Crawler	1/16	D	Ertl	546	1965	USA	Yellow, with blade
JD-46b	(JD-500) Industrial Crawler	1/16	D	Ertl	554	1967	USA	Yellow, with blade & winch
*JD-46c	(JD-500) Industrial Crawler	1/16	D	Ertl	509	1973	USA	Yellow; with blade, winch & ROPS
*JD-47	(JD-350) Industrial Tractor	1/16	D	Ertl	589	1975	USA	WFE—with backhoe, loader & ROPS
*JD-48	(JD-350) Industrial Tractor	1/25	P.K.	Ertl	8015	1975	USA	WFE—with backhoe, loader & ROPS
*JD-49a	Four Wheel Loader	1/25	D	Ertl	503	1971	USA	
JD-49b	Four Wheel Loader	1/25	D	Ertl	507	1973	USA	With ROPS
*JD-50	(570) Motor Grader	1/25	D	Ertl	504	1971	USA	Road grader with cab; articulated
*JD-51	(690) Hydraulic Excavator	1/25	D	Ertl	505	1971	USA	Crawler tracks
*JD-52a	(860) Scraper	1/25	D	Ertl	506	1971	USA	Elevating scraper pan
JD-52b	(860) Scraper	1/25	D	Ertl	507	1973	USA	Elevating scraper pan with ROPS
*JD-53	Log Skidder	1/16	D	Ertl	590	1975	USA	4WD; articulated; with blade, winch & ROPS
JD-54	2020	1/16	P	Wader		1967	D	WFE—utility
JD-55	2120	1/43	P	Nacoral	2120	1973	E	WFE—utility; green with silver plating
*JD-56a	(3020)	1/32	P	Lee Toys	9716 1881		USA	Row crop—red & silver
*JD-56b	(3020)	1/32	P	Lee Toys	1135 1891		USA	Row crop—red, silver & brown; with cab & duals
*JD-57a	JD-Lanz 700	1/61	D	Lesney	50b	1963	GB	WFE—utility, gray tires
*JD-57b	JD-Lanz 700	1/61	D	Lesney	50b	1965	GB	WFE—utility, black tires
JD-58	JD-Lanz	1/61	D	Tiny Car		1968	BR	WFE—utility
*JD-59	JD-Lanz 2020	5"	P	Rex			D	WFE—utility
JD-60	JD-Lanz	5 1/2"	P	Rex			D	Crawler-loader; yellow
*JD-61	Skid Steer Loader	1/16	D	Ertl	569	1977	USA	4WD—skid steer

Code No.	Model	Scale or Size	Type of Material	Manufacturer	Stock No.	Year	Country	Remarks
JD-62a & b	(4230)	1/64	D	Minimac ?		1978	RA	Similar to JD-19 but without cab. Also, industrial model
JD-63a & b	(4230)	1/16	D	Minimac ?		1978	RA	Similar to JD-36 but without cab and has a three point hitch; was available with a five-bottom, 3 P.H. plow & wheel disk. Also, industrial model without 3 P.H.
JD-64	A-G.P.	1/16	C.M.	Dennis Parker		1979	USA-	Row crop—excellent detail *(C.M.—Custom Made)
JD-65	(4230)	1/64	D	Ertl	1619	1978	USA/ HK	WFE—cab

КОНСТРУКТО

Code No.	Model	Scale or Size	Type of Material	Manufacturer	Stock No.	Year	Country	Remarks
*KOH-1	Kohctpykto	5''	P	Apthkya		1956	SU	WFE—yellow & white, possibly Lanz Bulldog made under license in the U.S.S.R.

KUBOTA

Code No.	Model	Scale or Size	Type of Material	Manufacturer	Stock No.	Year	Country	Remarks
KUB-1a	Kubota	1/42	D	Tomica	92	1975	J	WFE
KUB-1b	Kubota	1/42	D	Tomica Aviva	C10	1978	J	WFE with comic character Charlie Brown in driver's seat
KUB-2a	L-150	1/23	D	Diapet	0381	1975	J	WFE with trailer
					0382	1975	J	WFE with disk
					0383	1975	J	WFE with Roto-tiller
					0386	1975	J	
KUB-2b	L-245	1/23	D	Diapet	0381	1978	J	WFE with trailer
					0382	1978	J	WFE with disk
					0383	1978	J	WFE with Roto-tiller
					0386	1978	J	WFE
KUB-3		1/17	P	Kubota— Jigyosha		1979	J	Well detailed mounted on base which serves as a coin bank—tractor is detachable.

LANDINI (Now A Part of Massey-Fersugon Ltd).

Code No.	Model	Scale or Size	Type of Material	Manufacturer	Stock No.	Year	Country	Remarks
*LAI-1	R-4000	1/43	D	Mercury	523	1961	I	WFE—hood hinged in front; blue & brown with yellow wheels
LAI-2	14500 4WD	1/43	D & P	Yaxon	063	1979	USA	4WD with ROPS; blue & gray; similar to MF-43

LAMBORGHINI

Code No.	Model	Scale or Size	Type of Material	Manufacturer	Stock No.	Year	Country	Remarks
*LAM-1	R 1056 4WD	1/43	D & P	Forma-Plast Mattel & Yaxon	.086	1977	I	Removable cab—similar in design to SAME Buffalo 130

LANZ

Code No.	Model	Scale or Size	Type of Material	Manufacturer	Stock No.	Year	Country	Remarks
*LAZ-1	Bulldog	1/86	P	Auguplas-Minicars	25	1959	E	WFE
LAZ-2	Bulldog	1/43	P	Marklin	8002	1950	D	WFE—has Lanz name on front; has exhaust stack, separate driver

Code No.	Model	Scale or Size	Type of Material	Manufacturer	Stock No.	Year	Country	Remarks
LAZ-3	Bulldog	1/43	D	Marklin	8029	1959	D	WFE—no stack, separate driver
*LAZ-4	Bulldog	5''	P	Rex			D	WFE—blue & red
*LAZ-5	Bulldog	1/87	P	Wiking	V-308	1973	D	WFE—antique style
LAZ-6	Bulldog	1/43	D	Marklin	8022/81	1939	D	WFE—has Lanz name; clockwork; exhaust stack (See also John Deere)

LEYLAND

Code No.	Model	Scale or Size	Type of Material	Manufacturer	Stock No.	Year	Country	Remarks
*LEY-1a	384	1/43	D	Dinky	308	1971	GB	WFE-Blue with white wheels; driver
*LEY-1b	384	1/43	D	Dinky	308	1971	GB	WFE—red with white wheels; driver
*LEY-1c	384	1/43	D	Dinky	308	1977	GB	WFE—orange with white wheels; driver

MASSEY-FERGUSON

Code No.	Model	Scale or Size	Type of Material	Manufacturer	Stock No.	Year	Country	Remarks
*MF-1	(44)	1/43	D	Dinky	300		GB	WFE—similar to MH-1 with driver
MF-2a	Massey-Ferguson	1/43	D	Micro-Models	8	1958	AUS	WFE
MF-2b	Massey-Ferguson Roller	1/43	D	Micro-Models	12	1958	AUS	Road roller-Modified MF-2a
MF-3	Massey-Ferguson	1/43	D	Budgie	306	1968	GB	WFE
MF-4	Massey-Ferguson	1/43	D	Vilmer	575	1959	DK	WFE
MF-5	Massey-Ferguson	1/43	D	Crescent	1203	1960	GB	WFE
MF-6	Massey-Ferguson	1/40	D	Peetzy-Roco	U-301		A	WFE
*MF-7	35	1/32	D	Lion-Molberg			DK	WFE—utility, hood hinged in front
*MF-8	35	1/25	D	Morgan Milton Ltd.	1035	1970	IN	WFE—utility, excellent detail
*MF-9	35	1/43	D	Mercury	510	1961	I	WFE—utility, also available with implements
MF-10	35	1/43	D	Gamda	30	1965	R	WFE—utility
*MF-11	(35)	1/32	D	Chico Toys	18	1976	CO	WFE—utility, similar to MF-7
*MF-12a	50-B Industrial	1/43	D	Corgi	50	1973	GB	WFE—yellow & black with cab
*MF-12b	50-B Industrial	1/43	D	Corgi	54	1974	GB	WFE—yellow & black with cab & loader
*MF-13a	65	1/43	D	Corgi	50	1959	GB	WFE—utility
*MF-13b	65	1/43	D	Corgi	53	1959	GB	WFE—utility with shovel loader

Code No.	Model	Scale or Size	Type of Material	Manufacturer	Stock No.	Year	Country	Remarks
*MF-13c	65	1/43	D	Corgi	57	1959	GB	WFE—utility with fork loader
MF-14a	165	1/43	D	Corgi	61	1967	GB	WFE—utility with four-furrow plow
*MF-14b	165	1/43	D	Corgi	66	1966	GB	WFE—utility
*MF-14c	165	1/43	D	Corgi	69	1969	GB	WFE—utility with shovel loader
*MF-14d	165	1/43	D	Corgi	73	1970	GB	WFE—utility with saw trimmer
*MF-15	165 Industrial	1/78	D	Corgi Jr.	43	1969	GB	WFE—utility with blade & cab
*MF-16	65	1/43	D	Triang Spot-On	137	1964	IRL	WFE—utility, yellow wheels; three point hitch
*MF-17a	65X	1/43	D	Jue		1972	BR	WFE—utility, excellent detail
MF-17b	65X	1/43	D	Minimac		1975	BR	WFE—utility, excellent detail; change in manufacturer ownership
MF-18a	275	1/43	D	Minimac		1975	BR	WFE—first type
*MF-18b	275	1/43	D	Minimac		1975	BR	WFE—second type
*MF-19	3366 Crawler	1/43	D	Jue		1972	BR	Industrial crawler with blade
*MF-20	135 Diesel	1/38	D	Reindeer	175	1969	ZA	WFE—utility
*MF-21	175 Diesel	1/20	D	Reindeer	175	1969	ZA	WFE—utility-Goodyear tires, excellent detail, rare
*MF-22a	135	1/32	D	Britains	9529	1969	GB	WFE—utility with fiberglass cab
*MF-22b	135 Industrial	1/32	D	Britains	9572	1970	GB	WFE—utility with cab & loader, yellow & red
MF-22c	135	1/32	D	Britains	9520	1976	GB	WFE—utility, no cab
*MF-23	595	1/32	D	Britains	9522	1976	GB	WFE—cab
*MF-24	165	1/43	D	Lesney	K-3	1970	GB	WFE—utility with cab & trailer, yellow wheels
*MF-25a	165	1/43	D	Joal	203	1970	E	WFE—utility, resembles MF-14; 'Fabricacion Ebro' on side
*MF-25b	165	1/43	D	Joal	206	1972	E	WFE—utility with loader
*MF-26	165	1/20	P.K.	Scale-Craft	S-523	1975	GB	WFE—utility with electric motor
*MF-27	300 Industrial Crawler	1/50	D	N.Z.G.	129	1974	GB	Yellow with blade

Code No.	Model	Scale or Size	Type of Material	Manufacturer	Stock No.	Year	Country	Remarks
*MF-28	450-S Hydraulic Excavator	1/50	D	N.Z.G.	106	1974	GB	Yellow, industrial crawler excavator
*MF-29a	175 Diesel	1/16	D	Ertl	175	1965	USA	WFE
*MF-29b	3165 Industrial	1/16	D	Ertl		1967	USA	WFE—yellow, with loader
*MF-30	275 Diesel	1/16	D	Ertl	1103	1975	USA	WFE with ROPS
*MF-31a	1080	1/16	D	Ertl	180	1970	USA	WFE—cab
MF-31b	1080 V-8	1/16	D	Ertl	180	1970	USA	WFE—cab; mis-labeled
*MF-31c	1150	1/16	D	Ertl	179	1970	USA	WFE—cab; mis-labeled
MF-31d	1150 V-8	1/16	D	Ertl	179	1970	USA	WFE—cab & dual rear wheels
*MF-32a	1105	1/16	D	Ertl	161	1973	USA	WFE—cab; red wheels
MF-32b	1105	1/16	D	Ertl	161	1975	USA	WFE—cab; gray wheels
*MF-33	1155	1/64	D	Ertl	1350	1973	USA	WFE—cab; two wheels size variations
*MF-34a	1155	1/16	D	Ertl	183	1974	USA	WFE—cab; red wheels
*MF-34b	1155	1/16	D	Ertl	183	1975	USA	WFE—cab; gray wheels
*MF-34c	1155	1/16	D	Ertl	183	1976	USA	WFE—cab; decal variation
*MF-35	1155	1/25	P.K.	Ertl	8007	1975	USA	WFE—cab
*MF-36	1155 Spirit of America	1/25	P.K.	Ertl	8016	1976	USA	WFE—cab; commemorative bicentiennial issue
*MF-37a	590	1/16	D	Ertl	1106	1977	USA	WFE-cab; European model; gray cab
*MF-37b	595	1/16	D	Ertl	1106	1977	USA	WFE—cab; European model; gray cab
*MF-38	165	1/16	D			Between 1965 & 1974	RA	Similar in size to MF-29a (Ertl) but has greater detail including a three point hitch, vertical muffler & air cleaner—rare
MF-39	2775 & 2800	1/64	D	Ertl	1622	1978	USA	WFE—cab
MF-40	Hanomag D600C Crawler	1/50	D	Cursor	1269	1978	D	Crawler with blade & cab
MF-41	Hanomag 66C Wheel Loader	1/50	D	Cursor	569	1978	D	Wheel loader with cab
MF-42a	2775	1/20	D & P	Ertl	1107	1979	USA	WFE—cab; "glass" windows
MF-42b	2800	1/20	D & P	Ertl	1108	1979	USA	WFE—cab; "glass" windows; dual rear wheels
MF-43	1134 4WD	1/43	D & P	Yaxon	067	1979	I	4WD—cab

Code No.	Model	Scale or Size	Type of Material	Manufacturer	Stock No.	Year	Country	Remarks
MASSEY-HARRIS								
*MH-1a	(44)	1/43	D	Dinky	27a	1948	GB	WFE—metal wheels/tires; separate tan painted driver
MH-1b	(44)	1/43	D	Dinky	310	1954	GB	WFE—rubber tires; separate painted driver
*MH-2	(55)	1/80	D	Dinky-Dublo	069	1959	GB	WFE—utility, blue
*MH-3	(44)	1/87	D	Wardie BJW	82	1950	GB	WFE with driver—fenders over rear wheels
*MH-4	(44)	1/87	D	A.H.I.			HK	WFE with driver—gray wheels
*MH-5	(44)	1/87	D	Fun-Ho	1	1976	NZ	WFE with driver—silver wheels
*MH-6	(44)	3"	D	Fun-Ho	309		NZ	WFE
*MH-7	(44)	6 1/2"	D	Fun-Ho	305		NZ	WFE
*MH-8	(44)	1/87	D	Lesney	4a	1954	GB	WFE—driver
*MH-9	745D	1/15	D	Moko—Lesney	1	1951	GB	WFE—excellent detail; steer; rare
*MH-10a	(44)	1/20	P	Raphael Lipkin	1091		GB	WFE—blue with red wheels
*MH-10b	745	1/20	P	Raphael Lipkin			GB	WFE—same as 10b except. Red with yellow wheels; has 745 model designation
MH-11	(44)	1/43	D	Micro-Models	4322	1954	NZ	WFE—also with front end loader
MH-12	(44)	1/16	D	Major-Models		1954	NZ	WFE—also with front end loader
MH-13	(44) Crawler	1/16	D	Major-Models		1957	NZ	Modified MH-12
*MH-14	745	1/38	D	P.M.I.	744		ZA	WFE
*MH-15	44 Standard	1/20	Pot	Lincoln Specialties	918	1950	CDN	WFE—with screw-in exhaust & air cleaner stacks, wide fenders over rear wheels
*MH-16a	44	1/16	D	Lincoln Specialties			CDN	WFE—with Dominion Royal Tires; also available with a loader
MH-16b	44	1/16	D	Lincoln Specialties			CDN	WFE—with Goodyear Tires; also available with a loader
*MH-16c	44	1/16	D	Lincoln Specialties			CDN	WFE—with wood wheels & rubber tires; also available with a loader
*MH-17a	44	1/16	D	Slik			CDN	Row crop

Code No.	Model	Scale or Size	Type of Material	Manufacturer	Stock No.	Year	Country	Remarks
MH-17b	44	1/16	Pot	Slik			CDN	Row crop with driver—similar to MH-17a
*MH-18	44	1/16	Pot	The King Co.			USA	Row crop with separate driver/hard hat
MH-19	44	1/16	Pot	The King Co.			USA	Row crop with separate driver/baseball type cap
*MH-20a	44	1/16	D	Ruehl Products			USA	Row crop with metal wheels, excellent detail
MH-20b	44	1/16	D	Ruehl Products			USA	Row crop with plastic wheels, excellent detail
*MH-21	(44)	1/87	D	Gitanes	1		F	WFE—gray metal wheels & tires, with trailer
*MH-22	Challenger	1/12	CA or Kor	Robert Gray			USA	Antique model on steel wheels
*MH-23	(745)	6''	D	Lincoln Micro-Models		c.1950	HK	WFE—steerable tred with yellow wheels & black & silver engine, 'Empire Made' on hood side
*MH-24	(55)	6 1/2''	P	Plasticum				WFE—clockwork, steerable, either red with yellow trim or yellow with red trim

MERCEDES-BENZ

Code No.	Model	Scale or Size	Type of Material	Manufacturer	Stock No.	Year	Country	Remarks
*MB-1	MB Trac	1/90	P	Wiking	V-385	1974	D	4WD with cab
*MB-2	Unimog	1/32	D	Britains	9569	1976	GB	4WD truck, used also as a tractor
*MB-3	MB Trac 1300		D	Gescha	3043	1977	D	4WD
*MB-4	MB Trac 1300	1/20	D & P	Gama	433	1977	D	4WD with cab

MINNEAPOLIS-MOLINE

Code No.	Model	Scale or Size	Type of Material	Manufacturer	Stock No.	Year	Country	Remarks
*MM-1	(Standard U)	1/12	Wood			W.W. II	USA	WFE—crude
*MM-2	(Row Crop Z)	1/12	Wood ***	Werner Wood & Plastic Co.		W.W. II	USA	Row crop—steer, crude—***Wood & Plastic
MM-3a	(U)	1/32	R	Arcor			USA	Row crop with molded-in driver, variety of colors; the MM-U is a 1938 model.
*MM-3b	(U)	1/32	R	Arcor			USA	Row crop with molded-in driver, yellow with white wheels
*MM-4a & b	(Z)	1/16	R	Arcor		1937	USA	Row crop with molded-in driver, variety of colors; molding variations
*MM-5	(UB)	1/16	D	Slik Toys	9853	1956	USA	Row crop with steering
*MM-6	(R)	1/32	D	Slik Toys	9816		USA	Row crop with steering, 'MM' on sides; green, yellow & red colors

Code No.	Model	Scale or Size	Type of Material	Manufacturer	Stock No.	Year	Country	Remarks
*MM-7	(4 Star)	1/32	D	Slik Toys	9871		USA	WFE
*MM-8	445	1/32	D	Slik Toys	9871		USA	WFE—different grill
MM-9	(R)	1/32	D	Lincoln Specialties			CDN	Row crop with cast-in driver; variety of colors, similar to MM-6
*MM-10	(Z)	1/16	D	Slik Toys		1950	USA	Row crop with cast-in driver having flat top hat
*MM-11	(Row Crop)	1/25	D	Ertl	15	1963	USA	Row crop—plastic wheels, bronze bottom
*MM-12	(Row Crop LPG)	1/25	D	Ertl	15	1965	USA	Row crop—plastic wheels, bronze bottom, pressure type fuel tank
*MM-13a	(Row Crop LPG)	1/25	D	Ertl	15	1967	USA	Row crop—rubber tires & wheels, steers, pressure type fuel tank
MM-13b	Thermogas	1/25	D	Ertl			USA	Promotional model distributed thru "Thermogas" dealers. MM was first manufacturer to equip a farm tractor with L.P.G.
*MM-14a	G-1000 Vista	1/16	D	Ertl	17	1968	USA	WFE—yellow wheels
*MM-14b	(G-1000 Vista)	1/16	D	Ertl	17	1972	USA	WFE—white wheels, no number decals
*MM-15	Mighty Minnie	1/16	D	Ertl	2702	1974	USA	WFE—modified G-1000 super rod pulling tractor
*MM-16	G-1355	1/16	D	Ertl	19	1974	USA	WFE—with dual rear wheels & ROPS

MUIR-HILL

Code No.	Model	Scale or Size	Type of Material	Manufacturer	Stock No.	Year	Country	Remarks
MUH-1a	Two Wheel Loader	1/43	D	Dinky	437	1962	GB	WFE—industrial with loader
*MUH-1b	Two Wheel Loader Backhoe	1/43	D	Dinky	967	1973	GB	WFE—industrial with loader & backhoe
*MUH-2	4WD	4 1/4"	D	Lesney	K-5	1972	GB	Industrial with blade & trailer

NORM

Code No.	Model	Scale or Size	Type of Material	Manufacturer	Stock No.	Year	Country	Remarks
*NOR-1	Norm	1/90	P	Wiking	38		D	WFE—red or green

NEW HOLLAND

Code No.	Model	Scale or Size	Type of Material	Manufacturer	Stock No.	Year	Country	Remarks
NH-1	1/2 H.P.	1/16		Alvin Ebersol		1977	USA	1920s-30s replica—not a tractor, but a gasoline engine for powering small farm equipment

NUFFIELD

Code No.	Model	Scale or Size	Type of Material	Manufacturer	Stock No.	Year	Country	Remarks
*NUF-1	Universal (M-IV)	1/16	D	Densil Skinner		1954	GB	WFE—excellent detail
*NUF-2	Nuffield BMC	1/15	P	Pippin Raphael Lipkin	1078	1963	GB	WFE

Code No.	Model	Scale or Size	Type of Material	Manufacturer	Stock No.	Year	Country	Remarks
*NUF-3	Nuffield No. 2 Minic	1/16	P	Minic	2	1954	GB	WFE—with driver & clock-work

OLIVER

Code No.	Model	Scale or Size	Type of Material	Manufacturer	Stock No.	Year	Country	Remarks
*OL-1	(60)	5 1/4"	C.I.	Arcade	359	1936	USA	Row crop with cast-in driver, red with rubber tires
*OL-2	70	7 1/2"	C.I.	Arcade	3560	1936	USA	Row crop with plated driver, red or green
OL-3	70 Orchard	5"	C.I.	Hubley	612	1938	USA	WFE with separately cast driver, fenders over rear wheels
*OL-4	70	1/16	D	Slik Toys			USA	Row crop—similar to OL-2
*OL-5a	77	1/16	D	Slik Toys		1948	USA	Row crop with separate driver
*OL-5b	77 Row-Crop	1/16	D	Slik Toys		1950	USA	Row crop with separate driver
*OL-6	77 Row-Crop Diesel Power	1/16	D	Slik Toys		1952	USA	Row crop—no driver, steers
*OL-7	Super 77	1/16	D	Slik Toys		1954	USA	Row crop—no driver, steers, open engine
*OL-8	Super 55	1/12	D	Slik Toys		1955	USA	WFE—no steering, utility with three point hitch
*OL-9	(880)	1/32	D	Slik Toys	9876	1960	USA	Row crop—no steering
*OL-10	880	1/16	D	Slik Toys		1958	USA	Row crop—no steering
*OL-11	OC-6 Crawler	1/16	D	Slik Toys	9851		USA	Row crop type crawler with separate driver; yellow
*OL-12	70	1/25	R	Arcor	543		USA	Row crop with molded-in driver; red
*OL-13	77 Standard	1/16	D	Lincoln Specialists		c.1950	CDN	WFE—no driver
*OL-14	70 Orchard	1/25	D	Fun-Ho	81		NZ	WFE—reproduction of OL-3
*OL-15	Hart-Parr 28-44	1/12	C.A. or Kor	Robert Gray		1971	USA	WFE—antique style
*OL-16a	70	1/16	C.A. or Kor	Robert Gray		1976	USA	Row crop with driver—steel wheels
OL-16b	70 Standard	1/16	C.A. or Kor	Robert Gray		1976	USA	Standard with driver—steel wheels
*OL-17a	1800 (Ser A)	1/16	D	Ertl	604	1963	USA	Row crop—steers, striped decal with Keystone on sides
*OL-17b	1800 (Ser B)	1/16	D	Ertl	604	1964	USA	Row crop—steers, striped decal

Code No.	Model	Scale or Size	Type of Material	Manufacturer	Stock No.	Year	Country	Remarks
*OL-17c	1800 (Ser C)	1/16	D	Ertl	604	1964	USA	Row crop—steers, large 1800 & red trim on decal
*OL-17d	1800 4WD	1/16	D	Ertl	606	1963	USA	WFE—cleated front wheels
*OL-17e	1850	1/16	D	Ertl	604	1965	USA	Row crop
*OL-17f	1850 4WD	1/16	D	Ertl	606	1965	USA	WFE—cleated front wheels
*OL-17g	1850	1/16	D	Ertl	604	1968	USA	Row crop—no fenders
*OL-17h	White 1855	1/16	D	Ertl	604	1970	USA	Row crop
*OL-17i	White 1855 4WD	1/16	D	Ertl	606	1970	USA	WFE—cleated front wheels
*OL-17j	White 1855	1/16	D	Ertl	609	1975	USA	WFE
*OL-17k	1855	1/16	D	Ertl	610	1974	USA	WFE with dual rear wheels & ROPS
OL-17l	1855	1/16	D	Ertl	604	1975	USA	Row crop—no fenders
*OL-18	(1955)	1/43	D	Tootsietoy	2435	1970	USA	WFE—comes with tandum spreader

OWATONNA

Code No.	Model	Scale or Size	Type of Material	Manufacturer	Stock No.	Year	Country	Remarks
*OW-1	Mustang Skid-Steer Loader	1/16	D	Ertl	725	1977	USA	Four wheel-skid steer loader with ROPS

PERPLEX

Code No.	Model	Scale or Size	Type of Material	Manufacturer	Stock No.	Year	Country	Remarks
*PER-1	7300	7 1/2''	Tin	Arnold			F	WFE—steers, battery electric motor

PANHARD

Code No.	Model	Scale or Size	Type of Material	Manufacturer	Stock No.	Year	Country	Remarks
PAN-1	Panhard	1/43	L	C.D.		1926	F	Antique style

P.G.S.-PIGIESSI

Code No.	Model	Scale or Size	Type of Material	Manufacturer	Stock No.	Year	Country	Remarks
*PGS-1	420 Diesel 4WD	1/10	P.K.	Protar Micro Modelli Provini		1976	I	Garden tractor—articulated, hood lifts

PORSCHE

Code No.	Model	Scale or Size	Type of Material	Manufacturer	Stock No.	Year	Country	Remarks
*POR-1	Porsche	2 3/4''	P & T	Gama			D	WFE—clockwork, came with wagon
*POR-2a	Diesel-T	1/60	D	Siku	218	1964	D	WFE—red or blue
POR-2b	Diesel-T	1/60	D	Siku	254		D	WFE with trailer
*POR-3	Porsche	1/90	D	Wiking	380	1958	D	WFE—orange or red
*POR-4	TB-20	7''	P & D	T-N	230		J	WFE—friction, with trailer
*POR-5	Diesel	12''	P					WFE
POR-6	Porsche	6 1/4''	Vinyl	Steho		1976	D	WFE with wagon

RENAULT

Code No.	Model	Scale or Size	Type of Material	Manufacturer	Stock No.	Year	Country	Remarks
*REN-1	(E-30)	1/32	D	CIJ	3-33		F	WFE—old style, orange
*REN-2	E-30	1/32	D	CIJ	3-33	1959	F	WFE—orange
*REN-3	E-30	1/32	D	CIJ	3-33	1959	F	WFE—red

Code No.	Model	Scale or Size	Type of Material	Manufacturer	Stock No.	Year	Country	Remarks
*REN-4a	(E-30)	1/16	T	CIJ Europarc	8-52		F	WFE—clockwork, with hay tender
*REN-4b	(E-30)	1/16	T	CIJ Europarc	3-34		F	WFE—red
REN-5	Renault	1/25	P	Cursor			D	WFE
*REN-6	R-86	1/43	P	Norev	117		F	WFE—orange or green
*REN-7	652 Industrial	1/16	P	Ruspa Ogni Terreno		1976	F	WFE—with cab & loader, battery operated
REN-8	651-4	1/32	D	Solido	510	1977	F	WFE—4WD
REN-9		1/87	P	Cursor	201	1979	D	WFE—orange
ROSENGART								
ROS-1	Super Traction	1/43	L	C.D.		1932	F	WFE—steam traction engine
RUMLEY								
*RUM-1	Oil Pull (20-35)	1/16	C.A.	Old Time Toys, Pioneer Tractor Works		1972	USA	WFE—represents a 1925 model antique style, serial numbered
*RUM-2	Oil Pull (20-30)	1/16	C.A.	Alvin Ebersol		1975	USA	WFE—antique style, represents a 1927 model
*RUM-3	Oil Pull	6 1/4"	C.A.	Irwin		1976	USA	WFE—antique style with canopy
SAME								
*SAM-1	Leone	1/80	P	Forma-Plast Politoys/Mattel & Yaxon	J-20		I	WFE—mod type tractor
*SAM-2	Centauro 4WD	1/15	D & P	Dugu	1	1966	I	WFE—rare, cleated front wheels, excellent detail
*SAM-3	Leone 70 4WD	1/12	P	Edizional Apis		1975	I	WFE—cleated front wheels
*SAM-4	Buffalo 130 4WD	1/43	D & P	Forma-Plast	.085	1977	I	WFE—removable cab, similar to Lamorgnini R1056
SATOH								
SAT-1	Beaver	3 1/2" + 1 1/2"	P			1978	J	Compact 15 H.P. tractor—miniature has battery operated motor; rear mounted roto-tiller
SHEPPARD								
*SHE-1	SD-3 Diesel	1/12	D	Sheppard Mfg. Co.		1950	USA	Row crop—only about 200 made, a 1949 model, similar in design to the Allis-Chalmers WD
STEIGER								
*STE-1	Couger II 4WD	20"	C.I.			1975	USA	Dual wheels—cab, articulated, only 100 made
*STE-2a	Bearcat III 4WD	21"	C.I.			1976	USA	Dual wheels—cab, articulated, only 150 made

Code No.	Model	Scale or Size	Type of Material	Manufacturer	Stock No.	Year	Country	Remarks
STE-2b	Panther III 4WD	21"	C.I.			1976	USA	Dual wheels—cab, articulated; red, white & blue trim; several other decal variations
STEYR								
ST-1a	8160	1/43	D & P	Yaxon	059	1979	I	4WD—cab; red & white
ST-1b	B60507	1/43	D & P	Yaxon	0118	1979	I	4WD—cab; dual rear wheels; red & white
TWIN-CITY								
*TC-1	(60-90)	1/16	Kor	Robert Gray		1974	USA	WFE—model of 1918, largest internal combustion engine tractor ever made.
WALLIS								
*WAL-1	20-30	1/25	C.I.	Vindex			USA	WFE—rare, represents a 1927 model
WEATHERHILL								
*WH-1	Hydraulic Shovel	3 1/2"	D	Lesney	1		GB	Tractor with shovel
WHITE								
*WH-1a	2-135	1/16	D	Scale Models		1978	USA	WFE—cab; replaces the Oliver, Minneapolis-Moline & Cockshutt lines—There are also a limited number of commemerative models mounted on walnut plaques.
WH-1b	2-155	1/16	D	Scale Models		1978	USA	WFE with cab & dual wheels
WH-1c	2-135 Power Assist	1/16	D	Scale Models		1979	USA	4WD—cab
WH-2	2-180	1/16	D	Scale Models		1979	USA	WFE with dual rear wheels, cab—CAT V-8 engine
ZETOR								
*ZET-1	5511	1/80	D	Corgi Jr.	4	1970	GB/HK	WFE—Czechoslovakian tractor with cab; orange
*ZET-2	Super Diesel	3 1/2	P	U.S.U.D.	KCS-11	1973	CS	WFE—rare, friction motor

This price guide is not meant to be "absolute," but rather the opinion of a few experienced collectors of farm models. The prices given are for models in good condition with no breaks and little or no paint wear. Models "mint" and in the original boxes are, of course, worth more. While prices of certain models have been going for considerably more than those listed, it is felt that one or two "deals" should not establish the price of a certain model.

Listed Price: The prices listed in this guide are based upon average, played with condition with a minimum of 90% of paint and decals present, no casting or assembly defects, no breaks or repairs and all major parts present (rubber muffler or steering wheel may be missing.)

New-Boxed: New, in the original box models will command higher prices, particularly models from the '50s and '60s with colorful box designs.

Repaints: Professional quality repaints or repairs may command higher or lower prices than original condition models. Example: Cast iron repaints usually bring lower prices than original condition models, even if there is very little original paint remaining.

Damaged: Rough condition played with models with breaks, poor paint and decals, missing parts and defects bring much lower prices.

Other: There may be regional price differences, particularly where there is a great interest in a particular line of models. The price established on rare models may be well over the $500.00 mark, although this is not necessarily the rule. A rare model may not be as sought after as more common models, particularly those manufactured outside the United States. Supply and demand will dictate the prices finally established on the rare models only to the extent that they are also very much sought after.

Price in parenthesis (   ) indicates value of built-up model from kit.

The check list is presented as a convenience for collectors who want to keep a record of models they have in their collection. Additional spaces are provided to allow for new models.

ALLCHIN

☐	ALL-1	$ 40.00
☐	ALL-2	15.00
☐	ALL-2	(30.00)
☐	_____	
☐	_____	

ALLIS-CHALMERS

☐	AC-2	50.00
☐	AC-3	50.00
☐	AC-4	100.00
☐	AC-5	150.00
☐	AC-6	200.00
☐	AC-7	175.00
☐	AC-8	10.00
☐	AC-9	125.00
☐	AC-10	175.00
☐	AC-11a	150.00
☐	AC-11b	150.00
☐	AC-12	225.00
☐	AC-13	300.00
☐	AC-14	300.00
☐	AC-15	RARE
☐	AC-16a	350.00
☐	AC-16b	325.00
☐	AC-16c	225.00
☐	AC-17a	190.00
☐	AC-17b	175.00
☐	AC-18	25.00
☐	AC-19a	125.00
☐	AC-19b	100.00
☐	AC-20	90.00
☐	AC-21	210.00
☐	AC-22	90.00
☐	AC-23	100.00
☐	AC-24a	90.00

☐	AC-24b	80.00
☐	AC-24c	80.00
☐	AC-24d	80.00
☐	AC-25a	75.00
☐	AX-25b	40.00
☐	AC-26	40.00
☐	AC-27	35.00
☐	AC-28	45.00
☐	AC-29	20.00
☐	AC-30	15.00
☐	AC-31	20.00
☐	AC-32a	75.00
☐	AC-32b	75.00
☐	AC-33	90.00
☐	_____	
☐	_____	

AVERY

☐	AV-1	75.00
☐	AV-2	75.00
☐	AV-3	30.00
☐	AV-4	45.00
☐	_____	
☐	_____	

B.M. VOLVO

☐	BMV-1	20.00
☐	BMV-2	15.00
☐	BMV-3	5.00
☐	_____	
☐	_____	

BATES

☐	BAT-1	RARE
☐	_____	
☐	_____	

BEAUCE & FLANDRE

☐	BEA-1	100.00
☐	FLA-1	100.00
☐	_____	
☐	_____	

BELARUS (BYALARUS)

☐	BEL-1	250.00
☐	_____	
☐	_____	

BLAW-KNOX

☐	BK-1	75.00
☐	BK-2	90.00
☐	BK-3	125.00
☐	_____	
☐	_____	

BUFFALO-PITTS

☐	BP-1	75.00
☐	_____	
☐	_____	

BUKH

☐	BUK-1	30.00
☐	_____	
☐	_____	

CASE

☐	CAS-1	500.00
☐	CAS-2	35.00
☐	CAS-3a	210.00
☐	CAS-3b	250.00
☐	CAS-4	400.00
☐	CAS-5a	175.00
☐	CAS-5b	180.00
☐	CAS-6	125.00
☐	CAS-7a	125.00
☐	CAS-7b	175.00
☐	CAS-7c	600.00

☐ CAS-7d	400.00	
☐ CAS-8a	120.00	
☐ CAS-8b	150.00	
☐ CAS-8c	135.00	
☐ CAS-8d	65.00	
☐ CAS-8e	100.00	
☐ CAS-8f	145.00	
☐ CAS-9	50.00	
☐ CAS-9b	45.00	
☐ CAS-10	50.00	
☐ CAS-11	25.00	
☐ CAS-12	30.00	
☐ CAS-13	40.00	
☐ CAS-14	50.00	
☐ CAS-15	20.00	
☐ CAS-16	10.00	
☐ CAS-17	20.00	
☐ CAS-18	130.00	
☐ CAS-19	85.00	
☐ CAS-20	425.00	
☐ CAS-21a	45.00	
☐ CAS-21b	75.00	
☐ CAS-22	75.00	
☐ CAS-23	15.00	
☐ CAS-24	50.00	
☐ CAS-25a	50.00	
☐ CAS-25b	50.00	
☐ _____		
☐ _____		

CLARK MELROE

BOBCAT

☐ CL-1a	35.00	
☐ CL-1b	35.00	
☐ CL-2	30.00	
☐ CL-3	25.00	

☐ _____

☐ _____

CLETRAC

☐ CLE-1 RARE

☐ _____

☐ _____

COCKSHUTT

☐ COC-1	225.00	
☐ COC-2	450.00	
☐ COC-3	150.00	
☐ COC-4	150.00	
☐ COC-5a	150.00	
☐ COC-5b	125.00	
☐ COC-6	RARE	

☐ _____

☐ _____

COLORADO

☐ COL-1 150.00

☐ _____

☐ _____

CO-OP

☐ CO-1 275.00

☐ _____

☐ _____

DAVID BROWN

☐ DB-1	RARE	
☐ DB-2	150.00	
☐ DB-3	75.00	
☐ DB-4	RARE	
☐ DB-5	100.00	

☐ _____

☐ _____

DEUTZ

☐ DE-1	45.00	
☐ DE-2	25.00	

☐ DE-3a	25.00	
☐ DE-3b	25.00	
☐ DE-4	RARE	
☐ DE-5a	50.00	
☐ DE-5b	45.00	
☐ DE-6	25.00	
☐ DE-7	200.00	
☐ DE-8a	25.00	
☐ DE-8b	25.00	
☐ DE-9a	25.00	
☐ DE-9b	30.00	
☐ DE-9c	30.00	
☐ DE-9d	30.00	
☐ DE-10	25.00	
☐ DE-11	12.00	
☐ DE-12	20.00	
☐ DE-13	20.00	
☐ DE-14	40.00	

☐ _____

☐ _____

DUTRA

☐ DU-1 RARE

☐ _____

☐ _____

EICHER

☐ EI-1 60.00

☐ _____

☐ _____

ESCORT

☐ ES-1 20.00

☐ _____

☐ _____

FAHR

☐ FA-1	200.00	
☐ FA-2	10.00	

Item	Price	Item	Price	Item	Price
☐ FA-3	10.00	☐ FIA-1	100.00	☐ FOR-7	200.00
☐ ————		☐ FIA-2	100.00	☐ FOR-8	200.00
☐ ————		☐ FIA-3a	25.00	☐ FOR-9	100.00
FAIRBANKS-MOORSE		☐ FIA-3b	25.00	☐ FOR-10a	35.00
		☐ FIA-3c	25.00	☐ FOR-10b	35.00
☐ FMO-1	75.00	☐ FIA-3d	25.00	☐ FOR-11	35.00
☐ FMO-2	15.00	☐ FIA-4a	75.00	☐ FOR-12	15.00
☐ ————		☐ FIA-4b	75.00	☐ FOR-13	25.00
☐ ————		☐ FIA-5a	40.00	☐ FOR-14	50.00
FENDT		☐ FIA-5b	40.00	☐ FOR-15a	150.00
☐ FEN-1	200.00	☐ FIA-6a	10.00	☐ FOR-15b	150.00
☐ FEN-2	75.00	☐ FIA-6b	10.00	☐ FOR-15c	125.00
☐ FEN-3	25.00	☐ FIA-7a	100.00	☐ FOR-16a	100.00
☐ FEN-4	30.00	☐ FIA-7b	90.00	☐ FOR-16b	100.00
☐ FEN-5	25.00	☐ FIA-8	90.00	☐ FOR-17a	120.00
☐ FEN-6	25.00	☐ FIA-9	40.00	☐ FOR-17b	100.00
☐ ————		☐ FIA-10	15.00	☐ FOR-18a	85.00
☐ ————		☐ FIA-11a	100.00	☐ FOR-18b	60.00
FERGUSON		☐ FIA-11b	100.00	☐ FOR-19	100.00
☐ FER-1	25.00	☐ FIA-12	20.00	☐ FOR-20	100.00
☐ FER-2	50.00	☐ ————		☐ FOR-21	100.00
☐ FER-3	RARE	☐ ————		☐ FOR-22	100.00
☐ FER-4	600.00	**FIELD MARSHALL**		☐ FOR-23a	5.00
☐ FER-5	325.00	☐ FM-1a	65.00	☐ FOR-23b	10.00
☐ FER-6	135.00	☐ FM-1b	50.00	☐ FOR-24	10.00
☐ FER-7	100.00	☐ ————		☐ FOR-25	65.00
☐ FER-8	125.00	☐ ————		☐ FOR-26a	40.00
☐ FER-9	150.00	**FORD**		☐ FOR-26b	65.00
☐ FER-10	5.00	☐ FOR-1	200.00	☐ FOR-27	20.00
☐ FER-11	10.00	☐ FOR-2	175.00	☐ FOR-28a	20.00
☐ FER-12	150.00	☐ FOR-3	45.00	☐ FOR-28b	35.00
☐ FER-13	RARE	☐ FOR-4	225.00	☐ FOR-29a	100.00
☐ ————		☐ FOR-5a	275.00	☐ FOR-29b	40.00
☐ ————		☐ FOR-5b	400.00	☐ FOR-29c	30.00
FIAT		☐ FOR-6	500.00	☐ FOR-29d	30.00

☐	FOR-30	12.00	☐	FDN-3	80.00	☐	FDN-31c	175.00
☐	FOR-31	15.00	☐	FDN-4	100.00	☐	FDN-32a	50.00
☐	FOR-32	35.00	☐	FDN-5	100.00	☐	FDN-32b	50.00
☐	FOR-33	35.00	☐	FDN-6	50.00	☐	FDN-33	40.00
☐	FOR-34	15.00	☐	FDN-7	50.00	☐	FDN-34	RARE
☐	FOR-35	5.00	☐	FDN-8	RARE	☐	FDN-35	300.00
☐	FOR-36	5.00	☐	FDN-9	100.00	☐	FDN-36	200.00
☐	FOR-37	50.00	☐	FDN-10	60.00	☐	FDN-37	75.00
☐	FOR-38a	50.00	☐	FDN-11	70.00	☐	FDN-38	150.00
☐	FOR-38b	25.00	☐	FDN-12	250.00	☐	FDN-39	150.00
☐	FOR-38c	25.00	☐	FDN-13	RARE	☐	FDN-40	75.00
☐	FOR-39	75.00	☐	FDN-14	200.00	☐	FDN-41	15.00
☐	FOR-40	20.00	☐	FDN-15	140.00	☐	FDN-42	20.00
☐	FOR-41a	30.00	☐	FDN-16		☐	FDN-43a	50.00
☐	FOR-41b	40.00	☐	FDN-17	25.00	☐	FDN-43b	75.00
☐	FOR-41c	30.00	☐	FDN-18	10.00	☐	FDN-44a	50.00
☐	FOR-42	10.00	☐	FDN-19	10.00	☐	FDN-44b	75.00
☐	FOR-43	125.00	☐	FDN-20	25.00	☐	FDN-45	75.00
☐	FOR-44	5.00	☐	FDN-21	30.00	☐	FDN-46	65.00
☐	FOR-45	5.00	☐	FDN-22a	5.00	☐	FDN-47	5.00
☐	FOR-46	5.00	☐	FDN-22a	(10.00)	☐	FDN-48	50.00
☐	FOR-47	50.00	☐	FDN-22b	5.00	☐	FDN-49	15.00
☐	FOR-48	125.00	☐	FDN-22b	(10.00)	☐	FDN-50	15.00
☐	FOR-49	5.00	☐	FDN-23		☐	FDN-51	25.00
☐	FOR-50	20.00	☐	FDN-24	40.00	☐	FDN-51	(50.00)
☐	FOR-51	20.00	☐	FDN-25	50.00	☐	FDN-52	10.00
☐	FOR-52	30.00	☐	FDN-26	60.00	☐	FDN-53	RARE
☐	FOR-53	20.00	☐	FDN-27	50.00	☐	FDN-54	175.00
☐	FOR-54	30.00	☐	FDN-28	25.00	☐	FDN-55	200.00
☐	FOR-55	40.00	☐	FDN-29a	110.00	☐	FDN-56	200.00
☐	_____		☐	FDN-29b	100.00	☐	FDN-57	15.00
☐	_____		☐	FDN-30a	175.00	☐	_____	
	FORDSON		☐	FDN-30b	175.00	☐	_____	
☐	FDN-1	50.00	☐	FDN-31a	150.00		**FOWLER**	
☐	FDN-2	70.00	☐	FDN-31b	150.00	☐	FOW-1	40.00

FRICK

	Item	Price
☐	———	
☐	———	
☐	FRI-1	40.00

GRAHAM-BRADLEY

	Item	Price
☐	———	
☐	———	
☐	GB-1	25.00

GUIDART

	Item	Price
☐	———	
☐	———	
☐	GUI-1	200.00

HANOMAG (Now Part of Massey-Ferguson Ltd.)

	Item	Price
☐	———	
☐	———	
☐	HAN-1	35.00
☐	HAN-2	200.00
☐	HAN-3	RARE
☐	HAN-4	15.00
☐	HAN-5	40.00

HOLDER

	Item	Price
☐	———	
☐	———	
☐	HO-1	40.00

HUBER

	Item	Price
☐	———	
☐	———	
☐	HUB-1	200.00
☐	HUB-2a	40.00
☐	HUB-2b	40.00
☐	HUB-2	35.00
☐	HUB-4	50.00

McCORMICK-DEERING-I.H.

	Item	Price
☐	———	
☐	———	
☐	IH-1a	200.00
☐	IH-1b	200.00
☐	IH-2a	400.00
☐	IH-2b	400.00
☐	IH-3	500.00
☐	IH-4	500.00
☐	IH-5	75.00
☐	IH-6	150.00
☐	IH-7	200.00
☐	IH-8	375.00
☐	IH-9	RARE
☐	IH-10	50.00
☐	IH-11	35.00
☐	IH-12	35.00
☐	IH-13	50.00
☐	IH-14a	150.00
☐	IH-14b	150.00
☐	IH-14c	725.00
☐	IH-15	300.00
☐	IH-16a	400.00
☐	IH-16b	375.00
☐	IH-17	100.00
☐	IH-18a	150.00
☐	IH-18b	200.00
☐	IH-19	75.00
☐	IH-20	15.00
☐	IH-21	25.00
☐	IH-22	25.00
☐	IH-23	10.00
☐	IH-24	25.00
☐	IH-25	RARE
☐	IH-26	150.00
☐	IH-27a	50.00
☐	IH-27b	50.00
☐	IH-28a	25.00
☐	IH-28b	25.00
☐	IH-29a	25.00
☐	IH-29b	25.00
☐	IH-30a	20.00
☐	IH-30b	20.00
☐	IH-30c	20.00
☐	IH-30d	55.00
☐	IH-31a	30.00
☐	IH-31b	30.00
☐	IH-32a	250.00
☐	IH-32b	20.00
☐	IH-33	275.00
☐	IH-34	300.00
☐	IH-35	175.00
☐	IH-36a	80.00
☐	IH-36b	45.00
☐	IH-37	375.00
☐	IH-38a	225.00
☐	IH-38b	175.00
☐	IH-38c	175.00
☐	IH-38d	110.00
☐	IH-38e	100.00
☐	IH-38f	135.00
☐	IH-38g	85.00
☐	IH-38h	150.00
☐	IH-38i	160.00
☐	IH-39a	115.00
☐	IH-39b	35.00
☐	IH-39c	100.00
☐	IH-39d	40.00
☐	IH-39e	50.00

	Item	Price		Item	Price		Item	Price
☐	IH-39f	85.00	☐	IH-59	200.00	☐	JD-3	240.00
☐	IH-40	75.00	☐	IH-60	RARE	☐	JD-4	RARE
☐	IH-41a	35.00	☐	IH-61	240.00	☐	JD-5	700.00
☐	IH-41b	25.00	☐	IH-62	240.00	☐	JD-6a	700.00
☐	IH-42a	10.00	☐	IH-63	30.00	☐	JD-6b	700.00
☐	IH-42b	10.00	☐	IH-64	25.00	☐	JD-7	30.00
☐	IH-43a	200.00	☐	IH-65a	25.00	☐	JD-8	25.00
☐	IH-43b	175.00	☐	IH-65b	20.00	☐	JD-9	20.00
☐	IH-43c	175.00	☐	IH-66a	25.00	☐	JD-10	15.00
☐	IH-44a	150.00	☐	IH-66b	20.00	☐	JD-11	150.00
☐	IH-44b	160.00	☐	IH-67	70.00	☐	JD-12	10.00
☐	IH-44c	165.00	☐	IH-68	50.00	☐	JD-13	10.00
☐	IH-44d	175.00	☐	IH-69	45.00	☐	JD-14	10.00
☐	IH-45a	75.00	☐	IH-70a	12.00	☐	JD-15	10.00
☐	IH-45b	100.00	☐	IH-70b	12.00	☐	JD-16	10.00
☐	IH-45c	140.00	☐	IH-70c	12.00	☐	JD-17	10.00
☐	IH-45d	110.00	☐	IH-71	12.00	☐	JD-18	10.00
☐	IH-45e	100.00	☐	IH-72	15.00	☐	JD-19	5.00
☐	IH-46	225.00	☐	IH-73	30.00	☐	JD-20	10.00
☐	IH-47	35.00	☐	IH-74	25.00	☐	JD-21	RARE
☐	IH-48	100.00	☐	IH-75	50.00	☐	JD-22	100.00
☐	IH-49a	50.00	☐	IH-76	50.00	☐	JD-23	165.00
☐	IH-49b	45.00	☐	IH-77	35.00	☐	JD-24a	180.00
☐	IH-49c	20.00	☐	IH-78	20.00	☐	JD-24b	
☐	IH-50	100.00	☐	IH-79	15.00	☐	JD-25	60.00
☐	IH-51	50.00	☐	IH-80 Cub		☐	JD-26a	15.00
☐	IH-52	150.00	☐	IH-80 Farmall (C)		☐	JD-26b	85.00
☐	IH-53a	200.00	☐	IH-81	10.00	☐	JD-26c	85.00
☐	IH-54	40.00	☐	IH-82	130.00	☐	JD-26d	85.00
☐	IH-55	25.00	☐	IH-83	75.00	☐	JD-26e	85.00
☐	IH-56	350.00	☐	_____		☐	JD-26f	20.00
☐	IH-57a	30.00	☐	_____		☐	JD-27a	15.00
☐	IH-57b	25.00		**JOHN DEERE**		☐	JD-27b	15.00
☐	IH-58	25.00	☐	JD-1	650.00	☐	JD-28a	475.00
☐	IH-58	(50.00)	☐	JD-2	375.00	☐	JD-28b	450.00

☐	JD-29a	175.00	☐	JD-44b	225.00	☐	_____		
☐	JD-29b	195.00	☐	JD-45	200.00	**KUBOTA**			
☐	JD-30a	250.00	☐	JD-46a	70.00	☐	KUB-1a	5.00	
☐	JD-30b	225.00	☐	JD-46b	70.00	☐	KUB-1b	5.00	
☐	JD-31a	30.00	☐	JD-46c	40.00	☐	KUB-2a	20.00	
☐	JD-31b	40.00	☐	JD-47	30.00	☐	KUB-2b	20.00	
☐	JD-32a	20.00	☐	JD-48	40.00	☐	KUB-3	35.00	
☐	JD-32b	30.00	☐	JD-49a	50.00	☐	_____		
☐	JD-33	150.00	☐	JD-49b	40.00	☐	_____		
☐	JD-34	150.00	☐	JD-50	20.00	**LANDINI** (Now a			
☐	JD-34a	85.00	☐	JD-51	20.00	part of Massey-			
☐	JD-34b	85.00	☐	JD-52a	40.00	Ferguson Ltd.			
☐	JD-34c	65.00	☐	JD-52b	30.00	☐	LAI-1		
☐	JD-34d	100.00	☐	JD-53	25.00	☐	LAI-2	25.00	
☐	JD-34e	55.00	☐	JD-54	RARE	☐	_____		
☐	JD-34f	65.00	☐	JD-55	RARE	☐	_____		
☐	JD-34g	45.00	☐	JD-56a	10.00	**LAMBORGHINI**			
☐	JD-34h	45.00	☐	JD-56b	15.00	☐	LAM-1	25.00	
☐	JD-35	45.00	☐	JD-57a	30.00	☐	_____		
☐	JD-35a	45.00	☐	JD-57b	25.00	☐	_____		
☐	JD-35b	45.00	☐	JD-58	100.00	**LANZ**			
☐	JD-35c	45.00	☐	JD-59	RARE	☐	LAZ-1	20.00	
☐	JD-35d	80.00	☐	JD-60	RARE	☐	LAZ-2	150.00	
☐	JD-36	40.00	☐	JD-61	15.00	☐	LAZ-3	75.00	
☐	JD-37	15.00	☐	JD-62a	25.00	☐	LAZ-4	100.00	
☐	JD-38	40.00	☐	JD-62b	25.00	☐	LAZ-5	10.00	
☐	JD-39a	70.00	☐	JD-63a	85.00	☐	LAZ-6	RARE	
☐	JD-39b	60.00	☐	JD-63b	85.00	☐	_____		
☐	JD-40	125.00	☐	JD-64	175.00	☐	_____		
☐	JD-41	50.00	☐	JD-65	10.00	**LEYLAND**			
☐	JD-42a	200.00	☐	_____		☐	LEY-1a	35.00	
☐	JD-42b	300.00	☐	_____		☐	LEY-1b	35.00	
☐	JD-42c	190.00	**КОНСТРУКТО**			☐	LEY-1c	35.00	
☐	JD-43	250.00	☐	KOH-1		☐	_____		
☐	JD-44a	250.00	☐	_____		☐	_____		

MASSEY-FERGUSON

	Item	Price		Item	Price		Item	Price
			☐	MF-23	15.00	☐	MH-1b	50.00
			☐	MF-24	20.00	☐	MH-2	20.00
☐	MF-1	50.00	☐	MF-25a	15.00	☐	MH-3	20.00
☐	MF-2a	175.00	☐	MF-25b	15.00	☐	MH-4	10.00
☐	MF-2b	175.00	☐	MF-26	25.00	☐	MH-5	15.00
☐	MF-3		☐	MF-27	35.00	☐	MH-6	5.00
☐	MF-4	225.00	☐	MF-28	35.00	☐	MH-7	10.00
☐	MF-5	100.00	☐	MF-29a	50.00	☐	MH-8	20.00
☐	MF-6	75.00	☐	MF-29b	125.00	☐	MH-9	350.00
☐	MF-7	125.00	☐	MF-30	25.00	☐	MH-10a	30.00
☐	MF-8	40.00	☐	MF-31a	110.00	☐	MH-10b	175.00
☐	MF-9	250.00	☐	MF-31b	110.00	☐	MH-11	125.00
☐	MF-10	200.00	☐	MF-31c	190.00	☐	MH-12	125.00
☐	MF-11	75.00	☐	MF-31d	220.00	☐	MH-13	175.00
☐	MF-12a	20.00	☐	MF-32a	60.00	☐	MH-14	RARE
☐	MF-12b	25.00	☐	MF-32b	40.00	☐	MH-15	165.00
☐	MF-13a	50.00	☐	MF-33	100.00	☐	MH-16a	145.00
☐	MF-13b	60.00	☐	MF-34a	55.00	☐	MH-16b	145.00
☐	MF-13c	60.00	☐	MF-34b	35.00	☐	MH-16c	145.00
☐	MF-14a	30.00	☐	MF-34c	35.00	☐	MH-17a	100.00
☐	MF-14b	25.00	☐	MF-35	20.00	☐	MH-17b	100.00
☐	MF-14c	30.00	☐	MF-36	20.00	☐	MH-18	110.00
☐	MF-14d	30.00	☐	MF-37a	35.00	☐	MH-19	110.00
☐	MF-15	5.00	☐	MF-37b	40.00	☐	MH-20a	400.00
☐	MF-16	125.00	☐	MF-38	RARE	☐	MH-20b	400.00
☐	MF-17a	30.00	☐	MF-39	10.00	☐	MH-21	45.00
☐	MF-17b	15.00	☐	MF-40	35.00	☐	MH-22	50.00
☐	MF-18a	15.00	☐	MF-41	35.00	☐	MH-23	125.00
☐	MF-18b	15.00	☐	MF-42a	15.00	☐	MH-24	90.00
☐	MF-19	20.00	☐	MF-42b	15.00	☐	————	
☐	MF-20	100.00	☐	MF-43	20.00	☐	————	
☐	MF-21	250.00	☐	————		**MERCEDES-BENZ**		
☐	MF-22a	30.00	☐	————		☐	MB-1	5.00
☐	MF-22b	25.00	**MASSEY-HARRIS**			☐	MB-2	5.00
☐	MF-22c	30.00	☐	MH-1a	70.00	☐	MB-3	30.00

☐	MB-4	20.00	☐	_____		☐	OL-17f	140.00
☐	_____			**NEW HOLLAND**		☐	OL-17g	100.00
☐	_____		☐	NH-1	50.00	☐	OL-17h	85.00
	MINNEAPOLIS—		☐	_____		☐	OL-17i	130.00
	MOLINE		☐	_____		☐	OL-17j	100.00
☐	MM-1	100.00		**NUFFIELD**		☐	OL-17k	100.00
☐	MM-2	100.00	☐	NUF-1	RARE	☐	OL-17l	90.00
☐	MM-3a	25.00	☐	NUF-2	250.00	☐	OL-18	5.00
☐	MM-3b	50.00	☐	NUF-3	150.00	☐	_____	
☐	MM-4a	100.00	☐	_____		☐	_____	
☐	MM-4b	90.00	☐	_____			**OWATONNA**	
☐	MM-5	200.0		**OLIVER**		☐	OW-1	20.00
☐	MM-6	15.00	☐	OL-1	80.00	☐	_____	
☐	MM-7	150.00	☐	OL-2	175.00	☐	_____	
☐	MM-8	125.00	☐	OL-3	115.00		**PERPLEX**	
☐	MM-9	15.00	☐	OL-4	90.00	☐	PER-1	125.00
☐	MM-10	RARE	☐	OL-5a	200.00	☐	_____	
☐	MM-11	75.00	☐	OL-5b	200.00	☐	_____	
☐	MM-12	75.00	☐	OL-6	300.00		**PANHARD**	
☐	MM-13	45.00	☐	OL-7	400.00	☐	PAN-1	25.00
☐	MM-14a	200.00	☐	OL-8	500.00	☐	_____	
☐	MM-14b	175.00	☐	OL-9	20.00	☐	_____	
☐	MM-15	80.00	☐	OL-10	175.00		**P.G.S.-PIGIESSI**	
☐	MM-16	220.00	☐	OL-11	350.00	☐	PGS-1	70.00
☐	_____		☐	OL-12	40.00	☐	_____	
☐	_____		☐	OL-13	RARE	☐	_____	
	MUIR-HILL		☐	OL-14	25.00		**PORSCHE**	
☐	MUH-1a	35.00	☐	OL-15	50.00	☐	POR-1	25.00
☐	MUH-1b	30.00	☐	OL-16a	50.00	☐	POR-2a	10.00
☐	MUH-2	25.00	☐	OL-16b	50.00	☐	POR-2b	10.00
☐	_____		☐	OL-17a	275.00	☐	POR-3	20.00
☐	_____		☐	OL-17b	150.00	☐	POR-4	error
	NORM		☐	OL-17c	90.00	☐	POR-5	75.00
☐	NOR-1	15.00	☐	OL-17d	150.00	☐	POR-6	15.00
☐	_____		☐	OL-17e	100.00	☐	_____	

☐	_____	

RENAULT

☐	REN-1	125.00
☐	REN-2	80.00
☐	REN-3	80.00
☐	REN-4a	225.00
☐	REN-4b	175.00
☐	REN-5	200.00
☐	REN-6	10.00
☐	REN-7	50.00
☐	REN-8	20.00
☐	REN-9	20.00
☐	_____	
☐	_____	

ROSENGART

☐	ROS-1	20.00
☐	_____	
☐	_____	

RUMLEY

☐	RUM-1	75.00
☐	RUM-2	75.00
☐	RUM-3	45.00
☐	_____	
☐	_____	

SAME

☐	SAM-1	15.00
☐	SAM-2	RARE
☐	SAM-3	40.00
☐	SAM-4	25.00
☐	_____	
☐	_____	

SATOH

☐	SAT-1	50.00
☐	_____	
☐	_____	

SHEPPARD

☐	SHE-1	400.00
☐	_____	
☐	_____	

STEIGER

☐	STE-1	RARE
☐	STE-2a	140.00
☐	STE-2b	140.00
☐	_____	
☐	_____	

STEYR

☐	ST-1a	15.00
☐	ST-1b	15.00
☐	_____	
☐	_____	

TWIN-CITY

☐	TC-1	100.00
☐	_____	
☐	_____	

WALLIS

☐	WAL-1	RARE
☐	_____	
☐	_____	

WEATHERHILL

☐	WH-1	
☐	_____	
☐	_____	

WHITE

☐	WH-1a	35.00
☐	WH-1b	40.00
☐	WH-1c	40.00
☐	WH-2	60.00
☐	_____	
☐	_____	

ZETOR

☐	ZET-1	5.00
☐	ZET-2	35.00
☐	_____	
☐	_____	

MISCELLANEOUS

☐	MISC-1
☐	MISC-2
☐	MISC-3
☐	MISC-4
☐	MISC-5
☐	MISC-6
☐	MISC-7
☐	MISC-8
☐	MISC-9
☐	MISC-10
☐	MISC-11
☐	MISC-12
☐	MISC-13
☐	MISC-14
☐	MISC-15
☐	MISC-16
☐	MISC-17
☐	MISC-18
☐	MISC-19
☐	MISC-20
☐	MISC-21
☐	MISC-22
☐	MISC-23
☐	MISC-24
☐	MISC-25
☐	MISC-26
☐	MISC-27
☐	MISC-28
☐	MISC-29
☐	MISC-30

☐	MISC-31	☐	MISC-66	☐	MISC-101
☐	MISC-32	☐	MISC-67	☐	MISC-102
☐	MISC-33	☐	MISC-68	☐	MISC-103
☐	MISC-34	☐	MISC-69	☐	MISC-104
☐	MISC-35	☐	MISC-70	☐	MISC-105
☐	MISC-36	☐	MISC-71	☐	MISC-106
☐	MISC-37	☐	MISC-72	☐	MISC-107
☐	MISC-38	☐	MISC-73	☐	MISC-108
☐	MISC-39	☐	MISC-74	☐	MISC-109
☐	MISC-40	☐	MISC-75	☐	_____
☐	MISC-41	☐	MISC-76	☐	_____
☐	MISC-42	☐	MISC-77		
☐	MISC-43	☐	MISC-78		
☐	MISC-44	☐	MISC-79		
☐	MISC-45	☐	MISC-80		
☐	MISC-46	☐	MISC-81		
☐	MISC-47	☐	MISC-82		
☐	MISC-48	☐	MISC-83		
☐	MISC-49	☐	MISC-84		
☐	MISC-50	☐	MISC-85		
☐	MISC-51	☐	MISC-86		
☐	MISC-52	☐	MISC-87		
☐	MISC-53	☐	MISC-88		
☐	MISC-54	☐	MISC-89		
☐	MISC-55	☐	MISC-90		
☐	MISC-56	☐	MISC-91		
☐	MISC-57	☐	MISC-92		
☐	MISC-58	☐	MISC-93		
☐	MISC-59	☐	MISC-94		
☐	MISC-60	☐	MISC-95		
☐	MISC-61	☐	MISC-96		
☐	MISC-62	☐	MISC-97		
☐	MISC-63	☐	MISC-98		
☐	MISC-64	☐	MISC-99		
☐	MISC-65	☐	MISC-100		

Credits

Special thanks to the following people who contributed information and pictures for the book;

J.J. Allgaier, Deere & Company
Dave Bell, The Ertl Company
Paul Bender, collector
Robert S. Brennon, Miniature Toys Inc.
Jacky Broutin, antique dealer, Paris, France
Jim Brown, photography
Barb Burkholder, collector
Joseph Carter, former owner of Carter Tru-Scale, Illinois
Robert & Judy Condray, collector
Ken Conklin, collector & model maker, Illinois
James Coontz, mini-puller
Charles Cox, collector, Iowa
John Deyoe, collector, Illinois
Bill Drake, collector, New York
Dean Erie, collector, Iowa
Fred Ertl Jr., President, The Ertl Company
Gabriel Industries, Ms. Judith Sussman, manufacturer, New York
Robert Gray, collector & manufacturer, Iowa
Jim & Cindy Hamilton, collectors, Ohio
Rich Havens, photographer
Bob Hayes, photography
Bob Henke, collector
Leon & Jim Hosch, Lee Foundry, Iowa
Doug Jarvis, collector
Earl Jergensen, collector & manufacturer, Iowa
Howard M. Karslake, collector & model maker, Benfleet, England
Dale Kelly, The Antique Toy World
Jay Kobiske, collector, Wisconsin
Greg Lennes, International Harverster Inc.
Chris Lennard, photography
Neal Lininger, collector, Kansas
Tom Lucht, collector, Nebraska
Graham & Michelle Miller, collectors, Herts, England
Jim McCommons, photographer
Peter Neilson, collector, Michigan
Dennis Parker, collector, Colorado
Ken Reichert, collector, Ontario, Canada
John Sampson, collector, Indiana
David Sinclair, Sinclair's Auto Miniature
Gene Smiley, collector, Pennsylvania
Charles Souhrada, collector, Iowa
Rusty Sutherland, collector, New York
Mrs. R.J. Taylor, Britains Ltd.
Charles Tichenor, collector & manufacturer, Illinois
Eldon Trumm, collector & model builder, Iowa
Harry Van Woert, model builder
Steve Warters, mini-puller
Morgan Williams, collector, Kansas
Barry G.B. Young, Underwood Engineering Ltd.

Index

Miscellaneous Section is not Indexed.

AZTEX Corporation—Information:

This book is part of a continuing project. Please advise us of any additions or corrections which you come across in reading this volume. Any information, no matter how obscure or seemingly unimportant, is welcomed. In sending information, please make reference to the title and author and mail to:

Editor, AZTEX Corporation,
P O Box 50046, Tucson, AZ 85703